Sacra Corona
(Venice, 1656)

Recent Researches in Music

A-R Editions publishes seven series of critical editions, spanning the history of Western music, American music, and oral traditions.

Recent Researches in the Music of the Middle Ages and Early Renaissance
    Charles M. Atkinson, general editor

Recent Researches in the Music of the Renaissance
    David Crook, general editor

Recent Researches in the Music of the Baroque Era
    Steven Saunders, general editor

Recent Researches in the Music of the Classical Era
    Neal Zaslaw, general editor

Recent Researches in the Music of the Nineteenth and Early Twentieth Centuries
    Rufus Hallmark, general editor

Recent Researches in American Music
    John M. Graziano, general editor

Recent Researches in the Oral Traditions of Music
    Philip V. Bohlman, general editor

Each edition in *Recent Researches* is devoted to works by a single composer or to a single genre. The content is chosen for its high quality and historical importance and is edited according to the scholarly standards that govern the making of all reliable editions.

For information on establishing a standing order to any of our series, or for editorial guidelines on submitting proposals, please contact:

A-R Editions, Inc.
Middleton, Wisconsin

800 736-0070 (North American book orders)
608 836-9000 (phone)
608 831-8200 (fax)
http://www.areditions.com

RECENT RESEARCHES IN THE MUSIC OF THE BAROQUE ERA, 189

Sacra Corona (Venice, 1656)

Edited by Paolo Alberto Rismondo

A-R Editions, Inc.
Middleton, Wisconsin

To my mother

A-R Editions, Inc., Middleton, Wisconsin
© 2015 by A-R Editions, Inc.

All rights reserved. No part of this book may be reproduced or transmitted in any form by any electronic or mechanical means (including photocopying, recording, or information storage and retrieval) without permission in writing from the publisher.

The purchase of this edition does not convey the right to perform it in public, nor to make a recording of it for any purpose. Such permission must be obtained in advance from the publisher.

A-R Editions is pleased to support the use of *Recent Researches* material for study or performance. Please visit our website (www.areditions.com) to apply for permission to perform, record, or otherwise reuse the material in this publication.

Printed in the United States of America

ISBN 978-0-89579-805-3
ISSN 0484-0828

♾ The paper used in this publication meets the minimum requirements of the American National Standard for Information Sciences—Permanence of Paper for Printed Library Materials, ANSI Z39.48-1992.

Contents

Abbreviations and Sigla   vii

Acknowledgments   ix

Introduction   xi
   The Composers and Their Music   xii
   The Printer   xvi
   The Compiler   xvi
   The Dedicatee   xvii
   Contexts for the *Sacra Corona*   xvii
   The Music   xix
   Notes on Performance   xx
   Notes   xx

Texts and Translations   xxxii

Plates   xli

Sacra Corona (Venice, 1656)
   Dedication   2
     1. Nigra sum, *Giovanni Rovetta* (CC, B.c.)   3
     2. Dulce sit vobis pati, *Natale Monferrato* (CA, B.c.)   10
     3. O bone Jesu, *Francesco Cavalli* (CA, B.c.)   25
     4. Ad charismata caelorum, *Massimiliano Neri* (CA, B.c.)   33
     5. Jesu mi, Jesu benignissime, *Giovanni Battista Volpe* (CC, B.c.)   39
     6. Exsultate, gaudete, jubilate, *Pietro Andrea Ziani* (CT, B.c.)   46
     7. Surge propera, *Biagio Marini* (AB, B.c.)   53
     8. Salve mundi triumphatrix, *Maurizio Cazzati* (AB, B.c.)   61
     9. Spargite flores, *Orazio Tarditi* (CB, B.c.)   69
    10. Victoriam, victoriam, *Tarditi* (CB, B.c.)   81
    11. Stellae discedite, *Stefano Filippini* (CC, B.c.)   89
    12. Quis dabit mihi tantam charitatem, *Barbara Strozzi* (ATB, B.c.)   98
    13. O quando suavissimum, *Rovetta* (ATB, B.c.)   111
    14. Plaudite, cantate, *Cavalli* (ATB, B.c.)   123
    15. In virtute tua, *Cavalli* (ATB, B.c.)   133
    16. Peccator, si tu times, *Monferrato* (CABar, B.c.)   147
    17. Jesu mi dulcissime, *Marini* (ATB, B.c.)   163
    18. Obstupescite gentes, *Cazzati* (CCB, B.c.)   172
    19. Salve Regina, *Ziani* (ATB, B.c.)   186
    20. O Sacramentum, *Volpe* (ATB, B.c.)   197
    21. Salve Virgo benignissima, *Neri* (ATB, B.c.)   206
    22. O vos omnes, *Simone Vesi* (ATB, B.c.)   217
    23. Laetare Mater Ecclesia, *Filippini* (ATB, B.c.)   227

Critical Report   239
   Sources   239
   Editorial Methods   240
   Critical Notes   242
   Notes   246

Appendix
   Ad charismata caelorum: Version from *Motetti a due e tre voci* (1664)   251

Abbreviations and Sigla

In transcriptions from contemporary documents, the original orthography is maintained wherever possible, with slight adjustments to punctuation and silent corrections to some obvious errors. All dates are given in modern form (i.e., not *more veneto*).

Abbreviations

DBI	*Dizionario biografico degli italiani.* Rome: Istituto della Enciclopedia italiana, 1960–.
Gaspari	Gaetano Gaspari, *Catalogo della biblioteca del Liceo musicale di Bologna*, 5 vols. Bologna: Libreria Romagnoli dall'Acqua, 1892; repr., Bologna: Forni, 1961.
NG2	*The New Grove Dictionary of Music and Musicians*, 2nd ed. London: Macmillan, 2001.
MGG2	*Die Musik in Geschichte und Gegenwart*, 2nd ed., Personenteil. Kassel: Bärenreiter, 1994–2008.
RISM A/I	Répertoire International des Sources Musicales. *Einzeldrucke vor 1800.* Series A/I/7. Kassel: Bärenreiter, 1971–2003.
RISM B/I	Répertoire International des Sources Musicales, *Recueils imprimés XVIe–XVIIe siècles*, vol. 1, *Liste chronologique.* Munich: Henle Verlag, 1960.

Sigla

B-Bc	Brussels, Conservatoire Royal de Musique, Bibliothèque / Koninklijk Conservatorium, Bibliotheek
GB-Lbl	London, The British Library
GB-Och	Oxford, Christ Church Library
I-Baf	Bologna, Accademia Filarmonica
I-Bc	Bologna, Civico Museo Bibliografico Musicale
I-BGc	Bergamo, Biblioteca Civica "Angelo Mai," Consorzio della Misericordia Maggiore, Archivi Storici
I-BRs	Brescia, Biblioteca del Seminario
I-FZac	Faenza, Biblioteca Capitolare
I-Pas	Padua, Archivio di Stato
I-Pasd	Padua, Archivio Storico Diocesano
I-Pci	Padua, Biblioteca Civica
I-Pu	Padua, Biblioteca Universitaria
I-Rasv	Rome, Archivio Segreto Vaticano
I-RAaa	Ravenna, Archivio Storico Arcivescovile

I-Vas	Venice, Archivio di Stato
I-Vasp	Venice, Archivio Storico del Patriarcato
I-Vnm	Venice, Biblioteca Nazionale Marciana
I-Vmc	Venice, Biblioteca del Museo Civico Correr d'arte e storia veneziana
I-VIb	Vicenza, Biblioteca Bertoliana
PL-WRu	Wrocław, Biblioteka Uniwersitecka
S-Uu	Uppsala, Universitetsbiblioteket
US-Wc	Washington, D.C., Library of Congress, Music Division

Acknowledgments

The research for this edition was carried out at many institutions both in and outside of Italy. Thanks are therefore due to the staff of the following institutions: the Archivio di Stato (particularly Dr. Michela dal Borgo and Dr. Alessandra Schiavon), the Biblioteca Marciana, the Biblioteca Correr di arte e storia veneziana, the Archivio storico del Patriarcato, and the Archivio IRE, all in Venice; the Museo Internazionale e Biblioteca della Musica and Biblioteca dell'Archiginnasio, both in Bologna; the Archivio Storico Diocesano and Biblioteca Universitaria, both in Padua; the Library of Congress, Washington, D.C.; Christ Church Library, Oxford; the Universitetsbibliotek, Uppsala (particularly Kia Hedell, director of the Section for Manuscripts and Music); the Bodleian Library, Oxford (particularly Martin Holmes, Alfred Brendel Curator of Music); the Biblioteka Uniwersytecka, Wrocław (particularly Mirosław Osowski, director of the Music Department); and the Koninklijke Bibliotheek van België/Bibliothèque royale de Belgique, Brussels (particularly Karin Pairon).

Numerous scholars in Italy and beyond have contributed to the making of this work, providing everything from essential information to much-needed encouragement. I thank Michael Talbot (University of Liverpool) for assistance of various kinds with the Christ Church, Oxford, copy of the Phalèse edition of the *Sacra Corona*; Eleanor Selfridge-Field (Stanford University); Dr. Lavinia Prosdocimi (Biblioteca Universitaria, Padua) and Dr. Mariella Magliani (Biblioteca Civica, Padua), for help with the genealogical manuscripts held in the Biblioteca Civica; Dr. Francesca Fantini D'Onofrio (director of the Archivio di Stato, Padua); Prof. Arnaldo Morelli (University of L'Aquila), for help in identifying Roman musicians named in the records of the Venetian *procuratia*; Prof. Morelli and Prof. Patrizio Barbieri for discussions of the acoustical properties of wooden platforms used in early motet performances; Dr. Giuseppe Ellero (Istituti di Ricovero ed Educazione, Venice), for information on the history of the rebuilding of the Ospedaletto; Monsignor Pierantonio Gios (Archivio Storico Diocesano, Padua), for assistance in reconstructing the respective family histories of Federico Sculazzon and Bartolomeo Marcesso, the dedicatee and editor of the *Sacra Corona*; Don Marcello Bettin (parish priest of San Michele delle Badesse) and Don Lorenzo Biasion (parish priest at San Giorgio delle Pertiche), for allowing access to their parish records; and, for helpful information on local history, Silvano Rettore (at San Michele delle Badesse) and Bruno Caon (at San Giorgio delle Pertiche).

For help translating the original manuscript of this edition from Italian to English, I am grateful to Dr. Richard Bates and Dr. Elisabetta Zoni, and to Prof. Lorenzo Bianconi (University of Bologna) and Prof. Franco Piperno (University of Rome "La Sapienza") for referring me to these translators. For help with the motet texts, I thank Prof. Marco Leone (University of Salento) and Prof. Clizia Carminati (University of Bergamo), who offered numerous helpful suggestions, and Esther Criscuola de Laix, who prepared the English translations. Finally, I owe a great debt of gratitude to the staff of A-R Editions for their detailed advice and constant encouragement at every stage of the publication process.

Introduction

The anthology *Sacra Corona: Motetti a due, e trè voci di diversi eccellentissimi autori moderni* (Venice, 1656) contains twenty-three sacred works for two and three voices and basso continuo by twelve different composers: Giovanni Rovetta, Natale Monferrato, Francesco Cavalli, Massimiliano Neri, Giovanni Battista Volpe, Pietro Andrea Ziani, Biagio Marini, Maurizio Cazzati, Orazio Tarditi, Stefano Filippini, Barbara Strozzi, and Simone Vesi. All are represented by two compositions each except for Cavalli (three) and Strozzi and Vesi (one each).

Although the *Sacra Corona* has attracted recent scholarly attention,[1] it has yet to receive a specialized study of its own. One curious feature of the collection is the ordering of the works and composers within it, as given in the index (*tavola*) at the end of each partbook. The first six compositions are by the first six musicians in the list above, whose ordering within the collection—at least in the Basso Continuo partbook, which is the only partbook to include all twenty-three pieces—reflects the hierarchy of their positions at the ducal chapel of San Marco: Rovetta was chapelmaster, Monferrato was vice-chapelmaster, Cavalli and Neri were the two organists, Volpe held the position known as *organista de' nicchie* (organist of the niches),[2] and Ziani was a singer. In addition, Barbara Strozzi's composition (no. 12, "Quis dabit mihi tantam charitatem") is placed about halfway through the book as the first of the group of three-voice motets; its placement in the book may have been intended as an act of gallantry.

Another curious feature of the *Sacra Corona* is the presence of two distinct groups of composers within the collection: those who lived and worked in Venice (hereafter called "the Venetian group") and those from outside (the "non-Venetian" group). Besides the San Marco composers mentioned above, Biagio Marini and Barbara Strozzi can also be counted within the Venetian group. Marini had worked twice at San Marco, though he was employed at Vicenza Cathedral when the *Sacra Corona* was published.[3] He may have had a central role in the planning and conception of the anthology (see below); in any case, his name seems to form a link between the composers from San Marco and those of the non-Venetian group. Strozzi was a singer who worked and lived on her own, as well as a prominent figure in the musical academies of Venice; although she had no professional musical position in Venice, she had a connection to the San Marco composers by way of her musical studies with Cavalli.

The composers of the non-Venetian group—Maurizio Cazzati, Orazio Tarditi, Stefano Filippini, and Simone Vesi—all had either origins or positions in the easternmost part of the Po Valley, which at that time was part of the Papal States. All were clergymen and often prominent figures, and all had connections to the Romagna, though some also maintained ties with Venice (especially in having their compositions printed there).

In addition, two subgroups can be distinguished within the Venetian group of composers: those who were well established at San Marco and worked there for their entire career (Rovetta, Volpe, Cavalli, and Monferrato), and those who later worked outside of Venice with varying degrees of success (Neri, Marini, and Ziani). In general, the composers of the first subgroup had solid relations with prominent Venetian families (such as the Cavalli, the Lando, and the Grimani) and thus with the *procuratia de supra*, the governing body of the chapel. The three composers of the second subgroup were only a few of many members of the ducal chapel who sought employment elsewhere in the later decades of the seventeenth century, notably at princely courts in northern Europe. In contrast to the composers who remained at San Marco, they hailed primarily from cities of the Venetian Terraferma (Neri from Verona, Marini from Brescia)—a region with close historical and political ties to the Holy Roman Empire, which these composers exploited in later stages of their careers. Lacking strong support from the *procuratia*, these composers found it more convenient to seek positions elsewhere in and beyond Venetian territory, though often at institutions no less worthy than San Marco.[4]

One final intriguing feature of the collection is the relative obscurity of its compiler, Bartolomeo Marcesso, and its dedicatee, Federico Sculazzon; the latter in particular seems to have belonged not to Venice's patrician classes but to the mercantile class.[5] This edition brings to light new archival findings on these two figures, examining their ties to each other and to the composers and printer of the *Sacra Corona*. It further speculates on possible occasions for the collection's publication, based on both the background of the printer, Francesco Magni—heir to the prominent Gardano printing firm—and the political climate in Venice, then engaged in war with the Ottoman Empire.

The Composers and Their Music

The Venetian Group

Indeed, musical positions at San Marco were relatively undemanding compared to other major European musical chapels at the time. The duties of the chapelmaster were concentrated primarily around major feast days and special occasions, though musicians of lesser rank (such as singers, organists, and other instrumentalists) also had ample opportunities for music-making outside the chapel as well, most notably in theaters, other churches, the *scuole*, and the *ospedali*. All the positions were relatively stable; the *procuratori* typically only resigned themselves to dismissing musicians after repeated, unjustified, and important absences, or in cases of clear indiscipline. This situation contrasted vastly with that of court musical establishments like that of Vienna, where musicians—singers, instrumentalists, and chapelmasters—were called on almost constantly to perform at church services, in the emperor's private apartments, and at various special performances (such as operas) at court.[6]

Giovanni Rovetta's family probably had its roots in the town of the same name in Valle Seriana.[7] Many individuals with the name Rovetta—whose exact relationship to the composers of the same name is difficult to demonstrate today—are documented as working in the silk and wool industry in early-sixteenth-century Venice.[8] Possibly belonging to one of these families was Alberto Rovetta, a violinist whose activity is well documented at several Venetian institutions, especially the school of San Giovanni Evangelista,[9] located close to the district of San Giovanni Decollato (or San Zan Degolà, as it was known in Venetian dialect); he, and later his son Giacomo and his grandson Giovanni, lived in that district through the early seventeenth century.[10] Giacomo reached even greater renown than his father, eventually obtaining a permanent position in the ducal chapel as a violinist with important solo duties;[11] his son Giovanni, in turn, began his own career when his father was still at the height of his powers. When the *Sacra Corona* was published, Giovanni Rovetta had a stable position as chapelmaster at San Marco, and his tenure there proceeded calmly and without incident till his death in 1668. He seems to have attempted to extend his musical career to the theaters of Venice as well, though without success (perhaps because of the essentially undramatic nature of his music).[12]

Rovetta's motets in the *Sacra Corona* are good representatives of his overall style. Apart from the occasional borrowing of melodic and harmonic formulas, Giovanni Rovetta's musical output is quite distinct from that of his predecessor Claudio Monteverdi: while Monteverdi's works often consist of several strongly contrasting shorter sections, Rovetta's are built from longer, less contrasting blocks of musical material—an approach Cavalli would later take on an even larger scale in his sacred works.[13] Although the overall effect is less intensely expressive than Monteverdi, it is somewhat more relaxed, serene, and solemn—and thus particularly well suited to the desires of Rovetta's patrons, the *procuratori* of San Marco, who were keen to celebrate the virtues of Catholic orthodoxy and the power of the Most Serene Republic with suitably lengthy, solemn compositions.

Natale Monferrato. Recent biographical and bibliographical research has illuminated much about Monferrato's life, career, and music.[14] He too was employed by the ducal chapel for the bulk of of his musical career, though he also held positions at the Venetian *ospedali*, particularly the Mendicanti. After an early, unsuccessful attempt in 1639 to apply for the post of second organist, he was able to enter the chapel as a singer later that year, going on to become vice-chapelmaster in 1647 (though he seems to have carried out similar duties even earlier). When Cavalli died in 1676, Monferrato succeeded him as chapelmaster.

Monferrato's compositions are often quite lengthy, organized in long, clearly distinct sections for varying vocal forces according to the expressive content of the text, though he also probably intended in this way to display the vocal brilliance of the virtuoso performers at the *ospedali*. In this way, the formal structure of his compositions often resembles that of the cantata, eschewing the strictly contrapuntal texture and formal unity of the late Renaissance motet. "Peccator, si tu times" (no. 16), which numbers almost three hundred measures in the present edition, is a representative example of this style; its opening three text sections—each beginning with the word "Peccator" and ending with the words "curre ad Mariam"—are set as three strophes for canto (mm. 1–23), alto (mm. 24–43), and baritone (mm. 44–64). Even in the tutti passages, strict imitation between the voices is not always observed (see, e.g., mm. 65–86, mm. 140–239, and 240–76).

The life and works of *Francesco Cavalli* have been so thoroughly investigated elsewhere as to make any attempt to summarize them here superfluous.[15] Most scholarly investigation of his music thus far has centered on his operas and stage works, of which a complete edition is currently in progress.[16] Yet sacred music was an integral part of his oeuvre, and contemporary documentation attests to Cavalli's deep roots in the ducal chapel and the connections he formed with its members.[17] Furthermore, he is known to have worked occasionally in other important Venetian churches and *scuole*, making it likely that his sacred compositions—including the motets from the *Sacra Corona*—were performed outside San Marco as well.[18]

Massimiliano Neri was one of the major musical figures in mid-seventeenth-century Venice. He came from a prominent Veronese musical family whose members were active in the late sixteenth and early seventeenth centuries both in Verona's cathedral and at some important foreign courts (including Munich, Neuburg, Düsseldorf, and perhaps Vienna); he and his family came to Venice from Verona while he was still a boy, probably around 1631. Early in his Venetian career he was taken under the wing of Giacomo Soranzo, a member of a highly regarded aristocratic family.[19] In 1644 he was elected organist at the church of Santi Giovanni e Paolo, and he became first organist at San Marco later that year. Besides his activities at San Marco and Santi Giovanni e Paolo, Neri worked in several other prestigious musical institutions in Venice, which certainly offered ample performance opportunities for both his vocal and his instrumental works. One of very few documented records of Neri's performances comes down to us by accident: in 1658 Neri organized a festive vespers service for the patronal feast of the church of Santa Caterina but was tried by the Venetian authorities for making the service too long. One witness for the defense, Carlo Fedeli—also a musician at San Marco—testified that, "in order to finish quickly, he [Neri] left out of the vespers certain motets that should be performed, as well as sonatas."[20] Only thanks to this probably accidental evidence is it known that motets and sonatas—most likely composed by Neri—were performed at that service.

Neri is best known today as a composer of instrumental ensemble music, primarily by way of transcriptions made in the nineteenth and early twentieth centuries of sources now lost or damaged. His vocal music, on the other hand, seems to have been relatively neglected; he published only one single-author collection of vocal music (*Motetti a due e tre voci libro primo . . . opera terza* [Venice: Magni, 1664; RISM A/I N404]), dedicated to the *procuratori* of San Marco, and of which only one piece—"Dignare me" for two sopranos and basso continuo—has come down to us, albeit only in transcription.[21] Neri's two motets in the *Sacra Corona* are thus his only sacred vocal compositions that have come down to us from their original source, and they are his only known contributions to a contemporary anthology of vocal music. They, like the pieces in Neri's *Motetti a due e tre voci*, were most likely composed for performance at San Marco;[22] this seems confirmed by the fact that one of them, "Ad charismata caelorum," was later reprinted with significant variants in the *Motetti a due e tre voci* (see the appendix).

Giovanni Battista Volpe (known as "Rovettino") was Rovetta's nephew.[23] Although it was Rovetta who guided his nephew's first steps in the ducal chapel and sponsored his ordination as a priest,[24] Volpe was not Rovetta's pupil but Francesco Cavalli's, as stated in the dedicatory letter to Rovetta's *Madrigali concertati a due, tre, e quattro voci libro terzo* (Venice: Alessandro Vincenti, 1645), which Volpe collected and edited.[25] Relations between Giovanni Rovetta and Francesco Cavalli were both friendly and longstanding, as is borne out by a fortuitously surviving letter written by Rovetta to Cavalli's father, Giovanni Battista Caletti, in which Rovetta advocates the marriage of his sister Elena to Cavalli.[26] The marriage did not materialize; instead, many years later, Cavalli married Maria Loredan-Schiavina, while Elena married one "Antonio de Grandis d[ett]o Volpe q[uondam] Martin," from whom she later separated for unknown reasons (which perhaps explains why their son Giovanni Battista preferred to be known by his natural father's nickname, and not by the family name).[27] The letter provides eloquent testimony to the ways members of the ducal chapel sought to reinforce their positions by creating family ties with other members.

Volpe's motets in the *Sacra Corona* are among his few known compositions; he is also known to have composed an opera, *Gli amori di Apollo e di Leucotoe*, but little else survives from him.[28] Even these few compositions, however, demonstrate that he had remarkable musical talent, particularly an unusual harmonic and contrapuntal sensibility. He is remembered for these qualities by Francesco Gasparini in his basso continuo treatise, *L'armonico pratico al cimbalo* (originally published 1708),[29] and his two *Sacra Corona* compositions (nos. 5 and 20 in this edition) confirm this reputation.

Pietro Ziani served as one of the many singers at San Marco at the time of the publication of the *Sacra Corona*. His fairly average salary suggests that he did not have soloistic duties,[30] though he was active from around 1653 as an opera composer in Venetian theaters.[31] He was Venetian by birth,[32] and his lifelong residency in Venice is quite well documented: from 1640 he belonged to the Lateran congregation of Santissimo Salvatore (as did two brothers of the printer Francesco Magni),[33] and he also served as organist at the church adjacent to their monastery, located a short distance from the Magni print shop.[34]

Lacking an official professional title, *Barbara Strozzi* is given the courtesy title "Virtuosissima Signora" in the *tavola* of the *Sacra Corona*. Although she did compose one collection of sacred music (*Sacri musicali affetti*, op. 5, 1655), she lacked the direct professional ties to San Marco shared by most of the other composers; instead, her works were composed specifically for the Accademia degli Unisoni, founded by her adoptive father, the well-known poet and man of letters Giulio Strozzi.[35] Yet academies occasionally held meetings for devotional purposes in churches close to their usual meeting places, and such meetings could certainly include performances of motets, masses, and other sacred compositions, especially in academies like the Unisoni that placed particular emphasis on music.[36] Although there is relatively little specific documentation on the Unisoni compared to other academies of the time,[37] it is possible that they too may occasionally have engaged in prayer or quasi-liturgical activities, during which Strozzi's deeply devotional motet may have found a place.[38] The piece might also have been suitable for the musical performances that accompanied Holy Week observances at San Marco, which in 1656 featured "extraordinary" singers brought in from outside the chapel, just as had been done for the dogal entry earlier that year and for the celebration of the victory at the Dardanelles.[39] Finally, another possible connection to San Marco can be found in the ties between Giulio Strozzi and the circle of musicians around Monteverdi and later Cavalli, who had been Barbara Strozzi's teacher.

Although some members of both the Venetian and non-Venetian groups were firmly rooted in their home institutions (San Marco in Venice, various local cathedrals and churches in the Romagna), others were obliged to seek employment elsewhere. In the Venetian group, as we have seen, this was the case with Neri, Ziani, and Marini, who lacked the wholehearted support of the *procuratia* and thus had fewer career prospects within Venice. Within the non-Venetian group, Cazzati's position as a member of the secular clergy placed him in a similar situation of instability, since he—unlike Filippini and Tarditi—did not reside permanently within a monastic community.

In fact, composers from the two groups found themselves competing for the same positions. In 1656 and 1657, there was significant jockeying between Ziani, Marini, and Cazzati for the positions of chapelmaster at the cathedrals of Bergamo and Vicenza and at the Accademia della Morte in Ferrara. In 1656 Marini abandoned his position as chapelmaster of the cathedral in Vicenza.[40] Pietro Andrea Ziani, then employed as a singer at San Marco, applied for the position but failed to appear on both the dates on which he was called.[41] At the same time Maurizio Cazzati left his post in the cathedral of Bergamo and was succeeded by Ziani, who remained there till 1659.[42] In April 1653 Cazzati had taken over the direction of the Accademia della Morte, replacing Marini, who had worked there between October 1652 and April 1653.[43]

In 1662 Ziani resigned his position at San Marco[44] and moved to Vienna, where he worked as vice-chapelmaster of the dowager Empress Eleonora until 1669. After that, he returned to Venice to serve as first organist at San Marco;[45] as one slightly later but still fairly reliable document puts it, "although [in Vienna] he received one hundred thalers a month in wages due to the many ordinary and extraordinary duties . . . he returned again to this city for organ duties only, with less income but less work."[46]

The Non-Venetian Group

Maurizio Cazzati's early years were spent at the small court of Guastalla, where his father was a notary, and most of his career was spent in various parts of northern Italy (Bergamo, Ferrara, Bologna, and Mantua).[47] Between April 1653 and August 1657[48] Cazzati served as chapelmaster at the cathedral in Bergamo, and it seems likely that both of his motets in the *Sacra Corona*—"Salve mundi triumphatrix" (no. 8) and "Obstupescite gentes" (no. 18)—were composed for the remarkable and well-documented performances that took place yearly at the feast of the Assumption of the Virgin (15 August).[49] It is interesting to note, however, that "Obstupescite" was apparently intended for use at the feasts of other virgin saints as well, since it is headed "Per una Vergine, overo della Madona" (see plate 3); in fact, the name "Maria" appears only once in the source (Canto 1, mm. 38–39), while the generic "N." is used in most other cases to allow the substitution of another saint's name. The reappearance of "Obstupescite gentes" many years later in Cazzati's *Mottetti a due, tre e quattro . . . opera terza* (op. 3; Bologna, 1670)[50]—published after Cazzati had for some time already held the post of chapelmaster at San Petronio in Bologna—does not necessarily contradict the hypothesis that it was originally composed for the Marian festivities in Bergamo, for Cazzati seems to have maintained cordial relations with Bergamo even during his tenure in Bologna. On the title pages of several of his Bologna publications, he refers to himself as a member of the Accademia degli Eccitati, a prominent Bergamese academy,[51] and his *Salmi per tutto l'anno a otto voci brevi e commodi per cantare con uno o due organi* (Bologna: Antonio Pisarri, 1660)[52] is dedicated to two fellow members of the Eccitati, Ruggiero and Giovanni Battista Alessandri.

In contrast to the composers associated with San Marco, who felt the direct influence of Monteverdi and whose music usually has a monumental, grandiose quality commensurate with the elaborate musical and liturgical demands of the ducal chapel, the composers from outside Venice seem to have worked in more sober, less grandiose styles suited to the more modest forces available to them in the smaller institutions in which they worked.[53] Surviving documentation from these institutions and others nearby (i.e., in Rimini, Ravenna, Padua, and Bergamo, among others) does not suggest that a need was felt for particularly elaborate music; as a result, the compositions of the non-Venetian group tend to be shorter than those of the Venetian group, rarely exceeding one hundred measures.[54] One exception, Cazzati's monumental "Obstupescite gentes," probably composed for the feast of the Assumption, can be explained by the fact that this feast had particular prominence in Bergamo, while the length of Cazzati's other *Sacra Corona* composition, "Salve mundi triumphatrix," is compensated for by its repetitive, quasi-strophic formal structure (mm. 104–39 are essentially a repeat of mm. 68–103).

Cazzati initiated a general reorganization of the musical chapels in both Bergamo and Bologna. In both cases this led to a standardization of the instrumental ensembles, with strings given greater prominence than wind instruments.[55] As a result, Cazzati's numerous surviving compositions[56] feature highly standardized combinations of vocal and instrumental forces and an abundant use of stereotyped melodic and harmonic formulas, which in turn often results in somewhat slipshod harmonic and contrapuntal writing (a criticism leveled by some of his contemporaries).[57] Nevertheless, his music enjoyed great success during his lifetime, to judge from the many reprints of his numerous collections and the many manuscript copies of individual compositions; the standardized nature of his compositions made them adaptable to various vocal and instrumental combinations, and their organization into distinct lengthy sections also made it possible to make cuts as needed. These characteristics can be noted in Cazzati's two compositions in the *Sacra Corona*. "Obstupescite gentes" (no. 18) in particular shows his preference for sharp, sudden sonic contrasts over the contrapuntal niceties that were beginning to be regarded as somewhat old-fashioned at mid-century; as a result, the piece has a markedly sectional character. Furthermore, its organization into discrete, well-defined sections suggests the possibility of performance in a concertato style, with the triple-meter tutti sections (mm. 1–35, 50–84, and 136–235 respectively) entrusted to larger forces (with more than one singer to a part and possible instrumental doublings) and the more virtuosic duple-meter sections (mm. 36–49 and 85–135) to soloists.[58]

Orazio Tarditi. Recent research has uncovered much new biographical information on Orazio Tarditi, who held several positions throughout the Romagna during the course of his career but also maintained a fixed abode in Ravenna as a monk at the Camaldolite monastery.[59] Because of his connection to Ravenna, he is perhaps the one composer of the *Sacra Corona* most likely to have had personal contact with the Ravenna branch of the Magni family, to which the collection's printer, Francesco Magni, belonged, though much of his music was published instead by Magni's competitor Alessandro Vincenti.[60]

Besides a few youthful peregrinations, including a brief period of employment in 1629 as organist at the monastery of his order at San Michele di Murano (near Venice),[61] most of Tarditi's career was spent fairly close to his native town: he was chapelmaster at the cathedrals of Forlì (1639), Iesi (1644–45), and Faenza (1647–70). Like Filippini, he enjoyed the support of various high-ranking clergymen with connections to the Roman curia. In Iesi, for example, he was in the service of the "Most Eminent Card. Cenci," and in Faenza he served the archbishop, Cardinal Carlo Rossetti, "by whom, both for his virtue and for his pleasant nature, he was loved most warmly."[62] Rossetti was the dedicatee of Tarditi's *Sacri concertus duobus et tribus vocibus* (op. 35, 1655; RISM A/I T210).[63]

Like Neri and Cazzati, Tarditi later republished one his contributions to the *Sacra Corona*—"Victoriam, victoriam" (no. 10)—in one of his own collections, the *Concerto il trigesimo quinto di motetti a doi, e tre voci, alcuni con violini et una messa concertata a tre voci* (Venice: Alessandro Vincenti, 1663).[64] The inclusion of this warlike motet in a collection dedicated to the abbot-general of the Camaldolite order, Pietro Ferracci—especially on the occasion of the latter's election by Pope Alexander VII—seems at first slightly incongruous, though it is complemented by an elaborate metaphor in Tarditi's dedication comparing music to war and invoking the dedicatee's coat of arms: "Music [seems] but a harsh battle, in which there are some who flee, some who attack; some who sigh, some who delight; some who advance, some who fall; some who are still, some who are ever on the prowl"; thus, motivated by Isocrates's saying that "war is driven by iron and gold" (*Bella ferro, et auro animantur*), the collection is dedicated "to the gold and iron of your most noble coat of arms."[65]

Stefano Filippini's "Laetare Mater Ecclesia" (no. 23), a jubilant praise of St. Augustine as a destroyer of heresy, stands out in the *Sacra Corona* but can be explained by the composer's own biography. Since Filippini was an Augustinian friar and held a doctorate in theology, texts praising the energetic work of his order in quashing heresy are not at all exceptional in his motet output. His first collection, *Concerti sacri a 2.3.4. e 5. voci . . . libro primo, opera seconda* (Ancona, 1652),[66] includes three such motets: "Exultat hodie" (for cantus, altus, and tenor), "En fulget in summo populi vertice" (for two cantus voices and bass), and "Adeste, adeste dilectissimi Manicheorum filii" (for two cantus voices, altus, tenor, and bass):

> Exultat hodie caelorum caetus de triumpho Michaelis; nam signifer salutis in ima trusit tartara, & Princeps caelestis fulminavit rebelles. . . . In die tantae laetitiae canite laetantes ejus laudes, & victorias.
>
> (Today the host of heaven exults in the triumph of Michael, for the standardbearer of salvation has thrust the rebels into the depths of Tartarus, and the prince of heaven has struck them down . . . On a day of such great joy sing his praises and victories joyfully.)

* * *

> En fulget in sum[m]o poli vertice gloria Sa[n]ctorum Patrum decus haereticorum terror Augustinus . . .
>
> (Behold how Augustine shines forth at the highest summit of heaven: the glory of the people, the honor of the holy fathers, the terror of heretics . . .)

* * *

> Adeste, adeste dilectissimi Manichoorum filii ecce catholicae propugnator fidei Augustinus justitiae indutus lorica[m], et galea[m] salutis qua[m] fortiter certat, qua[m] viriliter pugnat ut antiquam nostrorum Religionem dissipet, diruat, disperdat . . .
>
> (Come forth, beloved children of the Manicheans; behold, Augustine, the champion of the Catholic faith, having put on the breastplate of justice and the helmet of salvation, fights so bravely, battles so manfully . . .)

Filippini spent two separate periods in Rome, from 1643 to 1648 and from 1655 to 1657, both of which were important for his musical career.[67] The first period saw the publication of his first surviving works, published in two anthologies collected by Canon Florido de Silvestris da Barbarano.[68] During Filippini's second stay in Rome, he published *Messe a tre voci . . . opera quinta* (Venice: Maurizio Balmonti, 1656; RISM A/I F741), dedicating it to Monsignor Carlo Antonio Dondino, one of the leading figures in the Roman curia, yet there is no evidence—either from the dedication to this collection or elsewhere—that he held an official position in Rome at this period. He may, however, have been in the entourage of the bishop of Ravenna, Luca Torreggiani, who was then in Rome and who recommended him as a replacement for the chapelmaster at Ravenna Cathedral, Giovanni Vincenzo Sarti.[69]

A context for Filippini's motet can be found in the theological debates that were raging at that time between Roman Catholicism and various Protestant factions that were attempting to gain ground in Italy. Of these, Jansenism was regarded as especially dangerous, since it attempted to insinuate itself into the church by way of specious interpretations of Augustine's positions (and, indeed, Jansen's most important and influential work was titled *Augustinus*). Specifically, Jansenism denied the role of free will in salvation and regarded acts of devotion as having little effect on salvation. In 1642, just before Filippini's first compositions appeared in Rome, Fabio Chigi (the future pope Alexander VII) published the papal bull *In eminenti*, which condemned Jansenism.[70] These themes were debated even within the Roman

Catholic Church, and especially between the Jesuits and the Augustinian order; even though the debate between the Jesuits and the Augustinians never reached the virulence of that between Jansenists and Catholics, it was latent in many publications of the period and periodically rose to the surface.[71] As an Augustinian, Filippini—perhaps influenced by senior figures in his order—may have wanted to make his own musical contributions to this ongoing debate against heresy. Even so, the presence of his Augustinian motet in the *Sacra Corona* is slightly puzzling given the miscellaneous nature of this and other contemporary motet collections, whose texts were often as general as possible in order to facilitate the widest possible dissemination (see, for example, Cazzati's "Obstupescite gentes" [no. 18], which offers the option of changing the name of the saint invoked in the text). Given the pride of place offered to Venetian composers within the *Sacra Corona*, the inclusion of this motet may have been intended as a testimony to the Venetian state's orthodox position in this theological debate.[72] In addition, given that music had become such an important feature of the sacramental and liturgical acts of which Jansenism disapproved, it is perhaps no coincidence that motets celebrating these acts—most specifically the Eucharist—are frequently to be found in motet collections from this period, including the *Sacra Corona* (nos. 4, 6, 13, and 20).

Simone Vesi was a canon at Padua Cathedral and worked as chapelmaster of the local bishop's private chapel from the beginning of his documented activity as a composer. His family roots and early musical training were in Forlì, in the Romagna;[73] his name is given as "Simon Vesi da Forlì capellano del Duomo di Padova" in his first musical publication,[74] and his other publications include similar references to his origins.[75] In Forlì he probably came into contact with other non-Venetian composers of the *Sacra Corona*, especially Filippini and Tarditi.[76] He mentions his "absence" from his native town in the dedication to his *Salmi concertati a 3. 4. 5. & a 6. con stromenti con il secondo choro ad libitum . . . opera quarta* (1656); although the numerous lacunae in the contemporary documentation from Padua make it difficult to know the details,[77] it is certainly possible that he made one or more short visits to Forlì during this period, as other surviving evidence suggests.[78]

Despite a failed bid to become chapelmaster of Padua Cathedral in 1647 (the position went instead to Francesco Petrobelli),[79] Vesi served (at least from 1648) as master of the private chapel of Giorgio Corner, bishop of Padua, who played an important role in the negotiations between Venice and Rome concerning the readmission of the Jesuits to Venice in 1657 (see "The Political Context" below). He probably began working for Corner shortly before 1648, since his dedication to the bishop in his *Motetti e salmi a voce sola* (1648) expresses gratitude "that Your Most Reverend Eminence has deigned to take me as your chapelmaster, choosing me above all others."[80] All Vesi's works were published in Venice by the publishing houses of Magni and Gardano.[81]

The Printer

As noted above, almost all the composers in the non-Venetian group of contributors to the collection either originated or worked in the Romagna, especially along the Adriatic coast. The family of the Venetian printer Francesco Magni had its origins in the same region, in Ravenna, and several recent and less recent studies have expanded our knowledge of this printer and his family history.[82] Various members of the Magni family are documented in late-sixteenth-century Ravenna as musicians (singers, organists, and composers), usually in monasteries in and near the city; most notable among these was Benedetto Magni (1574–1637), who served as organist of Ravenna Cathedral under Cardinal Pietro Aldobrandini.[83] In the first decade of the seventeenth century, Benedetto's brother Bartolomeo moved to Venice and became the trusted assistant of Angelo Gardano, whose daughter, Diamante, he later married.[84] In 1612 Benedetto Magni became involved in the "Arte de' Libreri, stampadori e ligadori" (the Venetian printers' and publishers' guild), and he eventually inherited his father-in-law's business.[85] Magni's increasing importance within Gardano's firm is reflected on the title pages of his publications, proceeding from "Stampa del Gardano" on his earliest publications to "Nella Stamperia del Gardano appresso Bartolomeo Magni" and finally "Stampa del Gardano Aere Bartolomeo Magni." Only once his son Francesco took over the business in 1650 did the name Gardano finally disappear from the firm's title pages, having been replaced with "Appresso Francesco Magni." At the time of the publication of the *Sacra Corona*, Francesco had been head of the firm for six years; five years before, he had purchased new, somewhat more upscale premises for the shop on the Piazza San Marco.[86]

Given that Bartolomeo and Francesco Magni published works by Benedetto Magni and other musicians from Ravenna, it seems that the Venetian branch of the Magni family remained in close contact with the Ravenna branch. In addition, many members of the Venetian branch kept up the family tradition of becoming canons regular of the Lateran congregation of Santissimo Salvatore, one of whose two Venetian monasteries was located close to the Gardano-Magni print shop.[87]

The Compiler

Bartolomeo Marcesso, the compiler and collector of the *Sacra Corona*, is named as one of the witnesses to the document formalizing Magni's purchase of a new workshop near San Marco.[88] Marcesso thus may have been an assistant to Magni just as Bartolomeo Magni had been several decades earlier to Angelo Gardano. But, although Marcesso, like Magni, married a close relative of his employer,[89] he seems not to have fared as well in the printing business. As music publishing declined in Venice in the last decades of the seventeenth century, the Gardano-Magni firm gradually reduced its activities, ceasing business in 1685, by which time Marcesso had set himself up as a hat seller (*baretter*) near the original Magni-Gardano print shop.[90] Other members of the Gardano family had similar businesses,[91] suggesting there were commercial relations between the two workshops.

Marcesso's family origins seem to have been near Padua in the small town of San Michele delle Badesse. Members of the Marcesso family are documented in even the earliest local parish records, which date from 1576, and the name appears continuously in local records well into the seventeenth century.[92] The Marcesso family seems to been an important presence in the community; they owned some land in the vicinity,[93] and one Bartolomeo Marcesso—possibly the grandfather of the Bartolomeo Marcesso who compiled the *Sacra Corona*—was, along with his wife, Felicita, frequently called on to serve as a sponsor at baptisms.[94] His many children included a Sebastiano Marcesso, who may have been Bartolomeo's father.[95] Other documents hint at relations between this Marcesso family and the Venetian patrician family of Tiepolo.[96]

The Dedicatee

The dedicatee of the *Sacra Corona*, Federico Sculazzon, seems to have been of similar social standing to Marcesso. He was certainly not a particularly prominent figure;[97] no Venetian genealogical register, either of this period or from later years, mentions a family of that name until well into the eighteenth century. Marcesso's dedication to Sculazzon (given on p. 2 of this edition) expresses a wish that his collection might "rest on the tips of the two spears, the worthy emblem of Your Excellency's house"; the reference is to the two crossed spears in the coat of arms appearing on the title page (see plate 1), which—especially together with the comment on the "worthiness" of the emblem—might suggest that Sculazzon had military connections.[98]

Sculazzon's family roots should probably be sought in the village of the same name located a few kilometers from the plateau of Asiago, now in the province of Vicenza but, then as now, under the ecclesiastical administration of the diocese of Padua.[99] The family did indeed have military connections with Padua from at least the early seventeenth century, though their activity does not seem to have produced any remarkable results.[100] However, they also possessed some land at Piazzola, on the border between Vicenza and Padua, which they probably inherited.[101]

In this region, at least, the Sculazzon family seems to have been fairly prominent, and its presence is well documented in and around Padua in the 1650s. At this period it consisted of Cesare Sculazzoni, who held the post of duty collector on meat (*datiaro delle Carni*);[102] his wife, Caterina; and several children.[103] It seems likely that Cesare was related to the Federico Sculazzon (Sculazzoni)[104]—more than likely the dedicatee of the *Sacra Corona*—whose residence in the same district as Cesare is documented by a few short but precise entries in the parish register.[105] One of these entries describes him as taking part in a celebratory ceremony at Luvigliano, a small town on the Euganean Hills whose main attraction is still the monumental sixteenth-century Villa dei Vescovi, once the summer residence of the bishops of Padua.[106] Perhaps significantly, a hatter named Angelo (Anzolo) Marcesso—possibly the brother of the compiler of the *Sacra Corona*—is known to have worked in the part of Padua where Federico Sculazzon and other members of his family lived.[107]

The Sculazzon family also seems to have owned a summer residence at San Giorgio delle Pertiche, a town to the north of Padua, though their presence there was only intermittent, and they left no trace in local records.[108] San Giorgio, however, was only a few kilometers from San Michele delle Badesse, home of the Marcesso family, and it is possible that this geographical proximity contributed to a connection between the two families. Indeed, a "Bartolomeo Marcesso di Andrea"—perhaps a nephew of the compiler of the *Sacra Corona*—is known to have managed the land owned by his family near their hometown, and may have performed a similar function for the Sculazzon family.

By the late eighteenth century the family, which by then owned vast areas of land near Padua,[109] changed their name to Scudolanzoni, and indeed one Gaetano Scudolanzoni seems to have achieved some distinction in the literary and aristocratic circles of Padua at that time.[110] Around this time the family seems to have taken specific measures to increase their social standing in the community, including the purchase or commission of an imposing villa in the village of Torre di Burri, near San Giorgio delle Pertiche, still known today as Villa Sculazzoni or Villa Scudolanzoni.[111] Some of the more prominent members of the family applied to join the nobility of Padua,[112] and later to the Imperial (Austrian) nobility;[113] their request was accepted, and their coat of arms—identical to that shown on the title page of the *Sacra Corona* (see plate 1)—was officially registered by the Italian state.[114] Thus it seems certain that the dedicatee of the *Sacra Corona* was a member of the same Paduan family.

Contexts for the *Sacra Corona*

Since the performance of motets in the mid-seventeenth century was often closely bound up with specific occasions and thus with specific venues, it is worth considering briefly under what circumstances the motets of the *Sacra Corona* may have been performed. Venice, of course, offered numerous opportunities for celebratory motets, and the composers who contributed to the *Sacra Corona* produced other collections of similar works that were dedicated to the *procuratori* of the chapel.[115] Motets and other sacred works—including some by composers in the *Sacra Corona*—are also known to have been performed frequently in charitable institutions such as the city's *ospedali*, *scuole*, and smaller churches, many of which were renowned for their musical ensembles. As noted above, Neri had motets performed at his festive vespers at Santa Caterina in 1658; similarly, Monferrato notes in the dedication to his *Motetti a voce sola . . . libro primo* (1655)[116]—addressed to the director of the Ospedale dei Mendicanti—that the proffered motets "were heard by Your Excellency with signs of the greatest pleasure" (*con segni di benignissimo compiacimento furono da V. S. Clarissima ascoltati*), and thus that the motets "that escaped my pen for the practice of the pupils of the place" (*scampati dalla mia penna per esercitio delle allieve del luogo*) could not have found a finer patron.[117] Furthermore, the non-Venetian composers of the *Sacra Corona* would also have had ample opportunities to perform celebratory motets, given that such works—composed by local composers—are known to have been frequently performed at the institutions in the Romagna at which they were employed.[118]

Possible Occasions

The *Sacra Corona* offers very few direct clues to what specific occasion, if any, may have prompted its publication. Although the dedication is notably shorter and more laconic than most others in similar contemporary collections, its curious reference to the "industrious wakefulness" (*industriosa veglianza*) with which "a sacred crown has been made out of such a worthy collection" (*di così degna raccolta, fattone una SACRA CORONA*) may be taken as a testimony that it was prepared quickly, in anticipation of an imminent event. At least two of the motet texts in the collection offer possible clues as to what this event might have been: Tarditi's "Victoriam, victoriam" and Cavalli's "In virtute tua."

Although it can certainly be interpreted metaphorically as well, the "victory" proclaimed in Tarditi's piece may refer to a Venetian military victory that took place during the very year the *Sacra Corona* was published; if so, it is one of several other motets published in Venice at this time to either celebrate or pray for Christian victories against the Turks.[119] On 26 June 1656, during what is now known as the Third Battle of the Dardanelles, the Venetian navy successfully defeated the Turks.[120] The victory was applauded widely in occasional pamphlets, paintings, literary works, and official historical works;[121] its effects may also have been felt in the private lives of the composers in the collection.[122] Special services and musical performances commemorating the victory were held at San Marco and various other Venetian churches; the records of San Marco include payments to various instrumentalists and singers who performed at a "mass sung for the victory won against the Turks on the third [of August, 1656]."[123]

Francesco Cavalli's motet "In virtute tua Domine laetabitur justus" (no. 15), may have been composed to celebrate the election of one of the three doges who succeeded each other in 1655 and 1656: Carlo Contarini (elected 27 March 1655), Francesco Corner (17 May 1656), and Bertucci Valier (15 June 1656).[124] The text of Cavalli's motet alludes to a "crown of precious stones" (*coronam de lapide pretioso*)—undoubtedly a reference to the *camauro*,[125] the headpiece placed on the new doge at the moment of his "entry" or "presentation."[126] For the elections of Contarini and Corner, significant payments are recorded for the maintenance of the "ducal crown" (*corona ducal*),[127] and for the elections of Contarini and Valier extraordinary payments are documented to Rovetta as chapelmaster for engaging extra musicians to accompany the ceremony.[128] Similar annotations for other dogal elections are very rare, and given Cavalli's important role as organist in the ducal chapel, it seems likely that "In virtute tua" was commissioned for one of those celebrations—perhaps most likely Contarini's, given the extra expenditures on the crown associated with his election.[129] At the same time, Francesco Corner cannot be ruled out as a possibility; he and his son, Giorgio Corner, bishop of Padua (for whom both Biagio Marini and Simone Vesi worked as musicians), played major roles in the political negotiations between Venice and Rome at this period (see "The Political Context" below).[130] If so, the motet would probably have been performed during the solemn mass at San Marco attended by the doge the day after the actual coronation.[131] Its presence in the *Sacra Corona* is one of many testimonies to the well-known close ties between Cavalli and the Venetian nobility.[132]

The extra musicians engaged for dogal entries and other major civic occasions were often well-known singers and instrumentalists in the employ of important personages and institutions, Venetian and otherwise, that sought to forge closer political or economic ties with the *procuratia* or the Venetian government. Thus the inclusion of outside musicians at San Marco—even if exceptional and temporary—could serve as a symbolic seal of a political alliance between Venice and another state. During Cavalli's tenure as chapelmaster (1669–73), musicians "borrowed" from various establishments in Rome, Florence, and the German-speaking lands—all areas where Venice sought allies in the battles against the Turks—were known to have served at San Marco on various occasions.[133] Outside musicians—perhaps some from musical chapels directed by the non-Venetian composers of the *Sacra Corona*—may thus have participated in the dogal entries and victory celebrations of 1655 and 1656.

The Political Context

Several other aspects of the political situation in Venice at this period, and particularly in the relations between Venice and the Holy See, suggest a possible milieu for the collaboration of the Venetian and non-Venetian composers of the *Sacra Corona*. As mentioned previously, all of the non-Venetian composers in the *Sacra Corona* came from territory that was part of the Papal States. Venice's relations with the Holy See had certainly improved since the *Interdetto* of 1605–7, but various points of contention still remained. Most notable among these were the questions of the repression of heresy, especially Jansenism; the suppression of minor religious orders (*conventini*) within Venetian territories, which had been ordered by Pope Innocent X in 1652 but never actually carried out;[134] and of the readmission of the Jesuits, who had been expelled from Venice during the *Interdetto*.[135]

During these years, Venice was desperately seeking funding for its naval campaign against the Turks, and the papal state was the sole source from which they could expect to receive such funding.[136] A concession from France or Spain was out of question, since either of these states would have demanded that Venice, in return, become its ally against the other, which in turn would place Venice in a difficult diplomatic position. But the

Holy See itself was in desperate financial straits,[137] and thus it agreed by special papal concession to offer Venice aid in their war against the Turks, granting Venice the proceeds from the sale of goods belonging to the Venetian *conventini* (which otherwise would have been appropriated by the papacy). The Venetian government eventually agreed to receive these funds but found it less easy to concede to the additional papal demand that the Jesuits be readmitted on Venetian territory.[138] Because of strong opposition in the Venetian senate,[139] most of the negotiations on these matters were carried out in secret between high-ranking churchmen and aristocrats in Venice, Rome, and elsewhere. Members of the Corner (Cornaro) family were especially instrumental in these negotiations; besides Cardinal Federico Corner in Rome and Francesco Corner, the doge of Venice,[140] Francesco's son, Bishop Giorgio Corner of Padua,[141] is known to have played an extremely important role in the proceedings that comes to light in the correspondence of Carlo Carafa, the Venetian papal nuncio.[142] These negotiations came to a head in 1656 and 1657, at which time Venice was just beginning to enjoy the benefits of the papal concessions: the Venetian treasury was starting to receive the proceeds of the sales of the goods belonging to the *conventini*;[143] the Roman fleet, as promised, took part in the naval campaign of the following year;[144] and the Venetian senate approved the readmission of the Jesuits in January 1657.[145] The publication at this critical moment of the *Sacra Corona*—a collaborative effort between musicians from Venice and from territories under the control of the papacy—hardly seems to be a coincidence, especially given that two of the composers (Marini and Vesi) were known to have been in Corner's employ.

Giorgio Corner, Bishop of Padua

The central role played by Giorgio Corner in the Venetian-Roman negotiations suggest that it may be worthwhile to investigate his patronage of music,[146] especially his possible relations with the composers contributing to the *Sacra Corona*. Unlike the well-known artistic patronage of his uncle, Cardinal Federico Corner (Cornaro),[147] Giorgio Corner's activities as a patron have received far less investigation.[148] Since 1 January 1653[149] he is known to have supported his own small, private musical chapel, which was distinct in both scope and function from that of the nearby cathedral,[150] even though both were headed by the composer Francesco Petrobelli.[151] The chapel consisted of the singers Bartolomeo Castello, Francesco Guerini,[152] and Filippo Marin; and the violinists Gasparo Rigola[153] and Tommaso Pergola; the activity of this small ensemble is documented, with a few lacunae, until at least March 1654.[154]

Corner's court chapel seems to have served a specifically ceremonial function that may have been closely intertwined with the bishop's own diplomatic activities. According to one contemporary description, the bishop "welcomed several princes, among them Cardinals Bichi and Carafa"[155] and "had a great court"; he also "added more rooms to the episcopal palace and embellished them with the richest adornments, paintings, and precious furnishings without equal" and "took pleasure in chamber music."[156] The reference to the Bishop's fondness for "chamber music" clearly alludes to the small-scale, private nature of his musical chapel, though the mention of such notable names as the Cardinals Antonio Bichi and Carlo Carafa—two of the leading figures in the aforementioned Venetian-Roman negotiations of the 1650s and 60s—hints that Corner may occasionally have turned his private music establishment toward diplomatic ends. One can imagine the motets of the *Sacra Corona* being performed in this milieu, especially in the presence of such notable visitors.

No monthly accounts from Corner's court survive from March 1654 through March 1657, but from that point through July 1657 Biagio Marini's name is listed as "chief chamberlain" (*maestro di camera*, the highest-ranking official position at court).[157] From July 1657 onward the names of the other musicians no longer appear in the court accounts, suggesting that the chapel was disbanded.[158] But Marini was apparently in the bishop's entourage much earlier, for his son, Giovanni Nicola,[159] is known to have been employed at court from at least January 1651.[160] Biagio's name first appears on a notarial document of 1654 from the bishop's court,[161] and in 1656 he and his son are named as beneficiaries of the bishop's will (perhaps in recognition of previous musical services, though this is not specified).[162] In the same year Corner authorized Biagio Marini to travel on his private boat from the Castello del Catajo, the summer villa of the Ferrarese nobleman and musical patron Pio Enea Obizzi, to the episcopal court at Padua.[163] This documentation indicates that Marini was an established and influential member of the Paduan episcopal court in the 1650s and 1660s, and it suggests that he played an instrumental role in establishing its musical organization. Although a detailed examination of Marini's career in Padua is beyond the scope of this study, the fact that he was in the employ of one of the major figures in the Venetian-Roman negotiations of the 1650s seems likely to be a significant factor in the genesis of the *Sacra Corona*.[164]

The Music

The compositions of the *Sacra Corona* are representative of the mid-seventeenth-century motet for solo voices and basso continuo—a genre whose flexibility, adaptability, and small-scale performing forces made it one of the most widespread and popular musical genres of its time. At the same time, these works illustrate—with some notable exceptions—the individual and often highly divergent stylistic characteristics typical of the music of their respective authors. Like many other solo motets of the period, these works are highly sectional in nature, consisting usually of relatively large sections according to the formal division of the text.[165] The sections often feature varying combinations of performers (e.g., solo "arias"—some quite lengthy—vs. tutti passages)[166] and are marked in the music in various ways, either by the use of double barlines or repeat signs (as in no. 1 and no. 6) or by tempo-change indications, some of which are quite expressive and varied (see, e.g., those in no. 13: "Tardo" at m. 15, "Presto" at m. 48, and "Prestissimo" at m. 113).

xix

Various formal strategies are in evidence throughout the collection, covering a wide range of formal possibilities for the midcentury solo motet. One of the simplest and most common of these—the repetition of an opening tutti refrain, either with or without variation, at the end of the piece, with one or more solo (or at least reduced) sections intervening—can be found in three motets (nos. 2, 10, and 14). Some motets feature strophic structures, which had been prevalent in opera for several decades but which by midcentury had taken hold in sacred vocal music and instrumental music as well. As mentioned above, Monferrato's "Peccator, si tu times" (no. 16), for canto, alto, and baritone, opens with three solo strophes, each sung by one of the three voices (mm. 1–64); after a brief, florid trio (mm. 65–86), they proceed with a triple-meter refrain (mm. 87–139) that is repeated with some variation at the end of the piece (mm. 187–239). Other motets feature several solo strophes—usually varied to a greater or lesser extent—that alternate with an unvaried tutti refrain. For example, in Filippini's "Laetare Mater Ecclesia" (no. 23), three solo strophes (mm. 58–65, 77–84, and 96–103, for alto, tenor, and bass, respectively) are separated by an eleven-measure tutti refrain based on the end of the opening tutti section (mm. 47–57). Given that this motet's text, as mentioned above, celebrates St. Augustine's triumph over heresy, the alternation of varied solo strophes with an unvaried tutti refrain seems to emphasize the flow of the individual expression of faith into the ideal unity of the Church. Finally, still other composers seem to have eschewed complex strophe-refrain structures in favor of a simpler succession of short contrasting sections; this procedure appears most prevalently in the works by the older composers (e.g., nos. 1 and 13, both by Rovetta), though composers of the later generation occasionally composed more compact works as well (e.g., nos. 3 and 5, by Cavalli and Volpe, respectively; and nos. 4 and 21, both by Neri).[167]

Notes on Performance

A wide range of continuo instruments were used at San Marco, including theorbo, portative organ, harpsichord, and even harp. Although the use of harp at San Marco is officially documented only after 1669, during Cavalli's tenure as maestro di capella,[168] there is evidence that it was used in the chapel as early as 1617, when a harpist was engaged to play during a display of relics.[169] Although the portative organ was not actually banned during Holy Week, harpsichord seems to have been the instrument of choice during that season,[170] and indeed there is particularly clear documentation of its use in 1656.[171] Harpsichord may thus be an especially appropriate option for the more austere, penitential motets in the *Sacra Corona*, such as those of Strozzi (no. 12), Volpe (nos. 5 and 20), and perhaps Monferrato (nos. 2 and 16).

An important consideration for the performance of motets for a few voices with basso continuo is the positioning of the performers relative to the listener. As Gastone Vio has noted, it was common in the mid-seventeenth century to set up temporary wooden platforms to accommodate musicians at special occasions involving music.[172] Such platforms seem to have served a twofold purpose: besides allowing unimpeded eye contact between performers and directors, they also had the acoustical effect of emphasizing higher frequencies, and thus their use was guided by the same principle as the traditional placement of organs in lofts well above ground level.[173] Several Venetian institutions even featured permanent structures for this purpose, either open or concealed by a grating, several of which still survive today; the one that is perhaps closest to its original configuration is that of the Ospedaletto, which was constructed during Neri's tenure there as *maestro* (1655–63).[174] There is ample documentation that such platforms were built at San Marco, exploiting the existing architectural configuration, and that a specialized builder was employed to construct them in the early seventeenth century.[175] Furthermore, the organs in most Venetian churches were usually placed on a platform above ground level, and it made good acoustic and visual sense for solo singers performing with the organ to be situated on the same platform.[176] Unfortunately, it is not easy to implement this practice today, except in custom-built spaces; a simple dais—which in fact often has the effect of increasing the low frequencies produced by the performers—is not an effective substitute.

Notes

The archival documents cited employ a variety of organizational systems. Most have standard folio numbering, though a few—usually "double-entry" financial records—feature opening numbering (with s referrring to the left side and *d* to the right; e.g., "4s" refers to the left side of the fourth opening). The following abbreviations are used in the notes:

- b. *busta* (envelope or bundle of documents, sometimes including one or more *registri*)
- D ducat (= 24 soldi)
- f. *filza* (loose papers originally held together by a string placed through a hole in the middle)
- £ lira (= 20 soldi)
- reg. *registro* (a bound archival volume)
- s. soldo

1. The most recent scholarly investigations of music from the *Sacra Corona* are Robert L. Kendrick, "Intent and

Intertextuality in Barbara Strozzi's Sacred Music," *Recercare* 14 (2002): 65–98, which examines briefly the general characteristics of the collection and then focuses on the piece by Barbara Strozzi; Daniele Torelli, " 'Sopra le tenebre del mio povero inchiostro': Biagio Marini e la musica sacra," in *Barocco padano 4: Atti del XII convegno sul barocco padano nei secoli XVII–XVIII; Brescia, 14–16 luglio 2003*, ed. Alberto Colzani, Andrea Luppi, Maurizio Padoan (Como: A. M. I. S., 2006), 147–204; and idem, " 'Ecce dedi verba mea in ore tuo': fonti liturgiche e non nei testi del mottetto seicentesco," *Musica tra storia e filologia: Studi in onore di Lino Bianchi* (Rome: Istituto Italiano per la Storia della Musica, 2010), 679–704. Both articles by Torelli focus on Marini's contributions to the *Sacra Corona*; in the second, Torelli remarks on the need for a specialized study of the collection as a whole (p. 198).

2. The *organisti de' nicchie* were two additional organists engaged to accompany singers and instrumentalists on a small positive organ in the side arches of the basilica, usually on major feast days and special occasions. These organists are designated variously in contemporary documents; I follow here the terminology of Reinmar Emans, "Die Musiker des Markusdoms in Venedig: 1651–1708," pts. 1 and 2, *Kirchenmusikalisches Jahrbuch* 65 (1981): 45–81; and 66 (1982): 65–82 (on the *organisti de' nicchie*, see especially pt. 1, 53).

3. Emans, "Musiker des Markusdoms," is probably the most reliable treatment of the subject. Other studies that include lists of the musicians working at the ducal chapel during this period include Eleanor Selfridge-Field, *Venetian Instrumental Music from Gabrieli to Vivaldi*, 3rd ed. (New York: Dover, 1994), 330–48; Paolo Fabbri, *Monteverdi*, trans. Tim Carter (Cambridge: Cambridge University Press, 1994), 296–98 n. 17; and James Harold Moore, *Vespers at St. Mark's: Music of Alessandro Grandi, Giovanni Rovetta and Francesco Cavalli* (Ann Arbor, Mich.: University Microfilms International, 1981).

4. Marini and Neri, for example, both held positions in northern European courts (Marini at Neuburg an der Donau and Düsseldorf, Neri at Cologne and Bonn) and were quick to exploit their connections with these courts in their own careers. On Neri, see Paolo Alberto Rismondo, "Massimiliano Neri (ca. 1618–dopo il 1670) e la famiglia Negri tra Italia e Germania," *Rivista internazionale di musica sacra*, n.s., 26 (2005): 57–109; and *DBI*, s.v. "Neri, Massimiliano" (pp. 260–62), by Paolo Alberto Rismondo. On Marini, see Marco Bizzarini, "Da Brescia a Varsavia: Le musiche policorali di Pietro Lappi con dedica a Sigismondo III (1605)," in *La musica policorale in Italia e nell'Europa centro-orientale fra Cinque e Seicento*, ed. Aleksandra Patalas and Marina Toffetti (Venice: Fondazione Levi, 2012), 208 n. 38.

5. Sculazzon's middling social rank is remarked on in Kendrick, "Intent and Intertextuality," 69; Torelli, " 'Sopra le tenebre del mio povero inchiostro,' " 198–200; and idem, " 'Ecce dedi verba mea in ore tuo,' " 695–98. Equally obscure, however, are the many dedicatees of miscellaneous collections published in this period; see, for example, *Arie a voce sola de diversi auttori* (Venice: Alessandro Vincenti, 1656; RISM B/I 1656⁴), which survives in a single copy in GB-Lbl (shelfmark K4 d 8) and whose compiler and dedicatee—Francesco Tonalli and one "Signor Santo Constanzi"—were certainly not leading figures of the time. This collection, which might be regarded as the secular counterpart of the *Sacra Corona*, contains songs by some of the same composers, including Barbara Strozzi, Francesco Cavalli, Orazio Tarditi, Maurizio Cazzati and [Pietro Andrea] Ziani, as well as other composers not included in the *Sacra Corona* (Giovanni Battista Chinelli, Francesco Lucio, Luigi Pozzi, and the otherwise unknown Giovanni Battista Agneletti). In contrast to the grand gestures of patronage made in many single-author musical collections of the period (such as Francesco Cavalli's *Musiche sacre* [1656], dedicated to Cardinal Giovan Carlo de' Medici), anthologies were often financed by the publishers and perhaps even individual authors themselves. See, for example, the twenty-two anthologies organized by the canon Florido de Silvestris da Barbarano between 1647 and 1672, whose dedicatees were not of particularly high standing and which are now thought to have been organized at the instance of their publishers.

6. See, for example, two oft-quoted letters by Monteverdi to the secretary of the Duke of Mantua (13 March 1620 and 10 September 1627, quoted in Fabbri, *Monteverdi*, 131–32).

7. See Paolo Guerrini, "I Rovetta nel bresciano," in *Giornale di Brescia*, 8 May 1960, later collected in *Appunti su argomenti diversi: curiosità linguistiche e dialettali, tradizioni e feste, folclore nomi e luoghi, notizie e personaggi di storia e cronaca*, ed. Antonio Fappani and Francesco Richiedei (Brescia: Edizioni del Moretto, [1987]), 484–85.

8. In one of the many notarial documents concerning individuals with the name Rovetta at this period, dated 17 November 1520, one "Andrea q[uondam] Bartolomeo da Rovetta, Hostes ad signum canevi" leaves a small sum to "m[aest]ro Francisco de Laude," of minor orders, whom the writer describes as "patri meo spirituali" (my spiritual father; I-Vas, Notarile, Testamenti, 1218 XII, fols. 66v–67r). The de Laude family of musicians was active at San Marco at that period; see Selfridge-Field, *Venetian Instrumental Music*, 336 and 347–48.

9. Alberto's name appears frequently in contemporary documents. See, for example, a petition of 17 December 1583, cited in Rodolfo Baroncini, "Contributo alla storia del violino nel sedicesimo secolo: I 'sonadori di violini' della Scuola Grande di San Rocco a Venezia," *Recercare* 6 (1994): 163 (document 63), which a mentions a group of musicians led by one "ser Berto de Bettin," who can be confidently identified as Alberto Rovetta. This Berto was probably the same musician who was employed by the school of San Marco after 1573 (ibid., 169 [document 79]).

10. For the most recent and reliable biographical account on Giovanni Rovetta, see Gastone Vio, "Nuovi elementi biografici su alcuni musicisti del Seicento veneziano," *Recercare* 14 (2002): 203–9. A biographical study of Rovetta is currently in preparation by the author.

11. A summary of Giacomo Rovetta's duties as a violinist with solo work from 1614 to 1641 can be found in I-Vas, Procuratia de Supra, reg. 52, opening 43s–d. A notice of Giacomo's death is given in I-Vasp, S Angelo, Registri dei morti, 4: Morti, Libro VIII, 1631–1649, p. 110: "Adi 28 [decem]brio 1641 / Il sig[no]r Giacomo Roetta d'anni 75 ammalato da febre, e cataro già giorni 11" (On 28 December 1641, Signor Giacomo Rovetta, aged 75 years, sick of fever and catarrh for eleven days). See also Selfridge-Field, *Venetian Instrumental Music*, 336.

12. Rovetta's opera *Ercole in Lidia* was performed in 1645 at the Novissimo theater. Although its music is lost, a short and enthusiastic description of the performance, written by the English traveler John Evelyn, still survives; see Ellen Rosand, *Opera in Seventeenth-Century Venice: The Creation of a Genre* (Berkeley: University of California Press, 1991), 9 and 107. Rovetta's *Argiope* (1649) seems to have been less successful, since his music was substituted by that of Alessandro Leardini, probably just before the first performance (see Moore, *Vespers at St. Mark's*, 15–16).

13. Most notably those published in *Musiche Sacre concernenti messa, e salmi concertati con istromenti, imni, antifone & sonate, a due, 3. 4. 5. 6. 8. 10. e 12. voci* (Venice: Vincenti, 1656; RISM A/I C1565).

14. See Luigi Collarile, "Natale Monferrato: Ritratto di un musicista veneziano del Seicento," *Rivista italiana di musicologia* 42 (2007): 169–234; and his article in *DBI*, s.v. "Monferrato, Natale" (pp. 643–47).

15. For an early attempt at a biography of Cavalli, see Jane Glover, *Cavalli* (London: B. T. Batsford, 1978); see also Moore, *Vespers at St. Mark's*, 18–28. Important biographical information may also be found in various articles by Gastone Vio, especially "Ancora su Francesco Cavalli: casa e famiglia," *Rassegna veneta di studi musicali* 4 (1988): 243–63.

16. Francesco Cavalli, *Opere*, ed. Ellen Rosand (Kassel: Bärenreiter, 2012–).

17. See, for example, the letter from Giovanni Rovetta to Cavalli's father, Giovanni Battista Caletti, cited in note 26 below.

18. On Cavalli's work in such institutions, see Vio, "Nuovi elementi biografici," 203; Moore, *Vespers at St. Mark's*, 21 and 337 n. 66 (at S. Caterina, 1645); Antonio Niero and Gastone Vio, *La chiesa dello Spirito Santo in Venezia* (Venice: Scuola tipografica Emiliana-Artigianelli, 1981), 76–77 (S. Spirito, 1637); Denis Arnold, "Francesco Cavalli: Some Recently Discovered Documents," *Music & Letters* 46 (1965): 50–55, esp. 53 (S. Rocco, 1627); and Jonathan E. Glixon, *Honoring God and the City: A Documentary History of Music at the Venetian Confraternities, 1260–1807* (New York: Oxford University Press, 2003), 212 (S. Domenico di Suriano).

19. Vio, "Nuovi elementi biografici," 211.

20. "P[er] fenir presto hà omisso nelli vesperi delli moteti che si dovevano dire[,] et sonate." Quoted in Rismondo, "Massimiliano Neri," 91.

21. Along with some of Neri's instrumental pieces, "Dignare me" was transcribed in the mid-nineteenth century by the German scholar Carl von Winterfeld; his transcription of the motet is given in Hugo Leichtentritt, *Geschichte der Motette* (Leipzig: Breitkopf & Härtel, 1908), 260, where Leichtentritt praises it as "ein Stück von feinem Gefüge" (a finely textured piece). Winterfeld's transcriptions of Neri's instrumental music were first noted in Selfridge-Field, *Venetian Instrumental Music*, 47 n. 8.

22. In the dedication to the *Motetti a due e tre voci*, Neri states that the pieces were "composed in the service of the ducal church of San Marco" (*composti per servitio della Chiesa Ducale di S. Marco*; Massimiliano Neri, *Motetti a due e tre voci libro primo . . . opera terza* [Venice: Magni, 1664], unpaginated).

23. Vio, "Nuovi elementi biografici," 205–6.

24. The "M[ol]to Ill[ust]re Sig[no]r Giovanni Roveta Maestro di Capella della ducal Chiesa di S. Marco," wanting "his nephew" Giovanni Battista Volpe, deacon of the church of San Fantin—who in the meantime had obtained a dispensation from Pope Innocent X "on account of his age, which does not meet the requirements of the sacred Council of Trent" (*sopra l'età, che le manca requisita del Sacro Concilio di Trento*)—to have a sufficient dowry for his ordination, provided the sum of 50D a year, the income of an investment made by Giovanni Rovetta "at the most distinguished office of the mint" (*dall'Offitio Illustrissimo della Cecca*) beginning 31 October 1639. I-Vas, Notarile, Atti, b. 3469: Claudio Paulini e soci, 1652, fols. 505v–506v (8 August 1652).

25. RISM A/I R2986; Gaspari, 3:164–65.

26. The letter, dated 22 November 1627, is given in its entirety in Vio, "Nuovi elementi biografici," 208–9.

27. I-Vas, Notarile, Atti, b. 3497: Protocolli Claudio Paulini e soci, 1662/I, fols. 49r–v, act dated 6 March 1662. Later documents detail the heirs to the notable investments made by Giovanni Rovetta (and perhaps by his father Giacomo before him) in the various state deposits in the Venetian Mint, a popular form of investment that was much used by other musicians of the time. See I-Vas, Provveditori in Zecca, b. 200: Terminazioni 14 maggio–13 agosto 1668, fols. 47r–v, 27 November 1668; and I-Vas, Provveditori in Zecca, b. 201: Terminazioni 12 dicembre 1668–8 giugno 1669, fols. 314r–v, 20 February 1669.

28. "Jesu mi, Jesu benignissime" (no. 5 in this edition) is also preserved in *Sacri concerti overo motetti a due, e tre voci di diversi eccellentissimi autori*, ed. Marino Silvani (Bologna: G. Monti, 1668; RISM B/I 1668[2]). The opera, which is preserved in manuscript at I-Vnm, is cited incorrectly in Robert Eitner, *Biographisch-bibliographisches Quellen-Lexikon der Musiker* (Leipzig: Breitkopf & Härtel, 1900–1904), 8:341–42. Eleanor Selfridge-Field describes it as surviving in *NG2*, s.v. "Volpe, Giovanni Battista." See also idem, *A New Chronology of Venetian Opera and Related Genres, 1660–1760* (Stanford, Cal.: Stanford University Press, 2007), 554 n. 14, where the survival of the opera is mentioned with less certainty, though it seems certain that the version surviving in I-Vnm corresponds to Volpe's composition (Eleanor Selfridge-Field, private communication). A brief excerpt appears in Rosand, *Opera in Seventeenth-Century Venice*, 665–67.

29. "Per altro non si biasima l'empire, o raddoppiare più che si può le Consonanze; Nè si osserva così esattamente, che nel mezzo non vi siano le Ottave, e le Quinte, benché procedino con l'istesso moto, perché si suppone siano salvate col cambiamento delle parti, come nelle Composizioni a 5. a 6. a 8. Voci, dove le parti Composte si raddoppiano le Consonanze una coll'altra, ma cangiandosi in modo, che tra di loro non vi siano i disordini proibiti dalle buone Regole del Contrappunto. E questo sentimento lo riporto dal famoso Ruettino di fel. mem. Organista della Ducale di S. Marco di Venezia, per averlo veduto da una sua lettera scritta a due Virtuosi, tra i quali verteva una simil Questione, circa il potersi conceder nel mezzo degli accompagnamenti più Quinte, e Ottave, e dalla medema lettera veniva decisa virtuosamente con l'istesse ragioni da me rapportate." Francesco Gasparini, *L'armonico pratico al cimbalo: Regole, osservazioni, ed avvertimenti per ben suonare il basso, e accompagnare sopra il cimbalo, spinetta, ed organo*, 4th ed. (Bologna: Giuseppe Antonio Silvani, 1722), 62.

30. He was recruited on 15 July 1650 with a salary of 70 D; see Emans, "Musiker des Markusdoms," pt. 1, 80 (no. 188), which also gives other details on his position at San Marco.

31. Ziani's operas *La guerriera spartana, Eupatra, Le fortune di Rodope e Damira*, and *L'incostanza trionfante* were performed at each of the Carnival theatrical seasons between 1653–54 and 1657–58; see Beth L. Glixon and Jonathan E. Glixon, *Inventing the Business of Opera* (New York: Oxford University Press, 2006), 39, 145, 158–60, and 327–29. He was active also as a harpsichordist in the same Venetian theaters where his operas were performed (ibid., 224, 350, and 351) and was ready to exploit his many Venetian relatives and acquaintances (ibid., 14 n. 36, 45 n. 48, 46 n. 50, 146 n. 21, 195, and 286 n. 36).

32. See Glixon and Glixon, *Inventing the Business of Opera*, 145–46.

33. Ziani is known to have been in residence in their community from 1640 through at least 1654, and again in 1659; see Oscar Mischiati, *La prassi musicale presso i Canonici Regolari del Ss. Salvatore* (Rome: Edizioni Torre d'Orfeo, 1985), 18, 40–42, and 77–78. The gap in the chronology probably corresponds to a lacuna in the documentary sources. In any case, other documentation confirms his residence in Venice during that period: see Glixon and Glixon, *Inventing the Business of Opera*, 45 n. 48, 46 n. 49, and 46 n. 51.

34. Ziani's first musical publications were printed by Magni; see Eitner, *Biographisch-bibliographisches Quellen-Lexikon*, 10:347–348; and Mischiati, *Prassi musicale*, 77–78.

35. The most important biographical studies of Strozzi are Ellen Rosand, "Barbara Strozzi, *virtuosissima cantatrice*: The Composer's Voice," *Journal of the American Musicological Society* 31, no. 3 (1978): 241–81, esp. 244–45; idem, "The Voice of Barbara Strozzi," in *Women Making Music: The Western Art Tradition, 1150–1950*, ed. Jane Bowers and Judith Tick, 168–90 (Urbana: University of Illinois Press, 1986); Beth L. Glixon, "New Light on the Life and Career of Barbara Strozzi," *The Musical Quarterly* 81, no. 2 (1997): 311–35; and idem, "More on the Life and Death of Barbara Strozzi," *The Musical Quarterly* 83, no. 1 (1999): 134–41.

36. On the performance of sacred music by the the Accademia degli Erranti in Brescia, see Rismondo, "Massimiliano Neri," 81–82, esp. nn. 146–49; and Paolo Guerrini, *Le cronache bresciane inedite dei secoli XV–XIX*, vol. 4 (Pavia: Brixia Sacra, 1929), 251, 268, 270–71, and 295. Sacred music was apparently also performed at meetings of the Accademia Filarmonica of Verona, which had been devoted to music since its founding; many of the printed works and manuscripts belonging to this academy (some of which still survive in its archive) contain compositions on sacred texts. See Giuseppe Turrini, *L'Accademia filarmonica di Verona: Dalla fondazione (maggio 1543) al 1600 e il suo patrimonio musicale antico; Annunziando il prossimo quarto Centenario* (Verona: La Tipografica Veronese, 1941), 191–93.

37. For example, as compared to the Accademia degli Erranti in Brescia or the Accademia Filarmonica of Verona (see note 36 above). In general, more documentation has been pre-

served from academies on the Venetian mainland (*Terraferma*) than from academies in Venice itself; one explanation is that the Venetian government kept a close watch on academic activity, because many of the Venetian academies were frequented by local nobles who were often reluctant to recognize the superiority of Venetian government. See Gino Benzoni, "Le accademie," in *Storia della cultura veneta*, vol. 4:1, *Il Seicento*, ed. Girolamo Arnaldi and Manlio Pastore Stocchi (Vicenza: Neri Pozza, 1983), 131–62, esp. 158–59.

38. A detailed textual and musical analysis of this motet is at the heart of Kendrick, "Intent and Intertextuality."

39. See Eleanor Selfridge-Field, "Rovetta's Music for Holy Week," in *La cappella musicale di San Marco nell'età moderna: atti del convegno internazionale di studi, Venezia, Palazzo Giustinian Lolin, 5–7 settembre 1994*, ed. Francesco Passadore and Franco Rossi (Venice: Fondazione Levi, 1998), 401–41 and 412–15. I-Vas, Procuratia de Supra, Chiesa, reg. 34 records a payment on 2 May 1656 of 11 s. to Giovanni Rovetta "for tuning the harpsichord and for additional musicians to sing and play the lessons during the days of Holy Week at matins" (*p[er] haver fatto accomodar il Clavicembalo, et per musici aggiunti p[er] cantar, è sonar le lettioni li giorni della sett[ima]na santa alli mattutini*). This entry is followed immediately by one for a payment to "Francesco Magini, organ repairman from Crema" (*Franc[esc]o Magini Crem[as]co conzaorgani*) for repairing "the old positive organ of the church of San Marco" (*l'organetto Vec[chi]o della Chiesa di S. Marco*).

40. Marini was appointed to the post on 31 August 1655, and on 20 August 1656 he organized musical performances in the cathedral (documented in I-VIb, Archivio Torre, Provisioni [del consiglio cittadino], no. 825, fol. 221r). Shortly afterward he was made musical director of the Accademia Olimpica (I-VIb, Archivio dell'Accademia Olimpica, fasc. 17: Parti dell'Accademia 1646 sino 1740, fol. 24r [26 February 1656]). By 4 November 1656 the canons were already complaining about his long absence, and on 14 December the position of chapelmaster was readvertised. See Giovanni Mantese, *Storia musicale vicentina* (Vicenza: Banca cattolica del Veneto, [1956]); 81–82; and Vittorio Bolcato, *Leone Leoni e la musica a Vicenza nei secoli XVI–XVII: catalogo tematico* (Venice: Fondazione Levi, 1995), xli. Soon afterward the Accademia Olimpica gained a new director in the figure of Carlo Grossi, since Marini was clearly no longer present (I-VIb, Archivio dell'Accademia Olimpica, fasc. 17: Parti dell'Accademia 1646 sino 1740, fol. 25r, 16 June 1657).

41. 28 November and 14 December. See Mantese, *Storia musicale vicentina*, 83, and the later corrections in Bolcato, *Leone Leoni*, xlii.

42. Ziani seems to have been chosen outright for the position, since he was not required to take any examination. See I-BGc, MIA 1283: Terminazioni dall'anno 1649 all'anno 1657, fol. 304v (15 May 1657).

43. See Giovanni Pierluigi Calessi, *Ricerche sull'Accademia della Morte di Ferrara* (Bologna: A. M. I. S., 1976), 28–29; in June 1653 Marini wrote a receipt for his payment.

44. Ziani's departure is not formally registered in the archival records of the *procuratia*. On 1 May 1661 he asked for a two-month leave of absence to go to Innsbruck (see Emans, "Musiker des Markusdoms," pt. 1, 80 n. 88); he likely did not return to Venice immediately after that leave, remaining instead at the imperial court until he entered the employ of the empress.

45. See I-Vas, Procuratia de Supra, Chiesa, reg. 146: Chiesa Actorum 1655–1675, fol. 146v, 20 January 1668.

46. " . . . benchè godesse Cento Tallari al mese di stipendio in riguardo alle molteplici obligationi ordinarie, et estraordinarie, e si ridusse di nuovo in questa Città al solo esercitio dell'Organo, con minor provento, mà con minor fatica . . ." I-Vas, Procuratia de Supra, Chiesa, b. 91, proc. 208, fasc. 2, fol. 6r. On 19 April 1677 the *procurator cassier* Alessandro Contarini had put to the vote his proposal that all musical personnel at San Marco undergo an ability test in their respective fields. His position was opposed by Giovanni Battista Corner Piscopia, a prominent *procuratore* who had specific financial interests in the Venice opera house. In his reply (also preserved in I-Vas, Procuratia de Supra, Chiesa, b. 91, proc. 208, fasc. 2, fols. 12r–15r), Corner claimed that if the members of the chapel refused en masse to take the test, it would be impossible to find suitable replacements for them, since the few good singers at the time had already found well-paid work at foreign courts. Contarini, giving Ziani as an example, replied that musical positions at San Marco were still desirable because they were less demanding than most courtly positions even though they paid less well. The *procuratia* eventually came to a decision in this matter: ability tests were reinstituted, but those who had served for more than twelve years were exempted (*fù fatta altra term[inatio]ne et dispensatti da fare la detta prova à quelli eletti dà 12 Anni in dietro*; see I-Vas, Procuratia de Supra, Chiesa, b. 91, proc. 208, fasc. 2, fol. 3r). It is not clear, however, that this decision—like many others made by the procuratia at this period—ever had any practical effects.

47. The best short biography of Cazzati is available in *DBI*, s.v. "Cazzati, Maurizio" (pp. 174–79), by Oscar Mischiati. See also Antonio Moccia, "Maurizio Cazzati e l'organizzazione musicale nel Seicento: un saggio biografico," in *Maurizio Cazzati (1616–1678) musico guastallese: Nuovi studi e prospettive metodologiche*, ed. Paolo Giorgi (Guastalla: Associazione culturale "Giuseppe Serassi," 2009), 11–28.

48. He was elected either on 25 April 1653 (see *DBI*, s.v. "Cazzati") or on 17 April (according to Maurizio Padoan, "Un modello esemplare di mediazione nell'Italia del Nord: S. Maria Maggiore a Bergamo negli anni 1630–1656," *Rivista internazionale di musica sacra* 11, no. 2 [1990]: 115–57, esp. 132).

49. See Maurizio Padoan, "Organici, eventi musicali e assetti spaziali della policoralità barocca: Santa Maria Maggiore a Bergamo e la cattedrale di Parma (1637–1659)," in *Barocco padano 5: Atti del XIII convegno internazionale sulla musica italiana nei secoli XVII–XVIII; Brescia, 18–20 luglio 2005*, ed. Alberto Colzani, Andrea Luppi, and Maurizio Padoan (Como: A. M. I. S., 2008), 568–73, which details the payments to musicians who took part in musical performances during Cazzati's time there.

50. RISM A/I C1581; Gaspari, 2:397.

51. On the Accademia degli Eccitati, see Michele Maylender, *Storia delle accademie d'Italia*, vol. 2 (Bologna, L. Cappelli, 1927), 232–35. Cazzati first mentions his connection to this academy in his *Antifone, letanie, e Tedeum a otto voci con organo e senza . . . opera XIX* (Venice: Magni, 1658; RISM A/I C1607; Gaspari, 2:196), which appeared after he had already been working in Bologna one year.

52. RISM A/I C1611; Gaspari, 2:196.

53. Good studies of stylistic trends in the seventeenth-century Roman school are few. See, for example, those in Ala Botti Caselli, ed., *Francesco Foggia: "Fenice de' musicali compositori" nel florido seicento romano e nella storia; Atti del primo convegno internazionale di studi del terzo centenario della morte (Palestrina e Roma, 7–8 ottobre 1988)* (Palestrina: Fondazione Giovanni Pierluigi da Palestrina, 1998).

54. Shorter compositions certainly had a place at San Marco as well; Neri's motets, for example, tend to be shorter than his instrumental works, even though both were probably composed for San Marco.

55. See *DBI*, s.v. "Cazzati."

56. Cazzati published at least three lists of his own compositions, which form the basis of the list given in *DBI*, s.v. "Cazzati"; this list, however, does not include the two works published in the *Sacra Corona*, and it may lack other compositions by Cazzati as well.

57. Particularly by the important Bolognese composer Giulio Cesare Arresti; see *DBI*, s.v. "Cazzati." Mischiati points out, however, that many of Cazzati's works seem to have been composed in great haste (possibly explaining some of these errors and infelicities). On the other hand, given that a comprehensive study of his many surviving compositions would be the task of a lifetime, a critical evaluation of his oeuvre as a whole is very difficult. He also seems to have been particularly interested in creating large-scale formal structures by way of

sectional contrast, an aspect of his compositions that deserves more complete analysis.

58. This possibility seems to be confirmed by the presence of the rubric "Tutti" at m. 220 of the Organo part of "Obstupescite gentes" in Cazzati's *Motetti a due, tre, e quattro . . . opera terza* (Bologna, 1670; see note 50 above and the critical report), even though all three vocal parts had already been sounding since m. 208. This marking may well be the one surviving annotation made by Cazzati for the work's performance in Bergamo.

59. Tarditi's descent from the Roman composer Paolo Tarditi is one particularly important new addition to his biography. See Daniele Torelli, "Orazio Tarditi e i compositori della congregazione camaldolese: Un modello della cultura musicale nel monachesimo seicentesco," in *Barocco padano 5*, ed. Colzani, Luppi, and Padoan, 150–55; and Paolo Fabbri, *Tre secoli di musica a Ravenna: Dalla Controriforma alla caduta dell'Antico Regime* (Ravenna: Longo, 1983), 34.

60. For details, see RISM A/I T183–T223. Tarditi's first publication with the Magni-Gardano publishing house was his *Concerto il vigesimo quinto: Musiche da chiesa diverse* (Venice: Gardano, 1647; RISM A/I T200; Gaspari, 2:501).

61. See Orazio Tarditi, *Celesti fiori musicali di varii concerti sacri a voce sola per cantare nell'organo . . . libro secondo, opera ottava* (Venice: Alessandro Vincenti, 1629; RISM A/I T186; Gaspari, 2:500).

62. " . . . da quali e p[er] la sua virtù, e p[er] la sua piacevole natura era con particolar affetto amato." See Torelli, "Orazio Tarditi," 154.

63. Rossetti was also the dedicatee of Simone Vesi's *Missa e salmi a 6. voci concertate & due violini* (Venice: Gardano, 1646; RISM A/I V1311).

64. RISM A/I T211; Gaspari, 2:502.

65. " . . . non sembrandomi altro la Musica che una inasprita battaglia, in cui appunto v'ha chi fugge, chi assale; chi sospira, chi gode; chi si avanza, chi cade; chi stà fermo, chi sempre s'aggira, e all'altra parte essendo verissimo il detto d'Isocrate, che 'Bella ferro, & auro animantur' non havrei saputo à chi rendere con più ragione questi inanimati miei corpi, ch'all'anima loro, cioè all'Oro, & al ferro della sua gentilissima Arma." Orazio Tarditi, *Concerto il trigesimo quinto di motetti a doi, e tre voci, alcuni con violini et una messa concertata a tre voci* (Venice: Alessandro Vincenti, 1663), unpaginated.

66. RISM A/I F738; Gaspari, 2:421.

67. See Giuseppe Ottavio Pitoni, *Notitia de' contrapuntisti e compositori di musica*, ed. Cesarino Ruini (Florence: L. S. Olschki, 1988), 331–32; and Fabbri, *Tre secoli di musica a Ravenna*, 40. Pitoni further notes that Filippini, during his stay in Rome, served as chapelmaster to two different chapters of the Augustinian order; see Pitoni, *Notitia de' contrapuntisti*, 332.

68. *Floridus concentus sacras continens laudes a celeberrimis musices erudites auctoribus, binis, ternis, quaternis, quinisque vocibus suavissimis modulis concinnatas, quas in unum collegit R. Floridus canonicus de Sylvestris a Barbarano* (Rome: Andrea Fei, 1643; RISM B/I 1643[1]; Gaspari, 2:360–61) and *R. Floridus canonicus de Sylvestris a barbarano has alteras sacras cantiones in unum ab ipso collectas suavissimis modulis ab excellentissimis auctoribus concinnatas binis, ternis, quaternis vocibus curavit in lucem edendas* (Rome: Lodovico Grignani, 1645; RISM B/I 1645[2]; Gaspari, 2:361). These volumes are the first two of the twenty-two anthologies collected by Florido de Silvestris between 1643 and 1672 (see note 5 above), which included works by leading Roman musical figures and some compositions by de Silvestris; both they and their collector deserve further specialized study. In de Silvestris's anthologies, Filippini's name is given as "P. Argentini," and he is described as "M[aest]ro di Cap[ella] & Organista in S. Agostino."

69. Fabbri, *Tre secoli di musica a Ravenna*, 39–40, cites autograph letters of 7, 14, 21, and 24 March 1657 (now held in I-RAaa) from Archbishop Torreggiani from Rome to his vicar concerning the "p[ad]re agostiniano" who was to fill in for Sarti, who was unwell and unable to carry out his duties satisfactorily.

70. See *DBI*, s.v. "Alessandro VII, papa" (pp. 205–15, esp. 205), by Mario Rosa. The episode is now recognized as having been decisive for the future pope's later approach to church governance; particularly important were his contacts at that time with the Jesuits.

71. For a general outline, see George L. Mosse, "Changes in Religious Thought," in *The Decline of Spain and the Thirty Years War 1609–48/59*, ed. John Phillips Cooper (Cambridge: Cambridge University Press, 1971), 169–201, esp. 187–88, 191–92, and 195. Some works by members of the Jesuit order were even put on the papal index of prohibited books in the seventeenth century (see, e.g., Paolo Sarpi, "Scrittura per informare la serenissima Repubblica sopra lo stato della controversia *de auxiliis*," in *Scritti filosofici e teologici editi ed inediti*, ed. Romano Amerio [Bari: Laterza, 1951], 146–54; original in I-Vas, Consultori in Jure, f. 7, fols. 49r–53r). Correspondence in 1656 between the Venetian ambassador in Rome and the Venetian government mentions plans to dismiss the Jesuit Giulio Clemente Scotti, who had published widely condemning papal authority, from his post at the University of Padua (I-Vas, Senato, dispacci degli ambasciatori e residenti, Roma, 139, fols. 33r–34r [from Rome, 15 January 1656] and fols. 65r–67r [from Rome, 5 February 1656]). On Scotti, see Cristoforo Poggiali, *Memorie per la storia letteraria di Piacenza*, vol. 2 (Piacenza: Nicolò Orcesi, 1789), 215–31; and Claudio Costantini, *Fazione Urbana: Sbandamento e ricomposizione di una grande clientela a metà Seicento*, rev. ed, (2008), under app. 1, sec. b3, "Giulio Clemente Scotti," http://www.quaderni.net/WebFazione/b3.htm.

72. In his dispatch of 15 January 1656 (see note 71 above), the Venetian ambassador, Girolamo Giustinian, informed the Venetian government of his response to the pope's concerns about Scotti: he had reassured him that the Venetian republic was "most zealous in keeping unharmed the purity of the dogmas of the holy faith" (*zelantissima nel mantener illeso il candore dei dogmi della santa fede*).

73. Because of the many lacunae in the documentary record from Forlì at this period, it is no longer possible to reconstruct the details of Vesi's early life. See Osvaldo Gambassi and Luca Bandini, *Vita musicale nella cattedrale di Forlì tra 15. e 19. secolo* (Florence: L. S. Olschki, 2003), 44–45.

74. *Missa e salmi a 6. voci concertate & due violini* (1646); see note 63 above.

75. For example, Vesi's *Salmi concertati a 3. 4. 5. & a 6. con stromenti con il secondo choro ad libitum . . . opera quarta* (Venice, Francesco Magni, 1656; RISM A/I V1315 and VV1315), is dedicated to Giacomo Teodoli, archbishop of Forlì ("all'ill[ustrissi]mo et rev[erendissi]mo monsignor arcivescovo Theodoli vescovo di Forlì"), and his *Motetti e salmi a voce sola concertati con istromenti, & in fine le lettanie della Madona à 4 . . . opera seconda* (Venice: "stampa del Gardano," 1648; RISM A/I V1312; Gaspari, 2:511) closes with a litany headed "Ad honore della Beatissima Vergine del Fuoco di Forlì," referring to an icon preserved and venerated at Forlì Cathedral. According to the late but reliable testimony of Giuseppe Ottavio Pitoni, Teodoli appointed Stefano Filippini chapelmaster of Forlì Cathedral in 1655 (see Fabbri, *Tre secoli di musica a Ravenna*, 40). On musical life at Forlì Cathedral at this period, see Gambassi and Bandini, *Vita musicale nella cattedrale di Forlì*, 43–45.

76. Both were at Forlì, Filippini in 1653–55 (just before the publication of the *Sacra Corona*) and Tarditi in 1639. See Gambassi and Bandini, *Vita musicale nella cattedrale di Forlì*, 44–45.

77. See, e.g., Antonio Lovato, "Tarquinio Merula 'musico' di Giorgio Cornaro vescovo di Padova (1642–1663)," *Rassegna veneta di studi musicali* 5–6 (1989–90), 187, esp. n. 32.

78. One such piece of evidence is the litany to the Madonna del Fuoco of Forlì published in his *Motetti e salmi* of 1648 (see note 75 above). On 22 April 1639, probably at the beginning of his tenure in Padua, he drafted a letter of attorney naming "Giacomo Vesi, his brother, a resident of the town of Forlì" (*il Sig.r Giacomo Vezi suo f[rate]llo habitante nella città di Forlì*) as his representative (*Procurator, Nontio, e Commesso*) within the city of

Forlì; see I-Pas, Notarile, b. 1696, fols. 308v–309v. The fact that Vesi was obliged to name his brother as his representative suggests that he went only rarely to Forlì but nevertheless still retained strong relations with that town.

79. See Lovato, "Tarquinio Merula 'musico,' " 200–201 (document 10).

80. " . . . che V. S. Illustrissima e Reverendissima s'è degnata di farmi, elegendomi, distintamente da ogn'altro, per suo Maestro di Capella." Vesi, *Motetti e salmi a voce sola*, unpaginated. As far as can be ascertained, there are no surviving records relating to Vesi's position in Corner's household, and nothing is known about his duties, his salary, or his date of departure (Lovato, "Tarquinio Merula 'musico,' " 186). Incidentally, Tarquinio Merula seems to have served as Corner's private chapelmaster between 1643 and 1645; see Lovato, "Tarquinio Merula 'musico,' " 187.

81. His *Motetti a voce sola . . . opera terza* (Venice: Magni, 1652), however, was reprinted in Antwerp in 1656 by the heirs of Pierre Phalèse (RISM A/I V1314).

82. See *DBI*, s.v. "Magni" (pp. 479–82), by Vittorio Bolcato.

83. See *DBI*, s.v. "Magni"; and Fabbri, *Tre secoli di musica a Ravenna*, 26–31.

84. See Elisa Bonaldi, "La famiglia Gardano e l'editoria musicale veneziana del pieno e tardo Cinquecento (1538–1611)," *Studi veneziani* 20, n.s., (1990): 273–302, esp. 293–94.

85. I-Vas, Arti, b. 163, reg. 2 (1597–1617), fol. 80r, 22 May 1612: "Comparse il mag[nifi]co Bortolamio Magni, et portò un'instrumento fatto con il q[uondam] sig[n]or Anzolo Gardano di haverlo servito nella sua professione sì di stamparia come di libraria, et però ricerca di esser matricolato come forestiero . . ." (The gentleman Bartolomeo Magni arrived, bringing an notarial deed he had drafted with the late Signor Anzolo Gardano, whom he had served in his profession of printer and bookseller, and so asks to be registered as a foreigner). The request was unanimously accepted by the *banca dell'arte*.

86. Francesco Magni purchased a new shop "in the district of San Giminiano behind the *procuratie vecchie,* namely, [the property] of Fortunato, a perfumer near the clock-tower of St. Mark's, which was previously the property of the most illustrious *procuratie*" (*in contrà di san Giminiano sotto le Procuratie Vechie cioè quella del Fortunato, proffumiero vicina all'orologlio* [sic] *di san Marco, era già di raggione delle Ill[ustrissi]me Procuratie*; I-Vas, Notarile, Atti, b. 5506: atti Giorgio Emo, 1651), fols. 210v–213r, 19 August 1651. These premises were sold to him by the aristocrat Marin Zorzi di Francesco in exchange for all Magni's property in Bagnarola, a small town in Friuli near the old abbey of Sesto al Reghena.

87. Biagio Marini described one of Bartolomeo Magni's sons, who may have been his pupil, as "a youth very promising on the violin" (*giovanetto di molta aspettatione nel violino*) and dedicated to him the opus 3 *Romanesca per violino solo e basso se piace* published in his *Arie, madrigale et corenti a 1, 2, 3* (Venice: Bartolomeo Magni, 1620). See *DBI*, s.v. "Magni" (pp. 479–80).

88. See note 86 above. Marcesso's name is given in this document as "D[omi]nus Bartholomeus Marcesso q[uondam] d[omini] Sebastiani Juvinis in Apothecca supras[crip]ti D[omini] Francisci Ma[g]ni."

89. See the testament of Antonia Marcesso, drawn up on 20 March 1673, in I-Vas, Notarile, Testamenti, Testamenti chiusi, 188a II, 368 (Atti Pietro Bozini), where she states that her husband, "signor Bortolamio, hatter in this city" (*s[igno]r Bortol[ami]o Baretter in q[ues]ta Città*), had probably set up his own business as a merchant some time ago (see note 90 below) and asks that what remains of her legacy be left "to my nieces, the daughters of the bookseller Francesco Magni" (*alle mie Nezze fig[lio]le di Franc[esc]o Magno librer*). The modest amount left by Antonia Marcesso to her nieces seems to confirm the humble social origins of the family. The identification is also confirmed by the death certificate; see Venice, Archivio Parrocchia di Santissimo Salvatore, Registri dei morti, 14: Liber mortuorum ab anno 1652 usque ab 1690, fol. 89v, which records, on 2 August 1673, that "Signora Antonia, wife of signor Bartolo Marcesso, around seventy years old, [died] of fever and catarrh six months ago" (*La sig[no]ra Antonia moglie del s[igno]r Bortolo Marcesso, d'anni 70 in c[irc]a, da febre, e cattaro, già mesi sei*).

90. See I-Vas, X Savi alle Decime, reg. 419: Anagrafi sestiere S. Marco, 1661, S. Giuliano, fol. 22v, no. 376 (in "Calle di Balloni"), which records a rent of 60D paid by "Bortolomio Marzesso Cappeller" (Bartolomeo Marcesso, the hatter); and I-Vas, X Savi alle Decime, reg. 419: Anagrafi sestiere S. Marco, 1661, S. Basso, fol. 58r, no. 69 ("In marzaria"), which records a payment of 46D from "Bortolo Marcesso Capeller alli quattro Giglij" (Bartolo Marcesso, hatter at [the sign of] the four lilies) to Francesco Magni "for part of the workshop . . . for which he used to pay sixty ducats" (*d'una portione di Bottega d[uca]ti 46 q[ua]le soleva pagare d[uca]ti 60*). Given the connection to Magni, it seems highly likely that this Marcesso is the same as the compiler of the *Sacra Corona*.

91. Matteo Gardano had previously traded in silk goods; see Bonaldi, "La famiglia Gardano," 292. Later, on 9 May 1664, "s[igno]ri Pietro et fratelli Gardani q[uondam] Francesco" are documented as having sold their "haberdashery shop at the sign of Venice on the Ponte de' Baretteri" (*bottega di Merzaria all'insegna della Venetia su'l ponte di Bareteri*; I-Vas, Notarile, Atti, b. 3503: Protocolli notaio Paulini e soci, 1664/I, fols. 168r–172r). The Ponte de' Baretteri is the only bridge on the customary itinerary from the Rialto to San Marco.

92. Unfortunately, the register covering the years 1600–1656, which could have provided information on the birthdate of the Bartolomeo Marcesso who edited the *Sacra Corona*, is missing.

93. On 20 March 1615 one "Bortholamio Marcesso" reported a rental "in the name of my son Bastian" (*a nome di Bastian mio fiolo*) at "S. Zorzi delle Perteghe in contrà del Bosco" (i.e., the area now known as the Bosco del Vescovo, where the Bishop of Padua had a Sunday villa, perhaps the one on which the present Villa Sculazzoni or Villa Scudolanzoni was later built; see note 111 below). I-Pas, Archivio Civico Antico, Estimi, Estimo 1615, b. 83, no. 40. With the help of a map in his possession that may date from the seventeenth century, the local historian Silvano Rettore has confirmed that the Marcesso family owned land in this region at this period (personal communication).

94. San Michele delle Badesse, reg. [Battesimi] 1. 1576 al '600, unfoliated, records Bartolomeo Marcesso as the husband of one Felicita, by whom he had various children: Laura (born 25 March 1582), Andrea (22 April 1584), Francesco (26 January 1589), Maria (28 March 1590), Caterina (23 September 1593), and Faustina (15 August 1598). The same register names Bartolomeo and Felicita frequently as godparents to various children born in the town. Unfortunately, no records survive between the years 1600 and 1656, though later documents list a younger Bartolomeo Marcesso ("Bortol[ome]o q[uondam] Andrea Marcesso") listed as a godfather (San Michele delle Badesse, reg. IA (1656–94), fols. 7r [23 October 1658] and 12r [28 April 1660]). This Bartolomeo was probably not the compiler of the *Sacra Corona* but rather his nephew.

95. Sebastiano was born on 14 September 1576; his godfather was "D. Simeone Boato patritio Pat[avin]o" (San Michele delle Badesse, reg. [Battesimi] 1. 1576 al '600, unfoliated, 14 September 1576). See also note 94 above.

96. I-Vas, Notarile, Atti, b. 2722/3: Atti Gian Francesco Crivelli, 1624, fol. 8v (17 May 1624) records a payment to "Bastian Marcesso q[uondam] s[er] B[artolo]mio da San Michiel dalle ba[de]sse sotto campo San Piero" from an "agent" (*fattore*) of Alvise Tiepolo di Francesco and his brothers, in the name of Alvise's widow, Lucrezia, for work carried out on the Tiepolo family home. The money was left by one Caterina, who had died in the Tiepolo family home, as a dowry for Maddalena Tiepolo di Lorenzo from Oderzo, who was probably not a member of the aristocratic Tiepolo family and who meanwhile had married Giacomo Marcesso, the son of the Bastian (Sebastiano) Marcesso named in the document.

97. The appellation used on the title page of the collection, "Molto Illustre" (as opposed to "Illustrissimo," which was used

xxv

only for the Venetian nobility and for particular prominent foreign figures), supports this conjecture.

98. In general, however, only the Venetian and especially the provincial nobility were allowed to draw attention to themselves in a military context. As an example, the captains of the militias documented in Padua in the late sixteenth and early seventeenth centuries are almost exclusively members of aristocratic families from Padua (Fracastoro, etc.), Vicenza (da Porto, etc.), Verona (Nichesola, Morando, Spolverini, Malaspina, etc.), and elsewhere in Venetian territory. See I-Pas, Milizie della repubblica veneta, b. 6 (Bande di genti d'arme, Rassegne e mostre generali), reg. 6 (1603).

99. This information was kindly supplied by Mons. Pierantonio Gios, director of I-Pasd. The family's military activity may be connected to the Venetian government's occasional need to defend the northern border of the *Terraferma*, north of Vicenza; see Ivone Cacciavillani, *I privilegi della reggenza dei Sette Comuni 1339–1806* (Limena: Signum, 1984), 105 and 109–16; and Michael Edward Mallett and J. R. Hale, *The Military Organization of a Renaissance State: Venice c. 1400 to 1617* (Cambridge: Cambridge University Press, 1984), 364–65.

100. In 1609 "the valiant [*strenuo*] Ludovico Sculazzoni da Padoa" was granted permission by the Venetian senate, as a "huomo d'arme" (man of arms), to join the Banda Portia, a militia led by a nobleman from Friuli, Count Fulvio (I) of Porcia (I-Vas, Collegio, Notatori, reg. 71, fol. 123v, under 22 October 1609). He did not remain long in that position, however, for on 28 October 1610 he was dismissed and "condemned to the loss of any residual sums" (*conden[n]ato alla p[er]dita dell'avanzi*); I-Pas, Milizie della repubblica veneta, b. 7 (Mostre generali delle bande), reg. 7, "Rassegna della banda del conte Fulvio (I) di Porcia," unpaginated. The Sculazzon family had an ancient link to the imperial (Austrian) noble family of the counts of Porcìa; in a document of 18 January 1550 (I-Pci, B.P. 1027 IX), the "prudens et circunspectus [the customary epithets for secretaries, clerks, and notaries] vir s. ALEXANDRINUS Sculazzonus s. Alexandri filius Patavinus" is granted the right to practice as notary by the authority of "FRANCISCVS PORCELLINUS PATAVIN[US] CIV[ES]," a member of the Porcìa family. (The counts of this family had the authority to confer notarial rights; see Francesco Schröder, *Repertorio genealogico delle famiglie confermate nobili e dei titolati nobili esistenti nelle provincie venete*, vol. 2 [Venice: dalla tipografia di Alvisopoli, 1831], 160.) The same document confirms that the Sculazzon family were already active as hatters: it was given "at Padua, in the alleyway where salt is sold publicly, in the shop of Giovanni Legerini, hatter" (*Patavij, in vico ubi sal publice venditur, in apotheca magistri Joannis legerini biretari*), and all three witnesses—all of whom resided in the same neighborhood of Padua as later members the Sculazzon family—are also referred to as "hatters" (*biretarijs*).

101. At that time Piazzola belonged to the Contarini family, whose splendid villa is still located there. See I-Pas, Archivio Civico Antico, Estimi, Estimo 1615, b. 52, no. 4735, an appraisal dated 4 June 1615 by "Vicenzo Scullazzoni q[uondam] m[esser] Orsilio" stating that the land possessed by Sculazzoni also bordered on land belonging to "the heirs of the late Antonio Sculazzon" (Eredi q[uondam] Ant[oni]o Sculazzon); and I-Pas, Archivio Civico Antico, Estimi, Estimo 1615, b. 132, no. 9996, another appraisal, dated 6 June 1615, concerning "D. Lod[ovi]co Sculazzoni fu del q[uondam] Baldesera" (probably the soldier mentioned above; see note 100).

102. This post also included military responsibilities; see I-Pas, Milizie della repubblica veneta, Dazieri e ministri pubblici, b. 70 (though this record mentions neither the historical period under consideration nor the Sculazzon family). Cesare Sculazzoni was at the center of a strange episode that was symptomatic of the social climate in Padua at that period: he was murdered in the street behind the cathedral of Padua on 12 June 1666 on his way from the Palazzo Pretorio to the palace of the aristocratic Paduan family of Mussato. I-Pas, Foro Criminale, Sentenze della corte pretoria, Raspe, b. 8 (24 March 1663–4 December 1666), reg. 3, "Arengo duodecimo," fols. 1v–3v; copies in I-Vas, Camerlenghi del Consiglio dei X, Raspe dei rettori, b. 38, Padova 1665–1773, 1665–66 / Padova, no. 22; and I-Pasd, Parrocchia dei Santi Fermo e Rustico, Registri di battesimi, matrimoni e morti, 1: Sanctorum Firmi et Rustici baptizatorum 1568–1736, matrimoniorum 1564–1736, mortuorum 1598–1734, 1624: Notta de' morti di San Fermo (13 June 1666). Galeazzo Mussato was head of the Padua cathedral chapter at the time the *Sacra Corona* was published, and remained in that post till at least 1663; see, e.g., I-Pasd, Cattedrale di Padova, Acta Capitularia, 57 (1652–1656), fols. 183v–184r (6 April 1655), fol. 197r–v (20 July 1655), and fols. 212r–v (6 December 1655); and DBI, s.v. "Gregorio (Gregorio Giovanni Gaspare Barbarigo) Barbarigo, santo" (p. 249), by Gino Benzoni.

103. Gianfrancesco Alessandro (born 21 April 1642), Federico Alessandro (born 12 September 1644), and Antonio (born 22 December 1646). I-Pasd, Parrocchia di San Clemente, Registri dei battesimi, 1 ("San Clemente. Battesimi 1590 sino 1627 e matrimoni 1603 sino 1637"), on 28 April 1642, 6 September 1644, and 4 January 1647, respectively. The baptismal sponsors also seem to have been members of the middle classes.

104. Cesare Sculazzon gave the name Federico to his second-born (see note 103 above), as was customary.

105. See the entries for 9 October 1639, 10 December 1639, and 15 December 1644 in I-Pasd, Parrocchia di Santa Lucia, Registri dei battesimi, 2 ("Santa Lucia. 159[4] sino [1]64[9]") in which "s[igno]r Fedrigo Sculazzon," residing "sotto S. Clemente," appears as godfather to children from important local families; also the entry for 8 November 1657 in I-Pas, Ufficio di Sanità, Morti, reg. 477 (1654–58), recording Sculazzon's death: "il signor Fedrigo Sculazzon di anni 56 amalato giorni 9 di febre continua visitato dall'eccellentissimo Marchetti et eccellentissimo Torre morto sotto san Clemente."

106. I-Pasd, Parrocchia di S. Lucia, Registri dei matrimoni, 1 (1570 usque 1684. Liber matrimoniorum ecclesiae Sanctae Luciae, 1570–1683), fol. 134r, 4 November 1655: the witnesses include "il s[igno]r Fedrigo Sculazzon q[uondam] Gasp[ar]o." The bride, as was customary, lived in the parish that kept the record, which explains why this documentation has survived; further research on this topic, however, is impeded by the fact that the parish registers of the church of Luvigliano for the period have been lost (information kindly supplied by the local priest, don Placido Verza).

107. I-Pasd, Parrocchia di S. Andrea, "Registri dei battesimi 1–2," reg. 2, (1632–1718), fol. 182v, records "s[ignor] Anzolo Marces[s]o di questa Parochia" (signor Anzolo Marcesso of this parish) as the godfather at a baptism on 26 September 1666. His profession is known from a document of 31 July 1669 recording his name as "Angielo Marcesso q[uondam] Bastiano" and his place of business as "the aforementioned wool-stocking shop and another nearby for hats of fur, wool, straw, and wood, all solid stuff for country folk" (*nela sud[et]ta Botega in Calce di lanna, et in altra confinante . . . in Cap[p]elli siove [sic] di Peli lana è di Paglia è legno tutta Robba grosa che serve à Contadinj*; I-Pas, Estimi, Estimo 1668, b. 46, no. 3587).

108. This building, probably used primarily as a holiday home, is visible on a map dated 1713 preserved in I-Vas, Provveditori sopra Beni inculti, disegni, Padova—Polesine, rotolo 386, mazzo 42A, disegno 5, catastico, fol. 61 v. The structure seems to have survived well into the nineteenth century, even housing the town council of San Giorgio delle Pertiche before being demolished in recent times (Prof. Bruno Caon, personal communication). See also I-Pasd, Mensa vescovile di Padova, Scritture del vescovado di Padova, 152 (Tomo CLII. San Zorzi), fasc. 1 (Pro episcopatu Padue contra Antonius Sculazonum, 1627–1693) and 2 (Reverendissimo vescovado contro Sculazzoni, 1688–1692), fols. 1r–176v; and fasc. 3 (Il reverendissimo vescovado contro il signor Antonio Sculazzon, sec. 17).

109. The family had holdings at San Giorgio delle Pertiche (several houses, shops, etc.), Campodarsego, Borgoricco, Villa d'Arsego, Legnaro, Bertipaglia, S. Giorgio di Carrara, Piazzola, Cittadella, "Mottinello sotto Cittadella," among others. See I-Pas, Archivio Civico Antico, Prove di nobiltà, 89: Prove de' req-

uisiti per aggregazione al Consiglio de' Nobili, Famiglie aggregate dal 1626 al 1805, vol. 88: Sculazzoni-Soncin, "Processo di carte per prove di Antonio Sculazzoni, Adi 14 Feb[ra]ro 1780."

110. *Saggi scientifici e letterari dell'accademia di Padova*, vol. 1 (Padua: A spese dell'Accademia, 1786), ciii, lists the "Nob. Sig. Gaetano Scudolanzoni" as an associate member of the academy; he was probably the author of an anacreontic ode composed "as a sign of true friendship, for the graduation of Luigi Paruta" (*In attestato di vera amicizia per laurea di Luigi Paruta*; Padua: Tipografia Bettoni, 1811), a copy of which survives in the library of the University of Padua. I am grateful to Prof. Bruno Caon for kindly supplying me with the text of his study of the Villa Scudolanzoni.

111. Various eighteenth- and nineteenth-century entries in the parish records of San Giorgio delle Pertiche—all from the summer months—record the presence of various members of the Scudolanzoni family at this villa, whose grounds include a small chapel. According to one local tradition, the villa was built over a previous structure belonging to the Bishop of Padua, though it is impossible to be certain (Prof. Bruno Caon and Silvano Rettore, personal communication).

112. See the "Processo di carte per prove di Antonio Sculazzoni, Adi 14 Feb[ra]ro 1780" cited above (note 109). This document provides the basis for the (typically sparse) information given in other, later genealogical manuscripts (e.g., I-Pci, ms. BP 1619, fasc. 25: Sculazzoni ora Scudolanzoni; I-Pci, ms. BP 1134, fasc. 12; and I-Pci, ms. BP 1376/4, 1134.12, 1619.25). See also Luigi Rizzoli, *Manoscritti della Biblioteca Civica di Padova riguardanti la storia nobiliare italiana* (Rome: Collegio Araldico, 1906), 6 n. 3, 26 n. 29, and 38 n. 57.

113. Schröder, *Repertorio genealogico*, 266–67.

114. Vittorio Spreti, *Enciclopedia storico-nobiliare italiana*, vol. 6 (Milan: Edizioni Enciclopedia Storico-Nobiliare Italiana, 1932), 222–23.

115. E.g., Neri's *Motetti a due e tre voci* (1664); see "The Venetian Group" above.

116. RISM A/I M3041; Gaspari, 2:465.

117. Natale Monferrato, *Motetti a voce sola . . . libro primo, opera quarta* (Venice: Vincenti, 1655), unpaginated.

118. See, for example, the account of Filippini's musical activities in Paolo Righini, "Stefano Filippini (Rimini 1616–ivi 1690): Nuove acquisizioni dalle fonti d'archivio," in *Stefano Filippini, Carlo Tessarini: Quaderno delle notti malatestiane 2007*, ed. Emilio Sala (Rimini: Raffaelli editore, 2007), 29–50, esp. 29–30 and 50. Orazio Tarditi often conducted his own musical works during services held at the churches of his order, the Camaldolites (see Torelli, "Orazio Tarditi," 154). In 1654 he likely contributed music for the titular feast of the church of Sant'Apollinare in Classe near Ravenna (see Fabbri, *Tre secoli di musica a Ravenna*, 34).

119. For another example, compare "Ad preces o cives" from Neri's *Motetti a due e tre voci*, which is given the heading "De V[irgine] M[aria] contro infedele" (to the Virgin Mary against the infidel) in the collection's table of contents. This heading, in conjunction with the motet's text, suggests that the motet may have been written for an extraliturgical devotional occasion, either at San Marco or elsewhere, to entreat the help of the Virgin in the conflict with the Turks. For a contemporary example of such a service, see the account of the German organist and instrument builder Paul Hainlein (1626–86), who described having heard a vespers service in 1647 at San Francesco della Vigna conducted by Giovanni Rovetta that culminated in a motet imploring the Virgin's help in the conflict against the Turks ("ein Motetten . . . von der Madona . . . daß sie deß Türcken macht zerstöhre, bögen und schildt zerbrechen"; quoted in Willibald Gurlitt, "Ein Briefwechsel zwischen Paul Hainlein und L. Friedrich Behaim aus den Jahren 1647–48," *Sammelbände der Internationalen Musikgesellschaft* 14 [1912–13]: 497).

120. On this battle, see Giuseppe Ferrari, *Le battaglie dei Dardanelli, 1656–1657* (Città di Castello: Unione arti grafiche, 1913); Silvio Romanin, *Storia documentata di Venezia*, vol. 7 (Venice: Pietro Naratovich, 1858), 427–28; and Roberto Cessi, *Storia della Repubblica di Venezia* (Florence: Giunti-Martello, 1981), 629.

121. On pamphlet prints celebrating the victory at the Dardanelles, see the examples listed in Emmanuele Antonio Cicogna, *Saggio di bibliografia veneziana* (Venice: G. B. Merlo, 1847), 136, no. 956; and Girolamo Soranzo, *Bibliografia veneziana in aggiunta e continuazione del saggio di Emmanuele Antonio Cicogna* (Venice: Pietro Naratovich, 1885), 102–3, nos. 1358–61. Many such pamphlets are preserved in I-Vnm, shelfmark Misc. 166. Pietro Liberi's painting *La battaglia dei Dardanelli* is still preserved in the Palazzo Ducale in Venice, and both it and the victory are celebrated in a poem composed by one of the leading librettists of that time (Gian Francesco Busenello, *Prospettiva del navale trionfo riportata dalla republica serenissima contro il Turco: Al signor cavalier Pietro Liberi pittore insigne, e famoso* [Venice: Gio. Pietro Pinelli, 1656]; Soranzo, *Bibliografia veneziana*, 102, no. 1358). On commemorative poetry celebrating the victory, see Antonio Medin, *La storia della repubblica di Venezia nella poesia* (Milan: Hoepli, 1904), 329–36 and 551. For an account of the victory in a contemporary historical work, see Francesco Sansovino and Giustiniano Martinioni, *Venetia città nobilissima, et singolare, descritta in XIIII. libri* (Venice: Stefano Curti, 1663), 730–31.

122. Massimiliano Neri, for example, gave the name Vittoria Francesca to one of his daughters, born 24 June 1658; see Rismondo, "Massimiliano Neri," 79 n. 133. On his motet "Ad preces o cives," entreating the help of the Virgin in the battle against the Turks, see note 119 above.

123. " . . . a Cassa D[uca]ti 5[oldi] sette cont[at]i al maestro di Capella p[er] doi trombe, doi trombette, un Violino, doi Contr'alti aggiunti in Capella p[er] la messa cantata p[er] la Vittoria ottenuta contro Turchi fu li 3 sta[n]te . . ." I-Vas, Procuratia de Supra, Chiesa, reg. 34 (Scontro, 9 [1648–58], 14 August 1656); see also other entries for the same date in Procuratia de Supra, Chiesa, reg 13 (Giornali Cassier, 16, 1648–59); and Procuratia de Supra, Chiesa, reg. 53 (Quaderni Chiesa, 8: 1639–1663), opening 431d. The victory was also celebrated every subsequent year at the Dominican church of Santi Giovanni e Paolo (the second most important church in Venice), since it coincided with the titular feast of the church (26 June); the doge visited the church on that date every year. See Sansovino and Martinioni, *Venetia città nobilissima*, 733; and Rismondo, "Massimiliano Neri," 79 n. 133.

124. Andrea da Mosto, *I dogi di Venezia* (Venice: F. Ongania, 1939; repr., Florence: Giunti, 2003), 383, 389, and 392, respectively. Valier in particular played an important role in the process of re-establishing good relations between Venice and the Papacy; see Gianvittorio Signorotto, "Il rientro dei gesuiti a Venezia. La trattativa (1606–1657)," *I gesuiti e Venezia: Momenti e problemi di storia veneziana della Compagnia di Gesù*, ed. Mario Zanardi (Venice: Giunta regionale del Veneto; Padua: Gregoriana libreria editrice, 1994), 401 and 415. Later, however, he is said to have displayed a "very eloquent coolness" (*freddezza molto eloquente*) toward the delegation of Jesuits who had been readmitted to Venice (Signorotto, "Il rientro dei gesuiti," 418–19).

125. On the *camauro*, see Agostino Pertusi, "*Quedam regalia insignia*: Ricerche sulle insegne del potere ducale a Venezia durante il Medioevo," *Studi veneziani* 7 (1965): 83–86.

126. As the real power of the doge gradually diminished over the course of the late sixteenth and early seventeenth centuries, the external, ceremonial splendor of the doge's election ceremony—which, significantly, was always called a "presentation" or "entry" instead of a "coronation"—increased to compensate. See Edward Muir, *Civic Ritual in Renaissance Venice* (Princeton: Princeton University Press, 1981), 263–88, esp. 286–88; Eugenio Musatti, *Storia della promissione ducale* (Padua: Tipografia del Seminario, 1888; repr., Venice: Filippi, 1983), 96–97; Agostino Pertusi, "*Quedam regalia insignia*," 121; and Iain Fenlon, *Music and Culture in Late Renaissance Italy* (Oxford: Oxford University Press, 2002), 15–16. Music certainly played a role in the ceremonies surrounding the dogal entry, though

specific documentation is scarce; for some early examples of music for dogal coronations, see F. Alberto Gallo, ed., *Antonii Romani Opera*, Antiquae musicae italicae monumenta veneta sacra, vol. 1 (Bologna: Università degli Studi di Bologna, 1965), vi–viii and 1–12.

127. See I-Vas, Procuratia de Supra, Chiesa, reg. 34, for payments on 2 April 1655 "to the jewelers-in-ordinary for delivery of the treasure" (*alli ordinari Zogelieri p[er] la consegna del Tesoro*) and "for the cleaning of the jewels of the ducal crown for the coronation of the *Serenissimo*" (*p[er] haver nettate le zogie della Corona Ducal p[er] la incoronation del ser[enissi]mo*); and on 23 March "for repairing the ducal crown's drawer, and having a key made for the same, having it painted again, and for crimson silk to cover said crown" (*p[er] accomodar la Cas[s]etta della Corona ducal, et far far una Chiave a d[ett]a farla depenzer da novo, et p[er] ormesino Cremesino p[er] coprir d[ett]o Corno*).

128. On 10 April 1655, for example, a payment of 3D 21 s. was made to Rovetta for "additional musicians for the solemn mass for the new *Serenissimo* [i.e., the doge]" (*p[er] Musici agionti p[er] la Messa solene del Novo Ser[enissi]mo*; I-Vas, Procuratia de Supra, Chiesa, reg. 53, opening 430s). Similarly, on 20 July 1656, "three ducats and thirteen soldi were paid to the chapelmaster; that is, fourteen lire for two theorbos and eight lire for two additional contraltos for the mass sung on the day of the entry of the *Serenissimo* Valier" (*D[uca]ti tre s[oldi] tredese cont[at]i al Maestro di Capella cioè £14 p[er] due tiorbe, et £8 p[er] due contralti aggiunti nella messa cantata il giorno dell'ingresso del Ser[enissi]mo Valier*; I-Vas, Procuratia de Supra, Chiesa, reg. 34). Other similar annotations can be found throughout I-Vas, Procuratia de Supra, Chiesa, reg. 13.

129. Another factor making Contarini the most likely candidate is the familial connection between the Contarini and Cavalli families established by the 1632 marriage of the doge's daughter, Lucrezia, to Cavalli's principal protector at that time, the nobleman Giovanni Cavalli (son of Federico Cavalli, the *podestà* of Crema, to whom the composer owed his first arrival in Venice and introduction to the ducal chapel). See da Mosto, *I dogi di Venezia,* 383. After Lucrezia's death, however, Giovanni Cavalli married Cecilia Soranzo in 1651; see I-Vas, Misc. Codici I: Storia Veneta, 18: Marco Barbaro, Arbori de patriti veneti, II, fols. 313r–v (family tree labeled "Cavalli 'B' ").

130. Francesco Corner was reportedly persuaded to accept the position of doge "by the efficacious prayers of his son, the Bishop of Padua" (*dalle preghiere efficaci del Vescovo di Padova suo figliuolo*). See Andrea Valiero, *Historia della guerra di Candia* (Venice: Baglioni, 1679), 396. In a letter of 25 May 1656 to Giulio Rospigliosi, the papal secretary of state, the Venetian papal nuncio, Carlo Carafa, not only mentions Giorgio Corner as one of the most important mediators between the Venetian republic and the Holy See in the affair of the readmission of the Jesuits to Venice, but also refers to Giorgio's father, Francesco, as "a gentleman of well-known piety and fervor ... who combines an indelible memory of many favors received with a devotion to the Holy See that is almost innate to his family" (*signore di quella pietà, e zelo, ch'è molto ben noto ... e che alla divozione quasi connaturale alla sua casa verso la Santa Sede porta congiunta una memoria indelebile delle tante grazie*). See Giuseppe Gullino, "Il rientro dei gesuiti a Venezia nel 1657: Le ragioni della politica e dell'economia," in Zanardi, *I gesuiti a Venezia,* 429.

131. See Sansovino and Martinioni, *Venetia città nobilissima,* 476–77; and da Mosto, *I dogi di Venezia,* xxvi.

132. See Giovanni Morelli and Thomas Walker, "Tre controversie intorno al S. Cassiano," in *Venezia e il melodramma nel Seicento,* ed. Maria Teresa Muraro (Florence: L. S. Olschki, 1976), 97–120.

133. To cite one instance that so far has not been mentioned in the scholarly literature: on 21 February 1670 payments of four *medaglie d'oro* and six sequins were made to "four additional musicians for the music last Christmas Eve" (*quattro musici aggionti p[er] la musica della notte di Natal prec[eden]te*), whose names are given as "D. Vicenzo del V. Granduca di Fiorenza," "sig. Fede del Prencipe Borghese" (i.e., the singer Francesco Maria Fede, active at the court of Giovan Battista Borghese, prince of Sulmona), "sig. Bortolamio Orga[nis]ta del sud[ett]o" (perhaps a misspelling of Bernardo [Pasquini], as suggested by Arnaldo Morelli, personal communication), and "s[igno]r Carlo Violinista del sud[ett]o" (i.e., Carlo Mannelli). I-Vas, Procuratia de Supra, Chiesa, reg. 15 ("Cassier Chiesa, 1663–1674") records similar payments for the following dates, though fewer precise details are given: on 23 January 1671 for "three temporary musicians" (*tre Musici istraordinarij*) engaged for the previous Christmas; on 5 January 1673 for "four musicians from outside" (*quatro musici forestieri*) and "three other additional musicians" (*tre altri musici agiunti*), also for Christmas; on 27 April 1673 to two "extraordinary musicians" (*musici estraordinarij*), Antonio Rivagni (known as Ceccolino, a well-known singer of the time) and one "s[igno]r Giulian di Bransuicke [i.e., Brunswick, Braunschweig]" for performing during Holy Week and Easter; on 4 July 1673 for "two musicians and two extraordinary players" (*due Musici et due concerti straordinarij*) who performed on the feast day of St. Peter (29 June) at a ceremony celebrating the ascent of Pietro Basadonna to the cardinalate; and on 12 January 1674 for "five sopranists and one contralto from outside" (*5 Sop[ra]ni et un contralto for[estie]ri*) as well as several "other musicians" (*altri musici*) for a Christmas performance.

134. With the bull "Instaurandae regularis disciplinae," issued on 15 October 1652; see Guerrino Pelliccia and Giancarlo Rocca, eds., *Dizionario degli istituti di perfezione,* vol. 8 (Milan: Edizioni paoline, 1988), 1815. The first request for the suppression of these communities by the papal nuncio was made before the Venetian senate in November 1652 but was badly received; see Emanuele Boaga, *La soppressione innocenziana dei piccoli conventi in Italia* (Rome: Edizioni di Storia e Letteratura, 1971), 115–18. It seems probable that Giorgio Corner, the bishop of Padua, played some role in the postponement of the application of the papal bull; see Boaga, *Soppressione innocenziana,* 117 n. 20.

135. Scholars have already noted the close relations between the these three fundamental causes of conflict between Rome and Venice, and that Venice entered into the negotiations with Rome with the specific goal of obtaining the finances it needed to continue its conflict with the Turks while also resolving the various outstanding disputes between the two states. See, for example, Ferrari, *Battaglie dei Dardanelli,* 21–23; Giuseppe Gullino, "L'opera del nunzio Carafa per il ritorno dei gesuiti nella Serenissima (1655–1657)," *Studi romani* 24, no. 2 (1976): 163–65; Gianvittorio Signorotto, *Inquisitori e mistici nel seicento italiano: L'eresia di Santa Pelagia* (Bologna: Il Mulino, 1989), 144–47; idem, "Il rientro dei gesuiti," esp. 402–5; and Boaga, *Soppressione innocenziana,* 115–30. On the effects of Venice's antiheretical efforts on the book trade, see Mario Infelise, "A proposito di 'Imprimatur': Una controversia giurisdizionale di fine '600 tra Venezia e Roma," in *Studi veneti offerti a Gaetano Cozzi,* ed. Gino Benzoni (Venice: Il Cardo, 1992), 287–99. An examination of the original documents shows fairly clearly that those involved were well aware of the close underlying connection between these issues; as soon as negotiations on one of them stalled, others were held back or delayed as well. In a letter of 27 May 1656, for example, Carafa advises Rospigliosi to postpone making a decision on the affair of the Jesuits "at least until all the goods belonging to the suppressed convents are sold, so that the great favor that His Holiness has granted the republic may be felt palpably by even the most ordinary people, and we [i.e., the papacy] can more easily arrange [matters] as we desire" (*fin tanto segua la vendita de parte de beni d[e]lle Religioni supresse, p[er]che conoscendosi in effetto, e toccandosi palpabilmente dalla gente più idiota la qualità della grazia, che S[ua] B[eatitudine] s'è degnata di fare alla rep[ubbli]ca si potrebbe più facilm[en]te disporre a q[ua]nto si desidera;* I-Vnm, Ms. It. Cl. VII, 386 [=8168]). In another letter of 9 December 1656, Carafa advised Rospigliosi to put off assigning the vacant diocese of Bergamo so that the clergymen hoping to be assigned to that

diocese might be all the more alert in assisting him with the affair of the Jesuits.

136. During his first meeting with the papal nuncio Carlo Carafa on 31 March 1655, the doge Carlo Contarini delivered a passionate speech that made specific mention of this urgent need: "Now that we are exhausted by so many years of war, we do not see what can be expected, if the pity of princes, and particularly that of the Holy See, does not hasten vigorously to us, [since we] have common interests" (*estenuati hormai da tant'anni di guerra non vedemo, che potersi promettere, se la pietà de P[ri]n[ci]pi, e della S[an]ta Sede in partic[ola]re non accorre vigorosam[en]te ai nostri, che sono communi interessi*; I-Vas, *Esposizioni Roma*, reg. 41 [1654, 17 marzo–1659, 21 febbr. m.v.], fols. 42r–v).

137. When he became pope as Alexander VII, Fabio Chigi inherited a debt of 48 million scudi from Innocent X; see *DBI*, s.v. "Alessandro VII." This fact was communicated to the Venetian senate in a dispatch of 1 January 1656 by Nicolò Sagredo and Girolamo Contarini (I-Vas, Senato, Dispacci, Dispacci degli ambasciatori e pubblici rappresentanti, Roma, 139, fols. 12r–15r, esp. 12r–v).

138. See Gullino, "L'opera del nunzio Carafa"; and idem, "Rientro dei gesuiti."

139. See Gullino, "Rientro dei gesuiti," 431.

140. See *DBI*, s.v. "Corner, Federico" (pp. 185–88), by Giuseppe Gullino; and *DBI*, s.v. "Corner, Francesco" (pp. 198–202), by Claudio Povolo.

141. See *DBI*, s.v. "Corner, Giorgio" (pp. 218–19), by Giuseppe Gullino. According to one anonymous member of the Roman curia, Giorgio Corner was "the best and most cordial intermediary and leader we have there [i.e., in Venice]" (*il maggiore e più cordiale mezzano et istigante che habbiamo là*), and Federico and Francesco could do no more than back him up. See Signorotto, "Il rientro dei gesuiti," 396.

142. See especially the letter in code sent by Carafa on 3 July 1655 to Rospigliosi, which is transcribed in full in Ferrari, *Battaglie dei Dardanelli*, 127–29 (I-Rasv, Nunziature Diverse, 194). An extract of this document is provided in Gullino, "L'opera del nunzio Carafa," 168. On Carafa, see Ferrari, *Battaglie dei Dardanelli*; and Gullino, "L'opera del nunzio Carafa," 72 n. 12.

143. See Riccardo Predelli and Pietro Bosmin, eds., *I libri commemoriali della Repubblica di Venezia: Regesti*, vol. 8 (Venice: R. Deputazione Veneta di Storia Patria, 1914), 22 (document 37), a papal breve of 29 April 1656 ordering the papal nuncio Carlo Carafa to ensure that the suppressed proceeds of sales of goods belonging to the *conventini* were transferred to the Venetian state. On 4 May 1656 Carafa informed the doge and the Venetian college (I-Vas, Collegio, Esposizioni Roma, reg. 41, fols. 81r–82v); the actual sale of goods took place over almost three years, from 14 August 1656 to 6 June 1659. See Gullino, "Rientro dei gesuiti," 426–29.

144. See Alberto Guglielmotti, *La squadra ausiliaria della marina romana a Candia ed alla Morèa: Storia dal 1644 al 1699* (Rome, Tipografia vaticana, 1893), 150–59.

145. Gullino, "Rientro dei gesuiti," 431.

146. On Giorgio Corner's musical patronage, see Lovato, "Tarquinio Merula 'musico.'"

147. On the artistic patronage of Cardinal Federico Corner (Cornaro), see William L. Barcham, *Grand in Design: The Life and Career of Federico Cornaro, Prince of the Church, Patriarch of Venice and Patron of the Arts* (Venice: Istituto veneto di scienze, lettere ed arti, 2001); and idem, "Re-examining Federico Cornaro's Retirement to Rome," *Studi veneziani*, n.s., 35 (1998): 137–52. Cornaro's best-known legacy today is probably the commissioning from Gian Lorenzo Bernini of the Cappella Cornaro at Santa Maria della Vittoria, Rome, which contains Bernini's famous altarpiece depicting the ecstasy of St. Teresa of Ávila. Even though Giorgio seems to have taken greater interest in music than in visual art, he is known to have possessed a valuable collection of paintings, which is inventoried in I-Vmc, ms. P.D. C. 767/5, fols. 85r–90v and 92r–93v.

148. See Lovato, "Tarquinio Merula 'musico.'"

149. See the three mandates, signed and possibly written by Giorgio Corner, for the hiring of Bartolomeo Castello, Filippo Marin and Gasparo Rigola, all dated "p[ri]mo genaro 1653," in I-Pasd, MVP, SVP, reg. 212, unpaginated. Each of these three figures is explicitly referred to as a "Musico" admitted to the service of the "musical academy" (*la accademia di musica*), with Rigola hired specifically "to play violin in the musical academy" (*per sonar il Violino nell'accademia di musica*).

150. On music at Padua Cathedral at this period, see Antonio Lovato, "La cappella musicale della cattedrale di Padova nel secolo XVIII," *Note d'archivio per la storia musicale*, n.s., 2 (1984): 145–94; and idem, "Gli organisti della cattedrale di Padova nel secolo XVII," *Rivista italiana di musicologia* 17 (1982): 3–70.

151. See *NG2*, s.v. "Petrobelli, Francesco" (p. 510), by Thomas Walker. Petrobelli is first mentioned in the accounts of the bishop's court in December 1652, though without any specification of his position; see the monthly account in I-Pasd, MVP, SVP, reg. 212, fol. 42r. His name appears subsequently in all surviving monthly accounts for 1653 (January–May; see I-Pasd, MVP, SVP, reg. 212, fols. 291r, 313r, 314r, and 315r; and I-Pasd, MVP, SVP, reg. 213, fol. 80r). All of the monthly accounts list the names of all the members of the bishop's court, occasionally with indications of their positions. Petrobelli's monthly salary was £18 12 s.; the singers received £15 10 s., and the violinists £10 6 s.

152. Guerini's activity as a singer is well documented both at the Franciscan chapel in Padua, known as the Santo (see the account of 24 April 1653 cited in Antonio Sartori and Giovanni M. Luisetto, *Archivio Sartori: Documenti di storia e arte francescana*, vol. 4, *Guida della Basilica del Santo, varie, artisti e musici al Santo e nel Veneto* [Padua: Biblioteca Antoniana, Basilica del Santo, 1989], 378) and in Venice; see I-Vasp, Sezione antica, Monialium, Decreti e licenze, b. 6, reg. 6 (Monialium, 4 July 1644–21 June 1646), fol. 33r–v.

153. From 1 August 1648 Rigola served as violinist at the Santo; see Sartori and Luisetto, *Archivio Sartori*, vol. 4, 378.

154. As documented in the monthly accounts from the bishop's court from January through May 1653 (see note 151 above). The account records resume in January 1654 and continue through March of that year; see I-Pasd, MVP, SVP, reg. 213, fols. [388r], [374b], and [374a], respectively. Petrobelli is not mentioned in the surviving accounts for 1654, though those of the other five musicians (Castello, Guerini, Marin, Rigola, and Pergola) continue to appear.

155. "... accolse diversi Principi trà quali ... [il] Card. Bicchi, il Caraffa ..." Antonio Monterosso, "Compendio delle vite de vescovi di Padova di Antonio Monterosso nodaro padovano," I-Pasd, no shelfmark, p. CCXLV; partially quoted in Lovato, "Tarquinio Merula 'musico,'" 186 n. 28. Virtually identical copies of this document are held at I-Pci.

156. "Visse con reggia pompa, e gran Corte, amplificò perciò di stanze il Palazzo Episcopale, quale fornì di ricchissimi ornamenti, quadri, e pretiose suppellettili senza essempio. Si dilettò di musica Camerale forse per lenire i dolori della podagra, dalla quale fù lungamente travagliato ..." Monterosso, "Compendio," p. CCXLV. The references to "adornments" and "precious furnishings without equal" is confirmed by an inventory compiled shortly after Corner's death (see I-Vmc, ms. P.D. C., 767/5, fols. 85r–90v and 92r–93v) and especially by a petition brought by the bishop's brother, Federico, on 8 March 1664 ("Corner Giorgio | vescovo di Padova | Eredità | 1663," in I-Vas, Avogaria di Comun, 3767/15). The latter mentions numerous paintings owned by Corner, including dogal portraits by Tintoretto; a portrait of the bishop's uncle, Cardinal Federico Cornaro senior, by Tinelli; a small landscape by Titian; and four paintings by Bassano depicting Noah's Ark.

157. In the monthly accounts for March through July 1657 (I-Pasd, MVP, SVP, reg. 216, unfoliated), Marini received the highest salary of any member of the court, and his name is listed first. These accounts are dispersed among various miscellaneous papers, but those for March–July may be found,

respectively, at fols. 183v, 185v, 176r, 206r (for May–June) and at fol. 205r of the section labeled "4. 'Mensuali' di spese della 'famiglia,' 1656–1659" in the modern archival index. A more detailed study of Biagio Marini's career at the court of Giorgio Corner is in preparation by the author.

158. A Brescian property register of early 1661 describes Marini as still residing in Padua and occupying the post of *maestro di camera* (quoted in Paolo Guerrini, "Note d'archivio per la storia della musica a Brescia: Frammenti e documenti inediti," *Note d'archivio per la storia musicale* 11, no. 1 [1934]: 16–17). Although this document has been cited in several biographical sources on Marini (e.g., *DBI*, s.v. "Marini, Biagio" [pp. 440–46], by Franco Piperno), he almost certainly no longer held that position in 1661; the monthly account for February 1660 (I-Pasd, MVP, SVP, reg. 217, fol. [82r]) assigns the same salary previously paid to Marini (£155) to "the most reverend Vicar General" (Mons[igno]r Riv[erendissi]mo Vicario G[e]n[era]l[e]) instead, and the same is true in all subsequent surviving monthly accounts (same register, fols. [108r], [92v], and [90v], for August, November, and December 1660; fols. [34v] and [32v], for February and March 1661).

159. See *DBI*, s.v. "Marini" (p. 442).

160. See I-Pasd, MVP, SVP, reg. 211, fol. 275r, and all subsequent surviving account records. Giovanni Nicola Marini was actually one of the most permanent members of the court, but his position is only rarely specified in surviving documents; he is occasionally called either "aiutante" (assistant) or "Gentilhuomo" (gentleman). It is possible that he was active in the musical chapel as well (perhaps as organist, since no organist is listed in the account books; see notes 151, 154, 157, and 158 above).

161. See I-Pas, Notarile, b. 2576: Notaio Severini Francesco, 1651–1676, fols. 297r–301v for a document dated 7 September 1654 that records Marini's purchase of a house and substantial plots of land in Scaltenigo, a small town in the Venetian hinterland (which at the time was nevertheless under the civil and ecclesiastical administration of Padua). One of the witnesses was "Don Steffano dalla Torre ... capellano nel Domo di Pad[ov]a, bresciano" (Don Steffano Torre, chaplain of Padua Cathedral, from Brescia), a renowned singer at Padua Cathedral who may have helped Marini enter the entourage of Bishop Corner. On 18 July 1654 Torre obtained permission—most likely at the instance of the bishop himself—to move to Venice in order to enter Corner's personal service. See Lovato, "Tarquinio Merula 'musico,' " 189 n. 40 and 202 (document 12).

162. The first draft of the will, dated "17. Novembre 1656. In Venetia," is only known to exist in a printed copy (I-Vbc, Ms. Cicogna 2858/4, fols. 41r–44v). In it, the bishop bequeaths 100D each to Biagio and Giovanni Nicola Marini, though neither name appears in the second draft, dated 15 November 1661 (I-Vbc, Ms. Cicogna 2858/4, fols. 45v–47r).

163. In a letter of 18 October 1656 from Obizzi's palace, Carlo Talasso, Corner's confidant and factotum, ordered that the boat be prepared for the voyage, and that Marini be provided with food (see I-Pasd, MVP, SVP, reg. 225, unfoliated): "Havendo Mons[igno]r Ill[ustrissi]mo P[at]rone concesso il suo Burchiello al sig[no]r Cav[alie]r Marini perché possa di là condurre le sue robbe à Pad[ov]a" (my most illustrious lord and master having lent his boat to Signor Cavalier Marini, so that he may carry his things to Padua). The unspecified "things" may have included musical instruments. The purpose of this trip may have been to pay homage to Carlo Carafa, the Venetian papal nuncio, during his short stay in Padua in October 1656; see I-Vas, Collegio, Esposizioni Roma, reg. 41, fols. 98v–99r (14 October 1656).

164. Giovanni Nicola Marini was at the bishop's court until 1662, when he was arrested for the theft of a large sum of money from the bishop's coffers, though he was eventually released under pressure from both his father and the bishop. See the letters from Girolamo Giustinian, the Venetian governor (*podestà e capitano*) of Padua in I-Vas, Capi del Consiglio dei Dieci, Lettere di rettori e pubblici rappresentanti, b. 94 (Padova dall'anno 1662 all'anno 1667), nos. 14, 19, and 22 (dated respectively 14, 23, and 29 June 1662); and Biagio Marini's petition on behalf of his son, in I-Vas, Consiglio di X, Deliberazioni, Criminali, f. 95 (included in the deliberation of 20 July 1662). Later, Giovanni Nicola was involved in a trial in which the bishop's brother, Federico Corner the younger, asked for the cancellation of the second draft of his brother's will; details will be provided in the study currently in preparation by the author (see note 157 above).

165. Although the Latin motet for solo voices was one of the most significant and richly represented musical genres of the seventeenth century, relatively little has been written about its formal characteristics. One of the most important and accessible works on this topic is Joachim Steinheuer, "Musikalische Form bei Tarquinio Merula," in *Barocco padano 1: Atti del IX convegno internazionale sulla musica sacra nei secoli XVII–XVIII; Brescia, 13–15 luglio 1999* (Como: A. M. I. S., 2002), 103–39.

166. The label "Aria" is used in no. 12 to designate the lengthy solo section in mm. 143–66.

167. Remarkably, Neri adopted far more elaborate formal strategies in his purely instrumental compositions; see Willi Apel, *Italian Violin Music of the Seventeenth Century*, ed. Thomas Binkley (Bloomington, Ind.: Indiana University Press, 1990), 136–41; Selfridge-Field, *Venetian Instrumental Music*, 146–52; and *DBI*, s.v. "Neri."

168. The harpist Benedetto di Carli was given a permanent post on 17 January 1669 with the usual remuneration for musicians (15D); see Selfridge-Field, *Venetian Instrumental Music*, 340.

169. I-Vas, Procuratia de Supra, Chiesa, reg. 30, n.p., 20 June 1617, includes a payment to "Alvise Ferrari sonador d'arpa per haver sonato li 3 giorni, che stetero in Chiesa le Santiss[im]e reliquie" (the harpist Alvise Ferrari for playing for three days while the most holy relics were at the church).

170. See Selfridge-Field, "Rovetta's Music for Holy Week," 401–41 and 412–15.

171. See note 39 above.

172. Gastone Vio, "Ultimi ragguagli monteverdiani," *Rassegna veneta di studi musicali* 2–3 (1986–87): 360 n. 46. This was common practice for special performances of music involving singers and instrumentalists (such as the one led by Neri at Santa Caterina; see note 20 above), though such performances were relatively rare even in the city's largest and wealthiest churches.

173. Some interesting remarks on the positioning of choir lofts may be found in the writings of the eighteenth-century scholar, architect, and mathematician Count Giordano Riccati (1709–90), who ordered the lowering of several choir lofts that were apparently situated much higher at first. This lowering would have the effect of increasing the direct soundwaves and reducing the amount of the reflection from the ceiling, which he accordingly ordered to be raised. Although many of his calculations are suspect, his aim was clearly to diminish the acoustical effect of higher choir lofts in response to the demands of a new, more resonant repertoire that involved a larger number of performers than the more modest forces typical of the late seventeenth century. See Patrizio Barbieri, "Giordano Riccati fisico acustico e teorico musicale: Con una memoria inedita di acustica musicale," *I Riccati e la cultura della Marca nel Settecento europeo: Atti del convegno internazionale di studio (Castelfranco Veneto, 5–6 aprile 1990)*, ed. Gregorio Piaia and Maria Laura Soppelsa (Florence: Olschki, 1992), 279–304, esp. 289–90 and 301–4.

174. Rismondo, "Massimiliano Neri," 86–88. There is no mention of its modification in either Giuseppe Ellero and Jolando Scarpa, eds., *Arte e musica all'Ospedaletto: Schede d'archivio sull'attività musicale degli ospedali dei Derelitti e dei Mendicanti di Venezia (secc. XVI–XVIII)* (Venice: I. R. E., 1978); or Bernard Aikema and Dulcia Meijers, *Nel regno dei poveri: Arte e storia dei grandi ospedali veneziani in età moderna 1474–1797* (Venice: Arsenale, 1989), even though, as the latter notes, the apse of the church was undergoing almost continuous modification during that period (p. 155). Originally, however, the

raised musicians' platform in the apse was closed at the sides, resulting in a more focused sound; the acoustical problems created by the opening of the sides—done in order to accommodate a larger musical ensemble—are highlighted in some later accounts; see, e.g., Ellero and Scarpa, eds., *Arte e musica all'Ospedaletto*, 54 (28 July 1738), 62 (23 September 1748), and 63 (3 March 1749).

175. Particularly in the early years of the seventeenth century, when Monteverdi was at the height of his influence, the permanent supplier of materials for the construction of temporary platforms was Paolo Osmarin. See I-Vas, Procuratia de Supra, Chiesa, reg. 141 ("Chiesa Actorum 1614–1620"), fols. 119v–120r (reporting Osmarin's hiring on 19 November 1619); I-Vas, Procuratia de Supra, Chiesa, reg. 52 (Quaderni, 1613–38), openings 149s–d (reporting his earnings from 20 December 1619 to 31 August 1626), opening 421s–d (reporting his earnings from 5 May 1627 to 9 June 1636, always with the indication "sue provesion per far li Palchi in chiesa" [his payment for making platforms in the church]); and I-Vas, Provveditori alla Sanità b. 866: Necrologi 72 (reporting his death on 19 November 1635). A well-known Venetian *calle*, just behind San Marco, is named for him, or at least for his family, though it is now misspelled as *calle del Rosmarin*; see Giuseppe Tassini, *Curiosità veneziane, ovvero Origini delle denominazioni stradali di Venezia*, 2nd ed. (Venice: Cecchini, 1886; repr., Venice: Filippi, 1988), 466. Although later accounts are sparse and short on detail, they confirm that these 'platforms' were still in use in the 1650s and 1660s: on 19 December 1665, for example, a mason was paid "for setting iron supports in the walls to keep in place the new small platforms made for the musicians in the two vaults . . . in the choir" (*per haver incassato li ferri nella muraglia per assicurar li pergoletti fatti da novo per li musici nelle due volte . . . in Coro*; I-Vas, Procuratia de Supra, Chiesa, reg. 15). See also the documents collected in I-Vas, Procuratia de Supra, Chiesa, b. 92, processo no. 216, fol. [3]r, reporting the election on 4 January 1636 of one Giovan Antonio Biricci "to make the necessary decorations in the church of San Marco with a yearly salary of fifty ducats, as had the late Paulo Osmarin" (*p[er] far li Concieri necessarij nella Chiesa di s. Marco p[er] anni Cinque con salario de ducatti Cinquanta all'anno come haveva il q[uonda]m Paulo Osmarin*).

176. The practice of *cantare sull'organo* (lit., "singing on the organ") is mentioned in Italian documents from the early fifteenth through the late seventeenth century; see Arnaldo Morelli, " 'Cantare sull'organo': An Unrecognised Practice," *Recercare* 10 (1998): 183–208. However, this practice has nothing to do from the later practice of *concertare sull'organo*, even though both practices involve placing singers on the same platform or balcony as the organ (and thus well above ground level). It is plausible, given the surviving repertoire from the mid-seventeenth century, that small groups of singers and instrumentalists could perform motets in this manner. They seem to have done so at San Marco, in any case: an unusual annotation in the chapel's archival records details the distribution of candles "to the prince's players" (*alli sonadori del Prenc[ip]e*) and "to the players who perform concertos in the organ" (*alli sonadori, che fanno la Musica in organo*; I-Vas, Procuratia de Supra, Chiesa, b. 92, processo no. 210, fasc. 1 ["Custodi della soprasacrestia, e fornitori di cere"], fol. 28r). Another notable Venetian example comes from San Giovanni Decollato (San Zan Degolà), a parish located near Giovanni Rovetta's childhood home: a payment was made on 20 May 1604 "to the boy who served as musician in the organ [loft]" (*al putto ch[e] ha servito in organo p[er] musico*), and on 30 May of the same year there is reference to a new payment "for a packet of books for singing, including a score of Viadana" (*muda de libri da ca[n]tar co[n] la partidura del Viadana*)—possibly a reference to the musical repertoire sung by the boy in the organ loft. Venice, San Giovanni Decollato (now in the parish archive of San Giacomo dell'Orio), Cassa di fabbrica, reg. 2, unpaginated.

Texts and Translations

As was typical in the mid-seventeenth century, texts are treated with great inconsistency in the sources, even within individual works; such inconsistencies have been tacitly emended in accordance with modern Latin usage, and modern Latin orthography—based on the practice of the *Liber Usualis* (hereafter *LU*)—has been adopted for all texts. All shorthands and abbreviations (such as & for *et*) have been expanded, and accent marks (such as in the vocative ò) have been deleted. Punctuation is sparse in the source and has been added by the editor; for texts based on one or more biblical verses, either verbatim or paraphrased, the Clementine Vulgate Bible (available online at http://vulsearch.sourceforge.net) has been used as a guide for punctuation. References to the authorship, biblical origins, or liturgical function of texts or parts thereof—including page number in *LU* where applicable—appear in the comments below each text. Emendations to textual errors in the source are detailed in "Notes."

The English translations have been provided by Esther Criscuola de Laix and strive to be as literal as possible, though occasionally word order and syntax have been altered slightly to clarify the meaning in English.

1. Nigra sum, Giovanni Rovetta

Nigra sum, sed formosa, filiae Jerusalem; ideo dilexit me Rex, et introduxit me in cubiculum suum.

Trahe me post te; curremus in odorem unguentorum tuorum.

Veni sponsa Christi, accipe coronam quam tibi Dominus praeparavit in aeternum.

Alleluia.

I am black but beautiful, daughters of Jerusalem; therefore the king has loved me and brought me into his chamber.

Draw me after you; we will run in the scent of your perfumes.

Come, bride of Christ, accept the crown that the Lord has prepared for you forever.

Alleluia.

Comment. Based on Song of Songs 1:4 and 1:3, and the antiphons *Nigra sum* (for vespers on feasts of the Virgin Mary; *LU* 1259), *Trahe me post te* (for matins on feasts of virgin saints and other female saints; cf. *LU* 1321, where it appears as a vespers antiphon for the feast of the Immaculate Conception), and *Veni sponsa Christi* (for vespers on feasts of virgin saints; *LU* 1209, 1214, and 2628–2629).

2. Dulce sit vobis pati, Natale Monferrato

Dulce sit vobis pati, o fideles.

O fideles, modicum sustinete tempus; nam merces vestra copiosa est in caelis.

In hoc mundo perit vita, in hoc mundo cessant laeta; cuncta vana transeunt.

Flos aetatis presto floret, cito languet, statim cadit aridus.

Ibi igitur, nostra fixa sint corda, ubi vera sint gaudia.

O fideles, ad sedes beatas, ad aedes amatas, ad regna tonantis, ad dona amantis properemus, festinemus omnes.

Si opes sine metu, si pacem sine dolo, si laetitiam sine fletu nos mortales cupimus, ad caelum sit gressus, ad

Let it be sweet for you to suffer, O faithful ones.

O faithful ones, be patient a little while; for your reward is great in heaven.

In this world life perishes, in this world happy things cease; all vain things pass away.

The flower of [this] age blooms quickly, languishes quickly, suddenly falls down dry.

Therefore, let our hearts be fixed on the place where there are true joys.

O faithful ones, let us hurry, let us all hasten to the blessed abode, to the beloved shrine, to the realm of the Thunderer, to the gifts of the Lover.

If we mortals desire peace without deceit, wealth without fear, happiness without tears, let our steps be

caelum sit via et noster accessus; nam nostra conversatio in caelis est.

Dulce sit vobis pati, o fideles; nam merces vestra copiosa est in caelis.

Alleluia.

toward heaven, let our path and our approach be toward heaven; for our conversation is in heaven.

Let it be sweet for you to suffer, O faithful ones; for your reward is great in heaven.

Alleluia.

Comment. Includes references to Matt. 5:12, the collect for the Fourth Sunday after Easter (*LU* 826), and Phil. 3:20.

3. *O bone Jesu*, Francesco Cavalli

O bone Jesu, o Jesu amabilis, Virginis dulcissime fili, mea lux, meum cor, meum gaudium: te canant Angeli, te colant homines aeternum.

O pie, o care, o clemens, respice mundi crimina; nec tuos averte oculos, sed benignissime sana.

Vide bone, sana pie, vide care, sana clemens; o dulcissime, o amabilis.

Tu solus esto animae salus, vitae suspirium; animae quae te fugit, animae quae te sprevit, et graviter offendit.

Esto salus languidae, esto vita sauciae, esto medela miserae.

Salvator unice, quem nos diligimus, Jesu dulcissime, quem nos recolimus: veni placide, ac nos aerumnis libera.

Veni bone, veni care, veni amabilis.

Comment. Anonymous original text.

O good Jesus, O beloved Jesus, sweetest son of the Virgin, my light, my heart, my joy; let angels sing of you, let men worship you eternally.

O gentle one, dear one, kind one, behold the wrongdoings of the world; neither avert your eyes, but heal most kindly.

See, good one; heal, gentle one; see, dear one; heal, kind one, O sweetest one, O beloved.

May you alone be the salvation of the soul, the sigh of life, even of the soul that flees you, that spurns you, and that gravely offends you.

Be the salvation of the languishing [soul], the life of the sick [soul], the remedy of the wretched [soul].

Only Savior, whom we love; sweetest Jesus, whom we worship; come, placid one, and deliver us from hardships.

Come, good one; come, dear one; come, beloved.

4. *Ad charismata caelorum*, Massimiliano Neri

Ad charismata caelorum accedite fideles; ad mensam Angelorum accurrite devoti.

Veneramini Deum vestrum qui vos pascit, consolatur, vos enutrit, convivatur.

O quam suavis est Dominus! Pane suavissimo de caelo praestito, dulcedinem suam in filios demonstravit.

Accurrite laetantes, accedite venerantes, accurrite.

Alleluia.

Come forward, faithful people, to the graces of heaven; run, devout people, to the table of the angels.

Revere your God who feeds you; he comforts you, nourishes you, feasts you.

O how sweet the Lord is! Having granted the sweetest bread from heaven, he has shown his sweetness to his children.

Run forward, joyful ones; come forward, worshipers, run forward.

Alleluia.

Comment. Third section based on the antiphon *O quam suavis est Dominus* (for vespers on Corpus Christi; *LU* 917).

5. *Jesu mi, Jesu benignissime*, Giovanni Battista Volpe

Jesu mi, Jesu benignissime, piissime Jesu, quam dulcis es, quam misericors es, quam bonus es, mi care Jesu.

Tu vulnerasti cor meum, tu transfixisti viscera mea, Jesu mi piissime.

Confige animam sagittis caritatis, o amor, o vita, o cor, o spes, o vita mea.

O mi care Jesu, fac ut ardeam in te, nihil amem[1] nisi te, fac ut moriar pro te, nihil velim nisi te, mi care Jesu, mi bone Jesu, piissime Jesu, dulcissime Jesu, nihil velim nisi te.

Alleluia.

My most kind Jesus, most gentle Jesus, how sweet you are, how merciful you are, how good you are, my dear Jesus.

You have wounded my heart, you have pierced through my bowels, my most gentle Jesus.

Pierce my soul with the arrows of charity, O love, O life, O heart, O hope, O my life.

O my dear Jesus, let me love nothing but you, make me burn for you, make me die for you, let me desire nothing but you, my dear Jesus, my good Jesus, most gentle Jesus, most sweet Jesus, let me desire nothing but you.

Alleluia.

Comment. Anonymous original text, with reference to Song of Songs 4:9.

Note. 1. Source has "amen" (except in C2, m. 77).

6. *Exsultate, gaudete, jubilate,* Pietro Andrea Ziani

Exsultate, gaudete, jubilate, laetamini; exsultate esurientes, jubilate sitientes, festinate agni, properate cervi, festinate exsultantes, properate jubilantes, currite ad pascua, festinate ad fontes.

Ecce panis, ecce potus Angelorum, properate, festinate, saturamini esurientes, inebriamini sitientes; ecce panis, ecce potus Angelorum.

O bone Jesu, o care Jesu, accende me, inebria me, o bone Jesu.
O bone Jesu, o care Jesu, accende me, combure me, satura me, inebria me.
O bone Jesu, o care Jesu, exaudi me, intra tua vulnera absconde me.
Satura me, inebria me, o bone Jesu, o care Jesu, exaudi me.
Amen.

Exult, rejoice, delight, be glad; exult, hungry ones; delight, thirsty ones; hasten, lambs; hurry, deer; hasten as you exult, hurry jubilantly, run to the pastures, hasten to the springs.

Behold the bread, behold the drink of the angels; hurry, hasten, sate yourselves, hungry ones; inebriate yourselves, thirsty ones; behold the bread, behold the drink of the angels.

O good Jesus, O dear Jesus, inflame me, inebriate me, O good Jesus.
O good Jesus, O dear Jesus, inflame me, set me on fire, satiate me, inebriate me.
O good Jesus, O dear Jesus, hear me, hide me within your wounds.
Fill me, inebriate me, O good Jesus, O dear Jesus, hear me.
Amen.

Comment. Anonymous original text including references to Ps. 41:2 and verse 21 of the sequence *Lauda Sion salvatorem* (for Corpus Christi; *LU* 945–49).

7. *Surge propera,* Biagio Marini

Surge propera amica mea, audi vocem dilecti tui, aperi columba mea, inspice caput rore plenum, guttis noctium madentes cincinnos; attende dilectum amore languentem, amica mea.
Clamat, pulsat, madet, languet sponsus.
Surge, aperi, miserere.
Introduc in domum genitricis tuae; ecce, ecce venit, saliens in montibus, transiliens colles.

Suscipe amantem, exaudi precantem, fove languentem, columba speciosa; vulnerasti cor meum in uno crine colli tui, columba mea, formosa mea, immaculata mea, amore langueo.
Alleluia.

Awake, hurry, my love; hear the voice of your beloved; open, my dove; behold my head full of dew, dripping with the drops of the night; give heed to your beloved as he languishes with love, O my love.
The bridegroom shouts, knocks, drips, languishes.
Awake, open, have mercy.
Lead [me] into the house of your mother; behold, he comes, leaping upon the mountains, leaping over the hills.

Receive the beloved, hear the one who prays, show favor to the one who languishes, O beautiful dove; you have wounded my heart with one hair on your neck, my dove, my beauty, my spotless one, I languish with love.
Alleluia.

Comment. Based on Song of Songs 2:10, 5:2, 2:8, 5:2, 3:4, 4:9, 5:8, and 2:5.

8. *Salve mundi triumphatrix,* Maurizio Cazzati

Salve mundi triumphatrix,
Afflictorum consolatrix,
Salve spes credentium;
Salve mali reparatrix,
Depressorum sublevatrix,
Salve vita mortalium.

Tu Regina summi Regis,
Miserorum quae dolores
Audis item et clamores
Ex ovili tui gregis.

Ave parens magni Dei,
Nunc ad caelum sublevata,
Et corona decorata,
Dulcis vita cordis mei.

Hail, triumpher over the world,
consoler of the afflicted,
hail, hope of believers;
hail, repairer of evil,
who lifts up the downtrodden;
hail, life of mortals.

Queen of the highest King,
you who hear the sorrows of the wretched
and their cries
from the sheepfold of your flock:

Hail, parent of the great God,
now lifted up to heaven
and adorned with a crown,
sweet life of my heart.

In te sola refugium nostrum, potentissima Regina.
　In te gaudium afflictorum, piissima Maria.
　Per te salus mundi venit, per te gaudent omnes caelites, amantissima Maria.
　Ergo omnes unisonis vocibus, gaudentibus citharis, laetantibus cantibus collaudemus Mariam.
　Eia ergo, festantibus cordibus, ridentibus modulis, psallentibus musicis veneremur Mariam.

In you alone is our refuge, most powerful Queen.
　In you is the joy of the afflicted, most gentle Mary.
　Through you salvation came to the world; through you all the dwellers of heaven rejoice, most loving Mary.
　Therefore let us all in one voice, with happy harps and joyful songs, praise Mary.
　Hark therefore, with festive hearts, with cheerful melodies, with plucking musicians, let us revere Mary.

　Comment.　Anonymous original text.

9. *Spargite flores*, Orazio Tarditi

Spargite flores, fundite rosas, et date lilia Mariae semper Virgini.
　Attollite lumina, elevate oculos, auroram salutate Mariam.
　Tu aurora, tu stella, tu luna, tu sol.
　O amabilis aurora, aurora pulchrior, tu stellis clarior, tu luna purior, sole lucidior es Maria.

Tu es Virgo Maria a Patre summo[1] dilecta, a filio mater electa, inter mulieres una nobilis, inter matres unica Virgo, et inter virgines sola Maria.

Quod prima mater abstulit,
Tu reddis mirabiliter,
Dum paris nobis gratiam,
Illa[2] si culpam peperit.

O animae praesidium, peccatorum refugium, o Angelorum solatium, et Trinitatis gaudium; tu succurre, o clementissima mater:

O mater amorum,
Dulcedine plena,
Regina caelorum,
Lux semper serena:

Da Deum timere,
Da semper amare,
Da nobis gaudere,
Da tandem regnare.

Scatter flowers, pour forth roses, and give lilies to Mary, ever Virgin.
　Raise up your lights, lift up your eyes, salute Mary, the dawn.
　O you dawn, star, moon, sun.
　O beloved dawn, you are more beautiful than the dawn, brighter than the stars, purer than the moon, more radiant than the sun, O Mary.

You, Virgin Mary, are the beloved of the highest Father, the chosen mother of the Son, one noble [woman] among women, among mothers the only virgin, and among virgins the only Mary.

What our first mother took away
you miraculously give back,
since you bring forth grace for us,
even if she brought forth sin.

O defense of souls, refuge of sinners, solace of the angels, and joy of the Trinity; help, O most kind Mother:

O Mother of loves,
full of sweetness,
Queen of heaven,
ever-serene light:

Grant that we may fear God,
love always,
rejoice,
and reign at last.

　Comment.　The first two lines of the poetic quatrain are an altered version of verse 2 of the office hymn *O gloriosa Domina* (see http://www.preces-latinae.org/thesaurus/BVM/OGloriosa.html and cf. LLI 1314).

　Notes.　1. Source has "summi."　2. Source has "Ille."

10. *Victoriam, victoriam*, Tarditi

Victoriam, victoriam omnes cantemus, laudantes Deum et benedicentes Dominum.
　Quis Deus magnus sicut Deus noster, in majestate excelsus, in sanctitate magnificus, in bonitate dulcis, in misericordia suavis; ipsum adorant Angeli, ipsum collaudant Arcangeli in caelo, laudantes in caelo cantantes.
　Date voces, date plausus, date cantus triumphales.

Victory, let us all sing victory, praising God and blessing the Lord.
　What god is as great as our God, exalted in majesty, magnificent in holiness, sweet in goodness, gentle in mercy; the angels adore him, the archangels praise him together in heaven, singing and praising in heaven.
　Offer your voices, give applause, offer triumphant songs.

Sic caelum intonet, sic terra gaudeat, sic mare resonet, sic mundus jubilet, sic stellae rideant, sic flores germinent, triumphi gloriam sic omnes concinant.

Victoriam, victoriam omnes cantemus.

Comment. Second section based on Ps. 112:5.

Thus let the heavens thunder, let the earth rejoice, let the sea resound, let the world delight; let the stars laugh, let the flowers grow, let all sing together of the glory of triumph.

Victory, let us all sing victory.

11. *Stellae discedite*, Stefano Filippini

Stellae discedite, astra jam fugite, tetra caligine vultum abscondite; caelum obscuris tectum jam tenebris non amplius lumina serena ostendat.

Pereat dies, veniat nox, omnia confundant umbrae, caligo, nubila, tenebrae, et mortalium oculis lucem eripiant surgentis aurorae.

Nox enim jam praecessit, dies autem appropinquavit, dum Maria, in summo caeli cardine, pulchra ut luna, electa ut sol, sanctitatis emittit radios; illuminat sedentes in tenebris, et umbra mortis.

Stellae discedite, lunae jam cedite, astra jam fugite, solem effugite; Maria sol, Maria luna mundum illuminat, caelum exornat; fugite flores, narcissus, violae, pratorum risus, discedite, fugite.

Tellus jam extet horrida spinis, nec viridanti amoenitate coronata amplius appareat; rosae purpureae, candida lilia, ponite folia, linquite odores.

Silete, o Zephiri, vosque Riphaeis venite e montibus Euri furentes, floribus, herbis expoliate prata, montes, colles.

Jam enim hiems transiit; imber abiit, et recessit. Flores apparuerunt in terra nostra.

Maria flos campi, rosa sine spina, et lilium convallium, dat laeta odorem suavitatis.

Veni Auster, surge Aquilo, perfla hortum nostrum, et beatissimae Mariae fluant aromata.

Tu Virgo rosa pulchrior, et lilio candidior, et luna jucundior, tu sole splendidior, praebe odorem, mitte splendorem, ut nos stellae, nos et flores tua luce, et te duce splendere et florere possimus in perpetuas aeternitates.

Stars, disperse; constellations, flee now; hide your face from the gloom. Let the sky, now covered in thick darkness, show no more serene lights.

Let day perish, let night come; let shadows, gloom, clouds, and darkness confound all, and let them tear the light of the rising dawn away from mortal eyes.

For now the night is far gone, but the day is at hand on which Mary, at the highest point of heaven, beautiful as the moon, chosen as the sun, sends forth rays of holiness; she illuminates those who sit in the darkness and shadow of death.

Stars, disperse; give way to the moon; constellations, now flee, flee from the sun; Mary the sun, Mary the moon illuminates the world, adorns the heaven; flee, flowers, narcissus, violets; laughter of the meadows, disperse and flee.

Let the earth now stand forth horrid with thorns, and let it not appear crowned with green pleasantness; crimson roses, white lilies, put away your leaves, relinquish your odors.

Be silent, O zephyrs, and you, raging east winds, come forth from the Riphean mountains; strip the meadows, mountains, and hills of greenery.

For lo, the winter is past, the rain is over and gone. The flowers appear in our land.

Mary, the flower of the field, the rose without thorn, the lily of the valley, gives forth an odor of sweetness.

Come, South Wind, rise, North Wind, blow through our garden, and let the perfumes of most blessed Mary flow forth.

You, Virgin more beautiful than the rose, whiter than the lily, more delightful than the moon, more splendid than the sun, give forth your odor, send forth your splendor, so that we stars and flowers, with your light and you as our leader, can shine and flourish throughout all eternity.

Comment. Includes references to Song of Songs 6:9, 2:11–12, 2:1, and 4:16.

12. *Quis dabit mihi tantam charitatem*, Barbara Strozzi

Quis dabit mihi tantam charitatem, ut redamare possim amantem Jesum?

Quis mihi tribuet incendium amoris, ut langueat cor meum languente[1] Jesu?

Nonne tu Christe mi, qui es charitas ipsa?

O quam suavis, o quam jucundus, quam delectabilis est amor tuus, dulcissime Jesu, piissime Jesu, amabilis Christe, vera spes, vera salus, vera vita animae meae; in te vivit, in te sperat, in te credit, in te amor meus est; amore tuo abundanter reficitur anima mea.

Tu es solus, bone Jesu, vera spes et vita mea.

Who will give me such great charity that I might love the loving Jesus back?

Who will give me the fire of love, that my heart might languish along with the languishing Jesus?

Is it not you, my Christ, you who are charity itself?

O how sweet, O how pleasant, how delightful is your love, sweetest Jesus, most gentle Jesus, beloved Christ, true hope, true salvation, true life of my soul; in you it lives, in you it hopes, in you it believes, in you is my love; my soul is abundantly refreshed by your love.

You alone, good Jesus, are my true hope and my life.

Concupiscit cor meum te videre, et in te solo requiescere.

Tibi enim soli vivo,
Ad te solum heu suspiro,
Et in te solo respiro;
Tibi vivo, mea vita,
Te adoro, o bone Jesu.

    Alleluia.

My heart desires to see you and to rest in you alone.

For you alone I live,
to you alone I sigh "alas,"
and in you alone I breathe;
for you I live, my life;
I adore you, O good Jesus.

    Alleluia.

Comment. Includes references to Jer. 9:1–2 and Song of Songs 2:5 and 5:8. On this motet and its text, see Robert L. Kendrick, "Intent and Intertextuality in Barbara Strozzi's Sacred Music," *Recercare* 14 (2002): 65–98, especially pp. 72–81.

Note. 1. Source has "languentem."

13. *O quando suavissimum*, Rovetta

O quando suavissimum bibam sanguinem, o quando dulcissimas carnes comedam, quando pascar, quando fruar Salvatore Jesu meo?

    Illius sanguine sitis mea esuriet, illius corpore fames mea consumetur.

    Adjuro vos Cherubim, sitibundo ferte sanguinem; adjuro vos Seraphim, date carnes huic famelico.

    Meum panem, meum Deum, manducabo Jesum meum.

    Currite flumina sanguinis, flumina[1] sitis, in remedium mille plagis, in remedium mille spinis, meus Pastor vulneratus.

    O vere bonus Pastor, o vere carus Amor; accedite famelici, venite sitientes, inebriamini.

    O vere bonus Pastor, o vere carus Amor; edite ergo, bibite omnes, et jam non homines sed dii vivite, ex Deo dii.

    Alleluia.

O when will I drink the most sweet blood, O when will I eat the most sweet flesh, when will I feed on and enjoy Jesus my Savior?

    O, in his blood my thirst thirsts; my hunger is consumed in his body.

    I beseech you, Cherubim, bring the blood to the thirsty one; I beseech you, Seraphim, give flesh to this hungry one.

    My bread, my God, my Jesus will I feed upon

    Run, rivers of blood, rivers of thirst, as a remedy for a thousand wounds, for a thousand thorns, my wounded Shepherd.

    O truly good Shepherd, O truly dear Love. Draw near, hungry ones; come, thirsty ones, be intoxicated;

    O truly good Shepherd, O truly dear Love. Therefore eat and drink, all you people, and live now not human but divine, divine from God.

    Alleluia.

Comment. Anonymous original text; third section includes references to Song of Songs 2:7, 3:5, and 8:4.

Note. 1. Source has "flumine."

14. *Plaudite, cantate*, Cavalli

Plaudite, cantate cymbalis, laudate citharis, psallite organis, alleluia.

    Cantate, et auditam facite vocem laudis ejus; venite, et narrabo vobis qui timetis Deum, quanta fecit Dominus animae meae.

    Sperate in eo gentes, sperate, et collaudate eum populi.

    Plaudite, cantate cymbalis, laudate citharis, psallite organis, alleluia.

Applaud, sing with cymbals, praise with lyres, make music with organs, alleluia.

    Sing and make heard the voice of his praise; come, and I will tell you who fear God how many great things the Lord has done for my soul.

    Hope in him, nations; hope, and praise him, peoples.

    Applaud, sing with cymbals, praise with lyres, make music with organs, alleluia.

Comment. Based on Ps. 150, 65:8, 65:16, and 61:9

15. *In virtute tua*, Cavalli

In virtute tua Domine laetabitur justus, et super salutare tuum exsultabit vehementer.

    Desiderium animae ejus tribuisti ei, et voluntate labiorum ejus non fraudasti eum.

    Praevenisti eum in benedictionibus dulcedinis; posuisti in capite ejus coronam de lapide pretioso.

The just man shall rejoice in your strength, O Lord, and he shall exult greatly in your salvation.

    You have given him his soul's desire, and you have not withheld from him the request of his lips.

    You have come before him with blessings of sweetness; you have placed on his head a crown of precious stones.

Comment. Ps. 20:1–3.

16. *Peccator, si tu times*, Monferrato

Peccator, si tu times metu mortis, curre ad Mariam.

    Peccator, si in te fremit daemon fortis, curre ad Mariam.

    Peccator, si te perdere querit hostis, curre ad Mariam.

    Surge qui dormis, surge qui cadis, surge qui peccas, et invoca Mariam.

    Maria tu fons, tu vena, tu vita, tu spes, tu gratiarum mater, deliciarum mare.

    Amplectere me, o sanctissima Maria, me peccantem, me fugentem, inter brachia pietatis; praebe lactis ubera, sana mortis vulnera, dele nostra crimina, o Maria.

    Maria, tu es illa dulcis rosa, tu es illa gloriosa, pulchra nimis et formosa, o Maria.

    Tu es illa Virgo quae dedit caelis gloriam; tu es illa Virgo quae dedit terris Deum; tu es illa major caelo; tu es illa terra fortior, tu es illa orbe latior, quae sola cepit quem mundus non capit omnis.

    Ad Virginem ergo properemus, festinemus, curramus omnes, semper dicentes:

    Maria tu fons, tu vena . . .

    Alleluia.

Sinner, if you fear with the fear of death, run to Mary.

    Sinner, if the strong demon rages within you, run to Mary.

    Sinner, if the enemy seeks to destroy you, run to Mary.

    Rise, you who sleep, you who fall, you who sin, and call upon Mary.

    Mary, you fountain, you channel, life, hope, mother of graces, sea of delights.

    Embrace me, O most holy Mary, me, a sinner who flees, with the arms of gentleness; offer breasts full of milk, heal the wounds of death, remove our sins, O Mary.

    Mary, you are that sweet rose; Mary, you are that glorious one, exceedingly lovely and beautiful, O Mary.

    You are that Virgin who gave glory to the heavens; you are that Virgin who gave God to the earth; you are the one greater than heaven, stronger than the earth, more spacious than the globe, who alone conceived the One whom the whole world cannot contain.

    Let us all then hasten, hurry, run to the Virgin, ever saying:

    Mary, you fountain, you channel . . .

    Alleluia.

    Comment. Sixth section is based on Petrus Chrysologus, sermon 145.

17. *Jesu mi dulcissime*, Marini

Jesu mi dulcissime,
Spes suspirantis animae,
Te quaerunt piae lacrimae,
Te clamor mentis intimae.

Jesu dulcis memoria
Dans vera cordis gaudia;
Sed super mel et omnia
Ejus dulcis memoria.

Jesu decus angelicum,
In aure dulce canticum,
In ore mel mirificum,
In corde nectar caelicum.

Jesu sole serenior,
Et balsamo sublimior,
Omni dulcore[1] dulcior,
Et cunctis amabilior.

Jesu summa benignitas,
Mira cordis jucunditas,
Incomprehensa bonitas,
Tua me stringat charitas.

Alleluia.

My sweetest Jesus,
hope of the sighing soul,
pious tears
and the cry of the inmost mind seek you.

The sweet memory of Jesus
gives true joy to the heart,
but sweeter than honey and all things
is his sweet memory.

Jesus, glory of the angels,
sweet melody in the ear,
wondrous honey in the mouth,
heavenly nectar in the heart.

Jesus, more serene than the sun
and more sublime than balm,
sweeter than all sweetness,
and beloved above all.

Jesus, highest kindness,
wonderful delight of the heart,
incomprehensible goodness,
let your love draw me in.

Alleluia.

    Comment. Based on verses from Bernard of Clairvaux's *Jesu dulcis memoria*.

    Note. 1. Source has "dulsore."

18. *Obstupescite gentes*, Cazzati

Obstupescite gentes, imitamini mortales, populi deferte laudes; canite, canite Virginis triumphos.

    Properate in solemnitate, festinate in festivitate Sanctae Virginis N./Mariae.

Be astounded, you nations; do the same, you mortals; offer praises, you peoples; sing the triumphs of the Virgin.

    Hurry to the solemnity, hasten to the festivity of the holy Virgin N./Mary.

Obstupescite gentes . . .

Ista est, quae immundas delicias orbis certo pede calcavit; ista est, quae spretis Averni praemiis caelum amavit; ista est, quae regna terrena despiciens, ad sublimia regna evolavit.

Ridete flores, florete lilia, coronate Virginem N./Mariam.

Afferte laudes, legate preces, concelebrate festum; ut omnes cum ipsa laudare, cantare, regnare possimus, alleluia.

Comment. Anonymous original text.

Be astounded, you nations . . .

She it is who has trampled the impure delights of the world with a sure foot; she it is who has loved heaven, spurning the rewards of hell; she it is who, despising earthly realms, has flown up to sublime realms.

Laugh, flowers; bloom, lilies; crown the Virgin N./Mary.

Offer praises, send prayers, celebrate this feast, so that with her we may all praise, sing, and reign. Alleluia.

19. *Salve Regina*, Ziani

Salve Regina, mater misericordiae, vita, dulcedo, et spes nostra, salve.
Ad te clamamus, exsules, filii Evae.
Ad te suspiramus, gementes et flentes in hac lacrimarum valle.
Eia ergo, advocata nostra, illos tuos misericordes oculos ad nos converte.
Et Jesum, benedictum fructum ventris tui, nobis post hoc exsilium ostende.
O clemens, o pia, o dulcis Virgo Maria.

Comment. Marian antiphon (*LU* 276).

Hail, O Queen, mother of mercy, our life, sweetness, and hope, hail!
To you we cry, exiles and children of Eve.
To you we sigh, groaning and weeping in this valley of tears.
Therefore, O our advocate, turn those merciful eyes of yours toward us.
And after this exile show us Jesus, the blessed fruit of your womb.
O kind, O gentle, O sweet Virgin Mary.

20. *O Sacramentum*, Volpe

O Sacramentum, maximum opus unitae Triadis, pignus almum fidelium, onus trementis inferi, honos caelestis curiae. Alleluia.

Ave cibus salutaris,
Perjucundus singularis,
Vita virtus cordium.

O frumentum electorum,
Potus dulcis servatorum,
Totum replens hominem.

Fac nos esca tali pastos,
Tuti saecli nimis vastos
Pertransire vertices.

Alleluia.

Comment. Anonymous original text.

O Sacrament, greatest work of the united Trinity, kind pledge of the faithful, burden of trembling hell, honor of the heavenly court. Alleluia.

Hail, food of salvation,
uniquely and thoroughly pleasing,
life and strength of hearts.

O grain of the elect,
sweet drink of servants,
filling the whole man.

Make us, fed with such food,
to safely ascend
to the vastest peaks of the world.

Alleluia.

21. *Salve Virgo benignissima*, Neri

Salve Virgo benignissima, salve Virgo clementissima, quae nobis omnibus in te sperantibus misericordiae tuae sinum aperuisti, ut de plenitudine ejus accipiant universi.
Tu gratia plena, tu norma virtutis, tu stella refulgens.
Per te accessum habemus ad Filium, o Maria, per te Redemptor advenit in pretium, o Maria, inventrix gratiae, mater salutis, genitrix vitae.
Stella maris, dirige nos; porta caeli, excipe nos; turris David, protege nos; salus mundi, suscipe nos.
Alleluia.

Comment. Anonymous original text.

Hail, most kind Virgin; hail, most gentle Virgin, you who have opened the womb of your mercy to all of us who hope in you, so that all may partake of its fullness.
You, full of grace, model of virtue, radiant star.
Through you we have recourse to the Son, O Mary; through you the Redeemer comes as [our] reward, O Mary, founder of grace, mother of salvation, bearer of life.
Star of the sea, lead us; gate of heaven, accept us; tower of David, protect us; salvation of the earth, receive us.
Alleluia.

22. *O vos omnes*, Simone Vesi

O vos omnes ambulantes in tenebris et umbra mortis, surgite, properate ad lucem; et si fuistis aliquando tenebrae, eritis lux in Domino.

Eia agite, surgite, properate, venite ad Dominum; ille enim est, qui cor illuminat, mentem elevat, animam purificat.

Eia agite, surgite, properate, venite, currite, cantate, laudate eum dicentes: O quam suavis es Domine, laetantibus in te.

Ecce Deus, Salvator noster; accedite ad illum, et illuminamini; accedite ad illum, et facies vestrae non confundentur.

Accedite ad illum, et facies vestrae non confundentur; quia Dominus suavis est,[1] dulcis, misericors invocantibus eum.

Accedite ad illum, et facies vestrae non confundentur; hic est enim Deus, largitor bonorum omnium, salvans animas, perducens illas ad caelesti patriam.

Curramus ergo, properemus, festinemus, cantemus: O quam suavis es Domine, laetantibus in te.

O all you people who walk in the darkness and in the shadow of death, hasten to the light; and if at one time you were darkness, you will be light in the Lord.

O act, rise, hasten, come to the Lord, for it is he who enlightens the heart, raises up the mind, purifies the soul.

O act, rise, hasten, come, run, sing, praise him, saying: "O how sweet you are, Lord, to those who rejoice in you!"

Behold God, our Savior; come to him and be enlightened; come to him, and your countenances will not be confounded.

Come to him, and your countenances will not be confounded; for the Lord is gentle, sweet, merciful to those who call upon him.

Come to him, and your countenances will not be confounded; for he is God, the giver of all good things, saving souls and leading them to the heavenly homeland.

Therefore let us all run, hasten, hurry, and sing: "O how sweet you are, Lord, to those who rejoice in you!"

Comment. Includes references to the responsory *O vos omnes* (for the second nocturn of matins on Holy Saturday; *LU* 727); Ps. 106:10, 106:14, and 33:9 (and similar verses); and Eph. 5:8.

Note. 1. Source has "es."

23. *Laetare Mater Ecclesia*, Filippini

Laetare Mater Ecclesia,
exsulta filia Sion,
ducite choros filiae Jerusalem;
quia alterum Africa protulit Annibalem,
sed pro Roma strenue pugnantem.

Non hic aceto fregit Alpes,
sed suae matris fractus est lacrimis.
Alterum Africa . . .

Habuit[1] ille venenum in annulo,
hic antidotum in calamo;
habuit ille hic virus evomuit.
Alterum Africa . . .

Ille Romanos apud Cannas profligavit;
hic Pelagium convicit, et evertit Erebum.
Alterum Africa . . .

Laetus ergo triumphet in caelis,
qui tam fortis pugnavit in terris;
afferte palmas paeana canentes,
ejus tempora cingite laureis.
Gaudeat tellus, plaudant Angeli,
psallant fideles in sono tubae.
Gaudeat tellus, plaudant Angeli,
psallant fideles in chordis et organo.
Gaudeat tellus, plaudant Angeli,
psallant fideles in timpano et choro.
Omnis spiritus laudet Dominum.

Rejoice, Mother Church;
exult, daughter of Zion;
lead dances, daughters of Jerusalem;
for Africa has brought forth another Hannibal,
though one fighting staunchly for Rome.

This one did not break down the Alps with vinegar
but was broken by the tears of his mother.
Africa has brought forth . . .

That one had venom in a ring,
this one had an antidote in a pen;
that one had poison, this one spewed it out.
Africa has brought forth . . .

That one routed the Romans at Cannae;
this one refuted Pelagius and overturned hell.
Africa has brought forth . . .

Therefore let him triumph joyfully in the heavens
who so bravely fought on earth;
bring palms while singing paeans,
encircle his forehead with laurels.
Let the earth rejoice, let the angels applaud,
let the faithful make music with the sound of the trumpet.
Let the earth rejoice, let the angels applaud,
let the faithful make music with strings and organ.
Let the earth rejoice, let the angels applaud,
let the faithful make music with drum and dance.
Let everything that has breath praise the Lord.

Comment. Anonymous original text in honor of St. Augustine, including references to Ps. 150 in final section.

Note. 1. Source has "Aabuit."

BASSO Continuo

SACRA CORONA

MOTETTI A Due, e Trè voci Di Diuersi Eccelentissimi
Autori moderni, Nouamente raccolti & dati in luce
Da Bartolomeo Marcesso

DEDICATI
RE
AL MOLTO ILL. SIGNORE

SIGNOR E PATRON COL.^{mo}

IL SIG. FEDERICO SCVLAZZON

IN VENETIA MDCLVI   Apresso Francesco Magni   D

Plate 1. *Sacra Corona: Motetti a due, e trè voci di diversi eccellentissimi autori moderni* (Venice: Bartolomeo Magni, 1656), title page. Library of Congress, Washington, D.C. (shelfmark M1490.M185 S2 Case).

Plate 2. Giovanni Battista Volpe, "Jesu mi, Jesu benignissime," *Sacra Corona: Motetti a due, e trè voci di diversi eccellentissimi autori moderni* (Venice: Bartolomeo Magni, 1656), Canto Secondo partbook, page 20, showing handwritten repeat sign. Library of Congress, Washington, D.C. (shelfmark M1490.M185 S2 Case).

Plate 3. Maurizio Cazzati, "Obstupescite gentes." *Sacra Corona: Motetti a due, e trè voci di diversi eccellentissimi autori moderni* (Venice: Bartolomeo Magni, 1656), Canto Secondo partbook, page 58. Library of Congress, Washington, D.C. (shelfmark M1490.M185 S2 Case).

Sacra Corona
(Venice, 1656)

Dedication

MOLTO ILL.^{RE} SIGNORE | SIG.^{RE} E PATRONE COL.^{MO}

Se le cose più rare, sono più pregiate nel mondo, e se li fauori deuono esser compensati, con eguali, ò maggiori espressioni, riceuerò io da questo secolo, lodi d'ammiratione; mentre all'industriosa veglianza di cosi degna raccolta, fattone una SACRA CORONA; questa riposi soura i cuspidi delle due lancie, decorose insegne della Casa di V.S. Molto Illustre. Accetti il dono, come tributo delle mie vbligationi [*sic*], e con l'acclamationi di cosi rara, e singolare operetta, si suggelli la publicatione della mia seruitù, che mi fà sempre viuere.

 Di V.S. Molto Illustre | Devotissimo & Obligatissimo seruitore | Bartolomeo Marcesso

Most illustrious sir, most honorable lord and patron:

If the rarest things are the most prized in the world, and if favors are to be recompensed with equal or greater expressions, I shall receive from this world admiring praise; for by the industrious wakefulness with which a SACRED CROWN has been made from such a worthy collection; may it rest on the tips of the two spears, the worthy emblem of Your Excellency's house. Accept this gift as a tribute of my obligations, and, with the applause due to such a rare and singular work, may this public manifestation of my service be sealed, which will cause me to live forever.

 Your Excellency's most devoted and obliged servant, Bartolomeo Marcesso.

1. Nigra sum

Giovanni Rovetta

17
C1
-le- xit me Rex, et in- tro- du- xit __ me in cu- bi- cu-lum su- um,
C2
i- de- o di- le- xit me Rex, et in- tro- du- xit __
B.c.
21
C1
i- de- o di- le- xit me Rex,
C2
me, ⟨et in- tro- du- xit __ me⟩ in cu- bi- cu- lum su- um, i- de- o di- le- xit me
B.c.
25
C1
⟨i- de- o di- le- xit me Rex,⟩ et in- tro- du- xit __ me, ⟨et in- tro- du- xit __
C2
Rex, et in- tro- du- xit __ me, ⟨et in- tro- du- xit __ me⟩ in cu-
B.c.
29
C1
me⟩ in cu- bi- - cu- lum su- um. Tra- he, tra- he me post
C2
-bi- cu- lum su- um.
B.c.

33
C1
te; cur- re- mus, cur- re- mus in o- do- rem un- guen- to- - rum tu- o-
C2
B.c.
37
C1
-rum.
C2
Tra- he, tra- he me post te; cur- re- mus, cur- re- mus in o- do- rem un- guen- to-
B.c.
41
C1
Ve- ni spon- sa Chri- sti, ac- ci- pe co-
C2
- rum tu- o- rum.
B.c.
45
C1
-ro- nam, ac- ci- pe, ac- ci- pe co- ro- nam,
C2
Ve- ni spon- sa
B.c.

50
C1
C2
Chri- sti, ⟨ve- ni spon- sa Chri- sti,⟩ ac- ci- pe, ac- ci- pe co- ro-
B.c.
56
C1
ve- ni spon- sa Chri- sti, ac- ci- pe co- ro- nam, ac- ci- pe,
C2
-nam, ve- ni spon- sa Chri- sti, ⟨ve- ni spon- sa Chri- sti,⟩
B.c.
61
C1
⟨ac- ci- pe, ac- ci- pe, ac- ci- pe⟩ co- ro- nam
C2
ac- ci- pe, ac- ci- pe, ac- ci- pe co- ro- nam
B.c.
66
C1
quam ti- bi Do- mi-nus prae- pa- ra- vit, ⟨quam ti- bi Do- mi-nus, quam ti- bi Do- mi-nus⟩
C2
quam ti- bi Do- mi-nus prae- pa- ra- vit, ⟨quam ti- bi Do- mi- nus,
B.c.

70
C1
prae- pa- ra- vit in ae- ter- - num, in ae- ter- num,
C2
quam ti- bi Do- mi- nus,⟩ in ae-
B.c.
73
C1
quam ti- bi Do- mi- nus,
C2
-ter- - num, in ae- ter- num, quam ti- bi Do- mi- nus
B.c.
76
C1
⟨quam ti- bi Do- mi- nus⟩ prae- pa- ra- vit in ae- ter-
C2
prae- pa- ra- vit in ae- ter- - num,
B.c.
6
6
79
C1
- num, ⟨in ae- ter-⟩ - - num, in ae- ter- num.
C2
⟨in ae- ter-⟩ - - num, in ae- ter- num.
B.c.
6

82
C1
Al- le- lu- ia, al- le- lu- ia,
C2
Al- - - le-
B.c.
88
C1
al- le- lu- ia, al- le- lu- ia,
C2
- lu- ia, al- le- lu- ia, al-
B.c.
94
C1
al- - - - le-
C2
-le- lu- ia,
B.c.
99
C1
- lu- ia, al- le- lu- ia, al-
C2
al- le- lu- ia, al- le- lu- ia,
B.c.

105
C1
-le- lu- ia, al- -
C2
al- [le- lu- ia,]
B.c.
110
C1
- - [le- lu- ia,] al- le- lu- ia, al-
C2
al- - [le- lu- ia,] al- le- lu- ia, al-
B.c.
6
115
C1
-le- lu- ia, ⟨al- - le- lu- ia.⟩
C2
-le- lu- ia, al- le- lu- - ia.
B.c.

2. Dulce sit vobis pati

Natale Monferrato

25
C
fi- de- les. O fi- de- - les,
A
fi- de- les. O fi- de- les,
B.c.
30
C
mo- di-cum su- sti- ne- - te tem- pus; nam mcr-
A
mo- di-cum su- sti- ne- te tem- pus; nam mer- ces
B.c.
7 6
[♭]
35
C
- - ces ve- stra co- pi-
A
ve- - - stra co pi o sa est
B.c.
41
C
-o- sa est in cae- - -
A
in cae- - - - -
B.c.
6
6

47
C
- lis, co- pi- o- sa est in
A
- lis, co- pi- o- sa est, co- pi- o- sa est in
B.c.
[6]
6
53
C
cae- - - - - lis, in
A
cae- - - - - lis, in
B.c.
58
C
cae- lis, co- pi- o- sa est in
A
cae- lis, co- pi- o- sa est in cae- -
B.c.
6
64
C
cae- lis, mer- ces ve- stra co- pi- o- sa
A
- lis, mer- ces ve- - stra co- pi- o- sa
B.c.
4

13

C: est__ in__ cae- lis.__ In hoc mun- do pe- rit vi- ta,

A: est__ in__ cae- lis.__ in hoc mun- do ces- sant

C: cun- cta va- na trans- e- unt. pre- sto, pre- sto flo- ret, ci- to,

A: lae- ta, cun- cta va- na trans- e- unt. Flos ae- ta- tis, ⟨flos ae- ta- tis,⟩

C: ci- to lan- guet, flos ae- ta- tis pre- sto flo- ret, ci- to lan- guet, sta- tim ca- dit a- ri- dus, ci- to

A: flos ae- ta- tis pre- sto flo- ret, ci- to lan- guet, sta- tim ca- dit a- ri- dus, pre- sto flo- ret,

C: lan- guet, sta- tim ca- dit a- ri- dus, flos ae- ta- tis pre- sto flo- ret, ci- to lan- guet, sta- tim ca- dit a- ri-

A: sta- tim ca- dit, flos ae- ta- tis pre- sto flo- ret, ci- to lan- guet, sta- tim ca- dit a- ri-

87
C
-dus. I- bi i- gi- tur, no- stra fi- xa sint cor- da,
A
-dus. I- bi i- gi- tur, u- bi ve-
B.c.
92
C
u- bi ve- ra sint gau- di- a, u- bi ve-
A
-ra, u- bi ve- ra sint gau- di- a, u- bi ve-
B.c.
97
C
- ra sint gau- di- a, ve- - -
A
- ra sint gau- di- a, ve- - -
B.c.
102
C
- ra sint gau- di- a, u- bi
A
- ra sint gau- di- a, u- bi ve- - ra,
B.c.

107
C
ve- - ra sint gau- di- a, ve- -
A
ve- ra sint gau- di- a, ve- -
B.c.
112
C
- - ra sint gau- di- a, ve- ra, ve- ra, ve- ra,
A
- - ra sint gau- di- a, ve- ra, ve- ra,
B.c.
118
C
ve- ra sint gau- di- a. O fi- de- les,
A
ve- ra sint gau- di- a. O fi- de- les,
B.c.
123
C
ad ae- des a- ma- tas,
A
ad se- des be- a- tas, pro- pe-
B.c.

16

17

Lyrics:

C: si pacem sine dolo, si laetitiam sine fletu nos mor- -tales cupimus, ad caelum sit gressus, ad caelum sit vi- a et no- ster ac-

A: Si opes sine metu, si laetitiam sine fletu nos mortales cupimus, ad caelum sit gres- sus, ad caelum sit vi- a et no- ster ac-

-ces- sus, et no- ster, no- ster ac- ces- sus;

-ces- sus, et no- ster, no- ster ac- ces- sus;

nam no- stra con- ver- sa- ti- o in cae- lis, in cae- lis

nam no- stra con- ver- sa- ti- o in cae- lis, in cae- lis

est,

est, no- stra con- ver- sa- ti- o in cae- lis, in

no- stra con- ver- sa- ti- o in cae- lis, in

205
C
cae- lis est, in cae- - lis est.
A
cae- lis est, in cae- - - lis est.
B.c.
209
C
Dul- ce sit vo- bis pa- ti,
A
Dul- ce sit vo- bis pa- ti, o fi- de-
B.c.
215
C
o fi- de- les, o, o fi-
A
- - les, o, o fi-
B.c.
221
C
-de- les, dul- ce sit vo- bis pa- ti, fi-
A
-de- les, dul- ce sit, dul- ce sit vo- bis pa- ti, fi-
B.c.

227
C
- de- les; nam mer- - - ces ve-
A
- de- les; nam mer- ces ve- - -
B.c.
♮ 7 ♭ 6 [4 3]
233
C
-stra co- pi- o- sa est in
A
-stra co- pi o sa est in cae- -
B.c.
6
239
C
cae- - - - lis,
A
- - - lis, co pi o sa
B.c.
6
245
C
co- pi- o- sa est in cae- - -
A
est, co- pi- o- sa est in cae- -
B.c.
6 [6] [♭]

251
C
A
B.c.
- - lis, in cae- lis, co- pi-
- - lis, in cae- lis, co- pi- o- sa
[♭]
256
-o- sa est in cae- lis, mer- ces
est in cae- - - lis, mer- ces ve-
6 [♭] [4 ♯]
262
ve- stra co- pi- o- sa est in cae- lis.
- stra co- pi- o- sa est in cae- lis.
268
Al- le- lu- ia, al- le- lu- ia, al- le- lu- ia,
Al- le- lu- ia, al- le- lu-

272
C
A
B.c.
al- le- lu- ia, al- le- lu- ia, al- le- lu-
-ia, al- le- lu- ia,
276
ia, al- le- lu- ia, al- le- lu- ia,
al- le- lu- ia, al- le- lu- ia,
279
al- le- lu- ia, al- le- lu- ia, al- le- lu- ia,
al- le- - lu- ia, al- le- lu- ia, al- le- lu-
283
al- le- lu- ia, al- le- lu- ia, al-
-ia, ⟨al- le- lu- ia,⟩

24

286

C: -le- lu- ia, al- le- lu- ia, al- le- lu- ia, al- le- lu- ia, ⟨al- le- lu-

A: al- le- lu- ia, al- le- lu- ia, ⟨al- le- lu- ia, al- le- lu- ia,⟩ al- le-

290

C: -ia, al- le- lu- ia,⟩ al- le- lu- ia, al- le- lu- ia,___

A: -lu- ia, al- le- lu- ia,___ al- le- lu- ia, al- le- lu- ia,___

294

C: ___ al- le- lu- ia, al- le- lu- ia, al- le- lu- ia, al-

A: al- le- lu- ia, al- le- lu- ia, ⟨al-

298

C: -le- lu- ia, al- le- lu- ia, al- le- lu- ia, al- le- lu- ia.

A: -le- lu- ia,⟩ al- le- lu- ia, al- le- lu- ia.

B.c.: 7 6 ♯

3. O bone Jesu

Francesco Cavalli

19
C
A
B.c.
- - di- um,
me- a lux, me- um cor, me- a lux, me- um cor, me- um
23
me- a
gau- - - - di-
27
lux, me- um gau- - -
-um, me- um cor, me- um gau- -
31
- di- um: te ca- nant An- ge- li,
- di- um: te

36
C
co- lant ho- -
A
co- lant ho- mi- nes, co- lant ho-
B.c.
41
C
- mi- nes ae- - ter- num, te ca- nant An- ge-
A
- mi- nes ae- ter num, te ca- nant An- ge-
B.c.
46
C
-li, te co- lant ho- mi- nes ae- ter- num.
A
-li, te co- lant ho- mi- nes ae- ter- num.
B.c.
51
C
O pi- e, o ca- re, o cle- mens,
A
O pi- e, o ca- re, o cle-
B.c.

28

respice, ⟨respice⟩ mundi crimina; nec tuos averte oculos, sed benignissime, benignissime sana.

Vide bone, vide care, sana, sana pie, sana, sana clemens, sana pie, sana clemens, vide bone, vide sana, sana clemens; o amabilis, o amabilis.

care, sana, sana clemens; o dulcissime, o amabilis.

Tu solus esto animae salus, vitae, vitae suspirium; animae quae te fugit,

96
C
a- ni- mae quae te spre- vit, et gra- vi-
A
B.c.
6
♯
101
C
-ter, et gra- vi- ter of- fen- dit.
A
E- sto sa- lus
B.c.
4
♯
106
C
E- sto sa- lus lan- gui- dae, e- sto vi- ta sau- ci- ae,
A
lan- gui- dae, e- sto vi- ta sau- ci- ae, e- sto, ⟨e-
B.c.
♮
110
C
e- sto, e- sto me- de- la mi- se- rae.
A
-sto⟩ me- de- la mi- se- rae. Sal- va- tor u- ni-
B.c.

114
C
A
B.c.
Je- su dul- cis- si- me, quem nos re- co- li- mus, quem nos
-ce, quem nos di- li- gi- mus,
118
re- co- li- mus,
Je- su dul- cis- si-
Sal- va- tor u- ni- ce, quem nos di- li- gi- mus,
122
-me, quem nos re- co- li- mus, quem nos re- co- li- mus: ve- ni, ⟨ve- ni⟩
quem nos re- co- li- mus: ve- ni, ⟨ve- ni⟩
127
pla- ci- de, ac nos ae- rum- nis li- be- ra.
pla- ci- de, ac nos ae- rum- nis li- be- ra.

132
C
Ve- ni bo- ne, ve- ni, ⟨ve- ni, ve- ni⟩ a- ma- bi- lis,
A
ve- ni ca- re, ve- ni, ⟨ve- ni⟩ a- ma- bi- lis, ve- ni
B.c.
139
C
ve- ni ca- re, ve- ni, ve- ni a- ma- bi- lis,
A
bo- ne, ve- ni, ⟨ve- ni,⟩ ve- ni a- ma- bi- lis, ve- ni
B.c.
145
C
ve- ni ca- re, ve- ni, ve- ni a- ma- bi- lis.
A
bo- ne, ve- ni, ⟨ve- ni,⟩ ve- ni a- ma- bi- lis.
B.c.

4. Ad charismata caelorum

Massimiliano Neri

Ad cha-ri-sma-ta cae-lo-rum ac-ce-di-te, ac-ce-di-te fi-de-les, fi-de-les ac-ce-di-te; ad men-sam An-ge-lo-rum ac-cur-ri-te, ⟨ac-cur-ri-te⟩ de-vo-ti, ad men-sam An-ge-lo-rum ac-cur-ri-te, ⟨ac-cur-ri-te⟩ de-vo-ti, ac-cur-ri-te, ⟨ac-cur-ri-te⟩ de-vo-ti.

ad men-sam An-ge-lo-rum ac-cur-ri-te, ⟨ac-cur-ri-te⟩ de-vo-ti, ac-cur-ri-te, ⟨ac-cur-ri-te⟩ de-vo-ti.

15
C
A
B.c.
solo
Ve- ne- ra- mi- ni De- um ve- strum qui vos pa- - scit, con- so- la- tur, vos e-
4 3
18
[solo]
Ve- ne- ra- - mi- ni De- um ve- strum qui vos pa- scit, con- so-
-nu- trit, ⟨vos e- nu- trit,⟩ con- vi- va- tur,
4 3 6 5
22
-la- tur, vos e- nu- trit, con- vi- va- tur, ve- ne- ra- mi- ni De- um ve- strum
ve- ne- ra- - mi- ni De- um ve- strum qui vos pa- scit, con- so-
4 4 3 7 6
26
qui vos pa- scit, con- so- la- tur, ⟨qui vos pa- - scit, con- so- la- tur,⟩ vos e-
-la- tur, vos e- nu- trit, vos e- nu- trit, qui vos pa- - scit, con- so- la- tur, vos e-
4 ♭3

-nutrit, ⟨vos enutrit,⟩ convivatur. O_____ quam suavis est Dominus, o_____ quam suavis est, o,____ o_____ quam suavis est Dominus!

(A) -nutrit, vos enutrit, convivatur. O_____ quam suavis est Dominus, o_____ quam suavis est, o_____ quam suavis est Dominus!

Pane suavissimo de caelo__ praestito, dulcedinem

(A) Pane suavissimo de caelo__ praestito,

53
C
su- am, ⟨dul- ce- di- nem su- am⟩ in fi- li- os de- mon- stra- vit.
A
dul- ce- di- nem su- am in fi- li- os de- mon- stra- vit.
B.c.
57
C
Ac- cur- ri- te lae- tan- tes, ⟨ac- cur- ri- te lae-
A
ac- ce- di- te ve- ne- ran- tes,
B.c.
63
C
-tan- tes,⟩ lae- tan- tes, ac- - cur- ri- te
A
ac- ce- di- te ve- ne- ran- tes, ac-
B.c.
69
C
lae- tan- tes, lae- tan- - tes, ac-
A
-ce- di- te ve- ne- ran- tes,
B.c.

75
C
- cur- ri- te lae-
A
⟨ve- ne- ran- tes, ve- ne- ran- tes,⟩ ac- - ce- di-
B.c.
80
C
-tan- tcs, lac- tan- - tes, lae- tan- - tes, ac-
A
-te lae- tan- - tes, lae- tan- - tes, ac-
B.c.
85
C
- cur- ri- te.
A
- cur- ri- te. Al- le- lu- ia. ⟨al- le- lu-
B.c.
90
C
Al- le- lu- ia, al- le- lu- ia, ⟨al- le-
A
-ia,⟩ al- le-
B.c.

95
C
A
B.c.
-lu- ia, al- le- lu- ia,⟩ al- le- lu- ia, ⟨al- le- lu- ia, al- le-
-lu- ia, ⟨al- le- lu- ia,⟩ al- le- lu- ia,
100
-lu- ia,⟩ al- le- lu- ia, ⟨al- le- lu- ia,⟩ al-
⟨al- le- - lu- ia,⟩ al- le- lu- ia, ⟨al-
105
-le- lu- ia, ⟨al- le- lu- ia,⟩ al- le- lu- ia.
-le- lu- ia, al- le- lu- ia,⟩ al- le- lu- ia.
4 3

5. Jesu mi, Jesu benignissime

Giovanni Battista Volpe

17
C1
-xi- sti vi- sce-ra me- a, tu vul- ne- ra- sti cor me- um, trans- fi- xi- sti vi- sce- ra
C2
tu vul- ne- ra- sti cor me- um, trans- fi- xi- sti vi- sce- ra
B.c.
20
me- a, Je- su mi pi- is- - si- me, vul- ne- ra- sti cor me- um, trans- fi-
me- a, Je- su mi pi- is- si- me,
24
-xi- sti vi- sce-ra me- a, Je- su mi pi- is- si- me. Con- fi- ge
Je- - su mi pi- is- - si- me.
28
a- ni- mam sa- git- tis ca- ri- ta- tis, o a- mor, o

41

60
C1
-fi- ge, o vi- ta me- - a, o
C2
o cor, o vi- ta me- - a,
B.c.
64
C1
vi- ta me- - a.
Allegro
O mi ca- re Je- su,
C2
o vi- ta me- a.
B.c.
68
C1
o mi ca- re Je- su, fac ut ar- de- am in te, ni- hil a- mem, ni- hil
C2
B.c.
71
C1
a- mem ni- si te. O mi ca- re Je- su, ca- re, ca- re
C2
O mi ca- re Je- su, ca- re, ca- re
B.c.

74
C1
Je- su, o mi ca- re Je- su, fac ut ar- de- am in te, ni- hil a- mem ni- si
C2
Je- su, o mi ca- re Je- su, ni- hil a- mem,
B.c.
78
Adagio
Allegro
C1
te, ni- hil ve- lim ni- si te, mi ca- re Je- su,
C2
fac ut mo- ri- ar pro te, mi bo- ne
B.c.
7 6
82
C1
pi- is- si- me Je- su, dul- cis- si- me Je- su, o mi ca- re
C2
Je- su, pi is si me Je su, dul cis- si- me Je- su, o mi ca- re
B.c.
85
C1
Je- su, fac ut ar- de- am in te, ni- hil ve- lim ni- si te, ni- hil ve- lim ni- si
p
C2
Je- su, fac ut ar- de- am in te, ni- hil ve- lim ni- si te, ni- hil ve- lim ni- si
p
B.c.
p

89
C1
te. Al- le- lu- ia, al- - le- lu- ia,
C2
te. Al- le-
B.c.
92
C1
al- le- lu- ia,
C2
-lu- ia, al- - le- lu- ia,
B.c.
95
C1
al- le- lu- ia, al-
C2
al- le- lu- ia, al- le- lu- ia, al-
B.c.
98
C1
- - - le- lu- ia,
C2
- - - le- lu- ia,
B.c.

45

6. Exsultate, gaudete, jubilate

Pietro Andrea Ziani

47

30
C
- - tes, cur- ri- te, ⟨cur- ri- te,⟩ cur- -
T
-lan- - tes, cur- ri- te, ⟨cur- ri- te,⟩ cur-
B.c.
36
C
- - ri- te, ⟨cur- ri- te, cur- ri- te⟩ ad pas- cu-
T
- - ri- te, cur- ri- te, ⟨cur- ri- te⟩ ad pas-
B.c.
7
41
C
-a, fe- sti- na- - - te, fe- sti- na- te ad
T
-cua, fe- sti- na- - te, fe- sti- na- te ad
B.c.
46
C
fon- tes. Ec-
T
fon- tes. Ec- ce pa- - nis, ec- ce po- - tus An- ge- lo-
B.c.
4 3

49

66
solo
C
An- ge- lo- rum. O bo- ne Je- su, o ca- re
T
-lo- rum.
3 4 3 ♯ 6
B.c.
71
C
Je- su, ac- cen- de me, o bo- ne Je- su, o ca- re
♯ 7 6 ♯
B.c.
75
C
Je- su, in- e- bri- a me, o ca- re Je- su, in- e- bri- a me, o bo- ne,
[♮]
5 6
B.c.
79
C
bo- ne, o bo- ne Je- su;
[solo]
T
O bo- ne Je- su,
♯
B.c.
84
T
o ca- re Je- su, ac- cen- de me, com- bu- re me, o bo- ne Je- su,
B.c.
89
T
o ca- re Je- su, ac- cen- de me, com- bu- re me, sa- tu- ra me,
B.c.

51

113
C
abs- con- de me. Sa- tu- ra me, in- e- bri- a me,
T
abs- con- de me.〉 in- e- bri- a me, sa- tu- ra
B.c.
117
o bo- ne Je- su, o ca- re Je- su, ex- au- di
me, o bo- ne Je- su, [o] ca- re Je- su, ex- au- di
122
me, 〈ex- au- di me,〉 ex- au- di
me, 〈ex- au- di me,〉 ex- au- - di
127
me. A- - - men.
me. A- - - men.

7. Surge propera

Biagio Marini

24
A
Cla-mat, pul-sat, ma-det, lan-guet, lan-guet, lan- - guet spon- sus.
B
Cla-mat, pul-sat, ma-det, lan-guet, lan-guet, lan- - guet spon- sus.
B.c.
29
A
Sur- ge, sur- ge, a- pe- ri, a- pe- ri, mi- se- re-
B
Sur- ge, sur- ge, a- pe- ri,
B.c.
35
A
-re, sur- ge, sur- ge, sur- ge, sur- ge, a- pe- ri, a- pe- ri,
B
a- pe- ri, mi- se- re- re, sur- ge,
B.c.
41
A
mi- se- re- re, sur- ge, sur- ge, a- pe- ri, a- pe- ri,
B
sur- ge, a- pe- ri, a- pe- ri, mi- se- re- re, mi- se-
B.c.

47
A
surge, surge, aperi, aperi, misere-
B
-re- re, mi- se- re- re, mi- se- re- -
B.c.
53
A
-re. In- tro- duc in do- mum ge- ni- tri- cis tu- ae; ec- ce, ec- ce ve- nit,
B
-re. ec- ce, ec- ce ve- nit, sa-
B.c.
57
A
ec- ce, ec- ce,
B
li- ens, sa- - li-ens, sa- li- ens in mon- ti-bus, tran-
B.c.
61
A
ec- ce, ec- ce, ec- ce ve- nit, sa-
B
-si- li-ens col- - - les, ve- nit, sa-
B.c.

-liens, sa- - liens in montibus, transiliens -liens, sa- - liens in montibus, transili-

col- les, transiliens col-
-ens, transiliens col- les, transiliens

-les, col- - les.
col- - les.

Suscipe amantem, exaudi precantem, fove languentem, co-

-lumba speciosa,

Suscipe amantem, exaudi precantem,

suscipe amantem,

fove languentem, columba speciosa, *exaudi precantem,*

fove languentem, columba speciosa; vulnerasti cor

columba speciosa;

meum *in uno crine colli tui, vulnera-*

vulnerasti cor meum, et in

94
A
- sti cor me- um, co- lum- ba me- a, for- mo- sa me- a, im-
B
u- no cri- ne col- li tu- i, vul- ne- ra- - sti cor me- um, a-
B.c.
98
A
-ma- cu- la- ta me- a, a- mo- re
B
-mo- re lan- gue- o, co- lum- ba me- a, for- mo- sa me- a, im- ma- cu- la- ta
B.c.
101
A
lan- gue- o, co- lum- ba me- a, for- mo- sa me- a, im- ma- cu- la- ta me-
B
me- a, a- mo- re lan- gue-
B.c.
104
A
-a, a- mo- re lan- gue- o, lan-
B
-o, co- lum- ba me- a, for- mo- sa me- a, im- ma- cu- la- ta me- a,
B.c.

107
A
- - gue- o, co- lum- ba me- a, for- mo- sa
B
lan- - gue- o, lan-
B.c.
110
A
me- a, im- ma- cu- la- ta, lan- -
B
- gue- o, co- lum- ba me- a, for- mo- sa me- a, im- ma- cu-
B.c.
113
A
- gue- o, lan- gue- o. Al- -
B
-la- ta me- - a. Al
B.c.
6 7 6
118
A
- - le- lu- ia, al-
B
- - le- lu- ia, al- -
B.c.

121
A
- - - le- lu- ia,
B
- - - le- lu- ia, al-
B.c.
124
A
al- - -
B
- - -
B.c.
127
A
- - -
B
- - -
B.c.
130
A
- - [le- - lu- ia.]
B
- - le- - lu- ia.
B.c.

8. Salve mundi triumphatrix

Della B. V. M.

Maurizio Cazzati

22
B
sal- ve vi- ta mor- ta- li- um, Sal-ve, sal-ve, sal-ve vi- ta, sal-ve vi- ta mor- ta- li-
B.c.
26
A
Tu Re- gi- na, tu Re- gi- na
B
-um, Sal-ve vi- ta mor- ta- li- um.
B.c.
31
A
sum- mi Re- gis, Mi- se- ro- rum quae do- lo- res Au- dis i- tem et cla- mo- res
B.c.
36
A
Ex o- vi- li tu- i gre- gis, Ex o- vi- li, ex o- vi- li tu- i gre-
B.c.
41
A
-gis.
B
A- ve pa- rens ma- gni De- i, Nunc ad cae- lum sub- le- va- ta, Et co- ro- na
B.c.

-de- co- ra- ta, Dul- cis vi- ta, dul- cis vi- ta cor- - - dis me-
-i, Dul- cis vi- ta cor- - - dis me- i.

In te so- la re- fu- gi- um no- strum, po- ten- tis- si- ma, po- ten- tis- si- ma Re- gi- -na.

Per te sa- lus mun- di ve- nit,

In te gau- di- um af- fli- cto- rum, pi- is- si- ma, pi- is- si- ma Ma- ri- a per te gau- dent om- nes cae- li- tes, a- man- tis- si- ma,

Adagio
Er- go, er- go om- nes
a- man- tis- si- ma Ma- ri- a. Er- go, er- go om- nes
u- ni- so- nis vo- ci- bus, gau- den- ti- bus ci- tha- ris, lae- tan- ti- bus
u- ni- so- nis vo- ci- bus, gau- den- ti- bus ci- tha- ris,
can- ti- bus, lae- tan- ti- bus can- ti- bus col- lau- de- mus,
lae- tan- ti- bus can- ti- bus, lae- tan- ti- bus can- ti- bus col- lau-
col- lau- de- - mus Ma- ri- am, col- lau- de- mus Ma- ri-
-de- mus, col- lau- de- - mus Ma- ri- am, col- lau- de- mus Ma- ri-

83
A
-am, u- ni- so- nis vo- ci- bus, gau- den- ti- bus ci- tha- ris, lae- tan- ti- bus
B
-am, u- ni- so- nis vo- ci- bus, gau- den- ti- bus ci- tha- ris, lae-
B.c.
87
A
can- ti- bus col- lau- de- mus, col- lau- de- mus Ma- ri- am,
B
-tan- ti- bus can- ti- bus col- lau- de- mus, col- lau- de-
B.c.
91
A
col- lau- de- - mus, col- lau- de-
B
- mus, col- lau- de- -
B.c.
94
A
- mus, col- lau- de- -
B
- mus Ma- ri- am, col- lau- de-
B.c.

97
A
- mus, col- lau- de- mus Ma- ri- am, col- lau- de- mus, col- lau-
B
- mus, col- lau- de- mus Ma- ri- am, col- lau- de- mus,
B.c.
100
A
-de- - mus, col- lau- de- mus Ma- ri- am.
B
col- lau- de- - mus, col- lau- de- mus Ma- ri- am.
B.c.
104
A
E- ia, e- ia er- go, fe- stan- ti- bus cor- di- bus, ri-
B
E- ia, e- ia er- go, fe- stan- ti- bus cor- di- bus, ri-
B.c.
109
A
-den- ti- bus mo- du- lis, psal- len- ti- bus mu- si- cis, psal- len- ti- bus
B
-den- ti- bus mo- du- lis, psal- len- ti- bus mo- du- lis,
B.c.

113
A
mu- si- cis ve- ne- re- mur, ve- ne- re-
B
psal- len- ti- bus mu- si- cis ve- ne- re- mur, ve- ne- re-
B.c.
117
- mur Ma- ri- am, ve- ne- re- mur Ma- ri- am, fe- stan- ti- bus cor di bus, ri
- mur Ma- ri- am, ve- ne- re- mur Ma- ri- am, fe- stan- ti- bus cor- di- bus,
121
-den- ti- bus mo- du- lis, psal- len- ti- bus mu- si- cis ve- ne- re- mur, ve- neri den ti bus mo du lis, psal- len- ti- bus mu- si- cis ve- ne- re- mur,
125
-re- mur Ma- ri- am, ve- ne- re- - mur,
ve- ne- re- - mur, ve- ne- re-

129
A
ve-ne- re- - mur, ve-ne- re- -
B
- - mur Ma- ri- am, ve- ne- re-
B.c.
133
A
- mur, ve- ne- re- mur Ma- ri- am, ve- ne- re- mur, ve- ne-
B
- mur, ve- ne- re- mur Ma- ri- am, ve- ne- re- mur,
B.c.
136
A
-re- - mur, ve- ne- re- mur Ma-ri- am.
B
ve- ne- re- - mur, ve- ne- re- mur Ma- ri- am.
B.c.

9. Spargite flores

Orazio Tarditi

21
C
fun- di- te rosas,
et da- te li- li- a Ma- ri- ae
B
et da- te li- li- a Ma- ri- ae sem- per Vir- gi- ni,
B.c.
26
sem- per Vir- gi- ni,
et da- te li- li- a Ma- ri- ae
et da- te li- li- a Ma- ri- ae sem- per Vir- gi- ni, et da- te
31
sem- per Vir- gi- ni, sem- per Vir- gi- ni, spar-
li- li- a Ma- ri- ae sem- per, sem- per Vir- gi- ni,
36
- - gi- te, spar- gi- te, spar- -
spar- - - gi- te, spar- -

41
C
- - gi- te flo- res. At- tol- li- te lu- mi- na,
B
- - gi- te flo- res.
B.c.
46
C
e- le- va- te o- cu- los, au ro ram sa lu ta te, au ro ram sa lu-
B
B.c.
49
C
-ta- te, sa- lu- ta- - te Ma- ri- am, au-
B
Tu au- ro- ra, tu stel- la, tu lu- na, tu sol,
B.c.
53
C
-ro- ram sa- lu- ta- te, sa- lu- ta- te Ma- ri- am.
B
tu au- ro- ra, tu stel- la, tu
B.c.

Tu au- ro- ra, tu stel- la, tu au- ro- ra, tu lu- na, tu sol, tu stel- la,
tu lu- na, tu sol, tu lu- na, tu sol, tu stel- la, tu au- ro- ra, tu lu- na, tu sol, tu lu- na, tu sol, tu lu- na, tu sol.

tu lu- na, tu sol, tu lu- na, tu sol, tu lu- na, tu sol.

O_____ a- ma- bi- lis, a-
O_____ a- ma- bi- lis, a- ma- bi- lis au-

-ma- bi- lis au- ro- ra,
-ro- ra, au- ro- ra___ pul- chri- or, tu stel- lis___

73
C
B
cla- ri- or, tu lu- na pu- ri- or, so- le lu- ci- di- or,
B.c.
78
C
au- ro- ra pul- chri- or, tu stel- lis cla- ri- or,
B
Ma- ri- a,
B.c.
83
C
tu lu- na pu- ri- or, so- le lu- ci- di- or, Ma- ri-
B
B.c.
88
C
-a, au- ro- ra pul- chri- or,
B
au- ro- ra pul- chri- or, es Ma- ri-
B.c.

93

C: tu stel- lis cla- ri- or, tu lu- na pu- ri- or,

B: -a, es Ma- ri- a, es

99

C: so- le lu- ci- di- or,

B: Ma- ri- a, es Ma- ri-

105

C: es Ma- ri- a, Ma- ri- a, es Ma- ri- a, Ma- ri- a,

B: -a, es Ma- ri- a, Ma- ri- a, es Ma- ri- a, Ma- ri- a, au- ro- ra

111

C: au- ro- ra pul- chri- or, tu stel- lis cla- ri- or, tu lu- na pu- ri- or, so- le lu-

B: pul- chri- or, tu stel- lis cla- ri- or, tu lu- na pu- ri- or, so- le lu- ci-

m. 115

C: -ci- di- or es Ma- ri- a, es Ma- ri- a, es Ma- ri- a.

B: -di- or es Ma- ri- a, es Ma- ri- a, Ma- ri- a.

m. 122

B: Tu es Virgo Maria a Patre summo dilecta,

m. 125

B: a filio mater electa, inter mulieres una nobilis, inter matres unica

m. 128

B: Virgo, et inter virgines sola_____ Mari-

m. 131

C: Quod prima mater abstulit, Tu reddis mirabiliter, Dum paris nobis

B: -a.

gra- ti- am, Il- la si cul- pam pe- pe- rit, Il- la si cul- pam pe- pe-

-rit. O a- ni- mae prae- si- di- um, pec- ca-
O, o a- ni- mae prae- si- di- um,

-to- rum, pec- ca- to- rum re- fu- gi- um, o,
pec- ca- to- rum, pec- ca- to- rum re- fu- gi- um, o,

o An- ge- lo- rum so- la- ti- um, et Tri- ni- ta- tis,
o An- ge- lo- rum so- la- ti- um, et Tri- ni-

et Trinitatis gaudium, Trinitatis, Trinitatis gaudium; tu succurre, succurre, succurre, o clementissima mater: O mater amorum, Dulcedine plena, Regina cae-

173
C: -lo- rum, Lux semper serena: Da nobis gaudere,

B: Da Deum timere, Da semper amare, Da nobis gau-

177
C: Da nobis gaudere, Da tandem re-

B: -dere, Da tandem regnare, Da nobis gaudere, Da tandem re-

180
C: -gnare,

B: -gnare, O mater amorum, Dulcedine plena, Regina cae-

183
C: Da Deum timere, Da

B: -lorum, Lux semper serena:

186
C
sem- per a- ma- re, Da no- bis gau- de- - - re, Da tan- dem re-
B
Da
B.c.
190
C
-gna- re, Da sem- per a- ma- re, Da no- bis gau- de-
B
De- um ti- me- re, Da no- bis gau- de- - re, Da
B.c.
193
C
- re, Da tan- dem re- gna- re, Da no- bis gau- de- re, gau-
B
tan- dem, da tan- dem re- gna- re, Da no- bis gau- de-
B.c.
196
C
-de- - -
B
- re, gau- de- - - re, Da
B.c.

199
C
- re, Da tan- dem, da tan- dem re- gna- re,
B
tan- dem, da tan- dem re- gna- re, Da tan- dem re- gna-
B.c.
203
C
Da tan- dem re- gna- -
B
- - re, Da tan- dem re-
B.c.
206
Adagio
C
- re, Da tan- dem re- gna- - re, re- gna- re.
B
-gna- - re, Da tan- - dem re- gna- re.
B.c.

10. Victoriam, victoriam

Orazio Tarditi

13
C
-mus, om- nes can- te- mus, om- nes can- te- - mus, om-
B
-nes can- te- mus, om- nes can- te- mus, om- nes can- te-
B.c.
16
C
-nes can- te- - - mus, om- nes can- te-
B
- - - mus, om- nes can- te-
B.c.
19
C
-mus, om- nes can- te- - mus, can- te- mus,
B
-mus, om- nes can- te- - mus, can- te- mus,
B.c.
23
Adagio
C
lau- dan- tes De- um et be- ne- di- cen- - tes Do- mi- num, et be- ne- di-
B
lau- dan- tes De- um et be- ne- di- cen- tes Do- mi- num, et be- ne- di-
B.c.

Sheet music, page 83.

Lyrics:
- -centes Dominum. Quis Deus magnus sicut Deus noster, in majestate excelsus, in sanctitate magnificus, in bonitate dulcis, in misericordia suavis; ipsum, ipsum adorant Angeli, ipsum, ipsum collaudant Arcangeli in caelo, laudantes in caelo, laudantes in caelo cantan-
- -centes Domi- num.
- -tes. Date voces, date plausus, date can-

48
C
B
B.c.
Da- te vo- ces, da- te plau-
- tus, da- te can- tus tri- um- pha- les, da- te
51
- sus, da- te can- -
vo- ces, da- te plau- - sus,
54
- tus tri- um- pha- les, da- te vo- ces, da- te plau-
da- te vo- ces, da- te plau- - sus,
57
- sus,
da- te can- - -

date voces, date plausus, date cantus triumphales, date cantus triumphales.

tus triumphales, date cantus triumphales.

Sic caelum intonet, sic terra gaudeat, sic mare resonet, sic mundus jubilet,

sic stellae rideant, sic flores germinent, triumphi

73
C
B
B.c.
sic cae- lum in- to- net, sic ter- ra gau- de- at,
glo- ri- am sic om- nes con- ci- nant, sic ma- re
76
sic stel- lae ri- de- ant, sic flo- res ger- mi- nent,
re- so- net, sic mun- dus ju- bi- let, tri- um- phi
79
tri- um- phi glo- ri- am, ⟨tri- um- phi glo- ri- am,⟩
glo- ri- am, sic om- nes con- ci- nant, tri- um- phi glo- ri- am, tri- um- phi
82
tri- um- phi glo- - ri- am, tri- um- phi
glo- ri- am, sic om- nes con- ci- nant, tri- um- phi glo-

85
C
glo- - - ri- am,
B
- ri- am, glo- - - ri- am, glo-
B.c.
88
C
glo- ri- am sic om- nes con- ci- nant.
B
- ri- am sic om- nes con- ci- nant. Vi- cto- ri- am, vi- cto- ri- am om- nes can- te-
p
f
B.c.
p
f
92
C
Vi- cto- ri- am, vi- cto- ri- am, vi- cto- ri- am, ⟨vi- cto- ri-
B
-mus, om- nes can- te- mus, vi cto ri am, vi cto ri am, vi-
B.c.
95
C
-am,⟩ vi- cto- - ri- am, vi- cto- ri- am, vi-
B
-cto- - ri- am, vi- cto- ri- am, vi- cto- ri- am
B.c.
♮

98
C
-cto- ri- am
B
om- nes can- te- mus, om- nes can- te-
B.c.
101
C
om- nes can- te- mus, om- nes can- te-
B
- mus, om- nes can- te- mus, om- nes can- te- mus, om-
B.c.
104
C
-mus, om- nes can- te- - mus, om- nes can- te-
f p
B
-nes can- te- mus, om- nes can- te- -
f p
B.c.
f p
107
C
f p f p f p
- mus, om- nes can- te- mus, om- nes can- te- mus.
B
f p f p f p
- mus, om- nes can- te- mus, om- nes can- te- mus.
B.c.
f p f p f p

11. Stellae discedite

Stefano Filippini

22
C1
nu- bi- la, te- ne- brae, et mor- ta- li- um o- cu- lis lu- cem e-
C2
nu- bi- la, te- ne- brae, et mor- ta- li- um o- cu- lis lu- cem e-
B.c.
25
C1
-ri- pi- ant sur- gen- - tis au- ro- rae.
C2
-ri- pi- ant sur- gen- - tis au- ro- rae.
B.c.
29
C1
Nox e- nim jam prae- ces- sit, di- es
C2
Nox e- nim jam prae- ces- sit, di- es au-
B.c.
35
C1
au- tem ap- pro- pin- - qua- vit, dum Ma- ri- a, in
C2
- tem ap- pro- pin- - qua- vit, dum Ma- ri- a, in
B.c.

40
C1
sum- mo cae- li car- di- ne, pul- chra ut lu- na, e- le- cta ut sol, san- cti-
C2
sum- mo cae- li car- di- ne, pul- chra ut lu- na, e- le- cta ut sol,
B.c.
43
C1
-ta- tis e- mit- tit ra- di- os; il- lu- mi- nat se- den- tes in
C2
san- cti- ta- tis e- mit- tit ra- di- os; il- lu- mi- nat se- den- tes in
B.c.
46
C1
te- ne- bris, et um- bra mor- tis. Stel- lae di-
C2
te- ne- bris, et um- bra mor- tis.
B.c.
52
C1
-sce- di- te, a- stra jam fu- gi- te so- lem ef-
C2
lu- nae jam ce- di- te, so- lem ef-
B.c.

58
C1
-fu- gi- te; Ma- ri- a sol, mun- dum il-
C2
-fu- gi- te; Ma- ri- a lu- na mun- dum il-
B.c.
64
-lu- mi- nat, cae- lum ex- or- nat; fu- gi- te flo- res, nar- cis- sus, vi- o- lae,
-lu- mi- nat, cae- lum ex- or- nat; fu- gi- te flo- res, nar- cis- sus,
68
pra- to- rum ri- sus, di- sce- di- te, fu- gi- te. Tel- lus jam
vi- o- lae, pra- to- rum ri- sus, di- sce- di- te, fu- gi- te.
72
ex- tet hor- ri- da spi- nis,
nec vi- ri- dan- ti a- moe- ni-

78
C1
ro- sae pur-
C2
-ta- te co- ro- na- ta am- pli- us ap- pa- re- at;
B.c.
84
C1
pu re ae, po- ni- te fo- li- a,
C2
can- di- da li- li- a, po- ni- te fo- li- a,
B.c.
89
C1
lin- qui- te o- do- res.
C2
lin- qui- te o- do- res. Si- le- te, o Ze- phi-ri,
B.c.
94
C1
C2
vos- que Ri-phae- is ve- ni- te e mon- ti- bus Eu- ri fu- ren- tes,
B.c.

floribus, herbis, expoliate prata, montes, colles.

Jam enim hiems transiit; imber abiit, et recessit. Flores apparuerunt in terra nostra. Maria flos campi,

Jam enim hiems transiit; imber abiit, et recessit. Flores apparuerunt in terra nostra. rosa sine

118
C1
et li- li- um con- val- li- um, dat lae- ta o- do- rem,
C2
spi- na, dat
B.c.
124
C1
o- do- - - - rem su-
C2
lae- ta o- do- - - - rem su-
B.c.
129
C1
-a- vi- - ta- tis. Ve- ni Au- ster, per- fla
C2
-a- vi- - ta- tis. sur- ge A- qui- lo, per- fla
B.c.
134
C1
hor- tum no- strum, et be- a- tis- si- mae Ma- ri- ae flu-
C2
hor- tum no- strum, et be- a- tis- si- mae Ma- ri- ae flu-
B.c.

137
C1
-ant a- ro- ma- ta. Tu Vir- go ro- sa pul- chri- or,
C2
-ant a- ro- ma- ta. et
B.c.
142
C1
et lu- na ju- cun- di- or,
C2
li- li- o can- di- di- or, tu
B.c.
6
148
C1
prae- be o- do- rem,
C2
so- le splen- di- di- or, mit- te splen-
B.c.
4
♯
154
C1
ut nos stel- lae, nos et flo- res tu- a lu- ce,
C2
-do- rem, ut nos stel- lae, nos et flo- res tu- a lu- ce,
B.c.

et te duce splendere et florere possimus in perpetuas, in perpetuas, ⟨in perpetuas⟩ aeternitates.

12. Quis dabit mihi tantam charitatem

Barbara Strozzi

21
A
-mo- ris, ut lan- gue- at cor me- um
T
-mo- ris, ut lan- gue- at cor
B
-mo- ris, ut lan- gue- at cor me- um lan-
B.c.
28
A
lan- guen- - - te, lan- guen- -
T
me- um lan- guen- - te, lan- guen- -
B
-guen- - te, lan- guen- - te, lan- guen- -
B.c.
36
Presto
A
-te, lan- guen- te Je- su? Non- ne, non- ne tu Chri- ste mi,
T
-te, lan- guen- te Je- su? Non- ne, non- ne tu Chri- ste mi,
B
- - te Je- su? Non- ne, non- ne tu Chri- ste mi, qui es
B.c.

43
A
qui es cha- ri- tas i- -
T
qui es cha- - ri- tas i- - - psa,
B
cha- ri- tas, qui es cha- ri- tas i- - -
B.c.
6 6 6 5
49
A
-psa, non- ne, non- ne tu Chri- ste mi, qui es
T
non- ne, non- ne tu Chri- ste mi, qui es cha- ri-
B
-psa, non- ne, non- ne tu Chri- ste mi, qui es cha- ri- tas, qui es
B.c.
55
A
cha- ri- tas i- - psa? O, o
T
-tas i- - - psa? O, o
B
cha- ri- tas i- - - psa? O, o
B.c.
6 6 6

62
A
quam su- a- vis, o, o quam su- a- vis,
T
quam su- a- vis, o, o quam su- a- vis,
B
quam su- a- vis, o, o quam su- a- vis,
B.c.
[6]
♯6
67
Presto
A
o quam ju- cun- dus, o, o
T
o quam ju- cun- dus, o, o, o quam ju- cun- dus,
B
o quam ju- cun- dus, o, o, o, o, o
B.c.
70
A
quam ju- cun- dus, o, o quam ju- cun- dus, quam de- le-
T
o quam ju- cun- dus, o, o quam ju-
B
quam ju- cun- dus, quam de- le- cta- bi- lis, o quam ju- cun- dus,
B.c.

73
A
-cta- bi- lis, o, est a- mor tu- us, quam de- le-
T
-cun- dus, quam de- le- cta- bi- lis est a- mor tu- us, quam de- le-
B
o, est a- mor tu- us, pi- is- si- me
B.c.
6
4
[5]
♯
76
A
-cta- bi- lis, dul- cis- si- me Je- su, a- ma- bi- lis, a-
T
-cta- bi- lis, dul- cis- si- me Je- su, a- ma- bi- lis, a-
B
Je- su, a- ma- bi- lis Chri- ste,
B.c.
79
A
-ma- bi- lis Chri- ste, ve- ra spes, ve- ra sa- lus, a-
T
-ma- bi- lis Chri- ste, ve- ra sa- lus, a- ma- bi- lis, a-
B
ve- ra spes, ve- ra sa- lus, a-
B.c.

82
A
-ma- bi- lis Chri- ste, a- ma- bi- lis, a-
T
-ma- bi- lis Chri- ste, ve- ra spes, ve- ra sa- lus, ve- ra vi- ta a-
B
-ma- bi- lis Chri- ste, ve- ra spes, ve- ra sa- lus, ve- ra vi- ta a-
B.c.
85
A
-ma- bi- lis Chri- ste, ve- ra spes, ve- ra sa- lus, ve- ra vi- ta
T
- ni- mae me- ae,
B
- ni- mae me- ae,
a-
B.c.
88
A
a- ni- mae me- ae, a- ma- bi- lis Chri- ste, a- - ni- mae me-
T
a- ma- bi- lis Chri- ste, a- - ni- mae me- ae,
B
-ma- bi- lis Chri- ste, a- ni- mae, a- - ni- mae me-
B.c.

91
A
-ae, a- - - - ni- mae
T
a- - - - ni- mae
B
-ae, a- - - - ni- mae
B.c.
95
A
me- ae; in te, in te vi- vit, in te, in te spe- rat, in te, in te, in te
T
me- ae; in te, in te vi- vit, in te, in te, in te
B
me- ae; in te, in te vi- vit, in te, in te
B.c.
99
A
cre- dit, in te, in te a- - mor me- us
T
spe- rat, in te, in te cre- dit, a- - - mor me-
B
spe- rat, in te, in te spe- rat, a- - mor me-
B.c.

103
Adagio
A
— est; a- mo- re tu- o a- bun- dan- ter, a- bun- dan- ter re- fi- ci- tur
T
-us est; a- mo- re tu- o a- bun- dan- ter, a- bun- dan- ter re- fi- ci- tur
B
-us est; a- mo- re tu- o a- bun- dan- ter, a- bun- dan- ter re- fi- ci- tur a-
B.c.
6
107
A
a- - ni- ma, a- -
T
a- ni- ma, a- ni- ma, a-
B
- ni- ma, a- - ni- ma, a- -
B.c.
110
A
- ni- ma me- a. Tu es so-
T
- ni- ma me- a.
B
- ni- ma me- a. Tu es so- lus, bo- ne Je-
B.c.

115
A
-lus, bo- ne Je- su, ve- ra spes, ve- ra spes et,
T
Tu es so- lus, bo- ne Je- su, ve- ra spes, ve- ra spes et
B
-su, ve- ra spes, ve- ra spes et vi- ta, et
B.c.
120
A
et vi- ta me- a, et vi- ta me- a.
T
vi- ta me- a, et vi- ta me- a.
B
vi- ta me- a, et vi- ta me- a.
B.c.
127
A
Con- cu- pi- scit cor me- um te vi- de- re, re- qui-
T
Con- cu- pi- scit cor me- um te vi- de- re, re- qui-
B
Con- cu- pi- scit cor me- um te vi- de- re, et in te so- lo,
B.c.
6 6 7 6

131
A
-e- sce- re, re- qui- e- sce- re, et in te so- lo,
T
-e- sce- re, re- qui- e- sce- re, et in te so- lo,
B
et in te so- lo, in te so- lo, et in te so- lo re- qui-
B.c.
135
A
et in te so- lo, in te so- lo, et in te so- lo, in te so- lo
T
et in te so- lo, in te so- lo, et in te so- lo, in te so- lo
B
-e- sce- re, re- qui- e- sce- re, et in te so- lo, in te so- lo
B.c.
139
A
p
re- qui- e- sce- re, ⟨re- qui- e- sce- re.⟩
T
p
re- qui- e- sce- re, re- qui- e- sce- re.
B
p
re- qui- e- sce- re, re- qui- e- sce- re.
B.c.
p

Solo. Aria
A
B.c.
Ti- bi e- nim so- li vi- vo, Ad te so- lum heu su- spi- ro,
Et in te so- lo re- spi- ro, in te so- lo re- -spi- ro;
Ti- bi vi- vo, me- a vi- ta, Te ad- -o- ro, o bo- ne Je- su,
Ti- bi vi- vo, me- a vi- ta, Te ad- -o- ro, o bo- ne Je- su,
Te ad- o- ro, te ad- o- ro, o bo- ne Je- su, bo- ne Je-
p
p

167
A
-su. Al- - le-
T
Al- - le-
B
Al- le- lu- ia, al- le- lu- ia,
B.c.
6 [5]
172
A
-lu- ia, al- le- lu- ia, al- le- lu-
T
-lu- ia, al- le- lu- ia, al- le- lu-
B
al- - le- lu- ia,
B.c.
6 5
177
A
-ia, al- le- lu- ia, al- le- lu- ia, al- le- lu- ia, al- le-
T
-ia, al- le- lu- ia, al- le- lu- ia, al- le- lu- ia,
B
al- le- lu- ia, al- le- lu- ia, al- le- lu- ia,
B.c.

110

13. O quando suavissimum

Giovanni Rovetta

13
Tardo
A
car- nes co- me- dam,
T
dul- cis- si- mas car- nes co- me- dam, quan- do pa- scar, quan- do
B
dul- cis- si- mas car- nes co- me- dam,
B.c.
♯
2
17
A
quan- do pa- scar, quan- do
T
fru- ar Sal- va- to- re Je- su me- o,
B
B.c.
22
A
fru- ar Sal- va- to- re Je- su me- o,
T
quan- do
B
quan- do pa- scar, quan- do
B.c.

27
A
quan- do pa- scar, quan- do fru- ar Sal- va- to- re Je- su me-
T
pa- scar, quan- do fru- ar Sal- va- to- re Je- su me-
B
fru- ar Sal- va- to- re Je- su me-
♯6 ♯6 ♮ [4] ♯
B.c.
32
A
-o, quan- do pa- scar, quan- do fru- ar Sal- va- to- re Je- su me-
T
-o, quan- do pa- scar, quan- do fru- ar Sal- va- to- re Je- su me-
B
-o, quan- do pa- scar, quan- do fru- ar Sal- va- to- re Je- su me-
B.c.
37
A
-o? Il- li- us san- gui-ne si- tis me- a e- su- ri- et,
T
-o? il- li- us cor- po-re
B
-o?
♯ ♯
B.c.

41
A
Ad- ju- ro vos Che- ru- bim, si- ti- bun- do
T
fa- mes me- a con- su- me- tur. Ad- ju- ro vos Che- ru- bim, si- ti- bun- do
B
Ad- ju- ro vos, vos Che- ru- bim, si- ti- bun- do
B.c.
44
A
fer- te san- gui- nem; ad- ju- ro vos Se- ra- phim, da- te
T
fer- te san- gui- nem; ad- ju- ro vos Se- ra- phim, da- te
B
fer- te san- gui- nem; ad- ju- ro vos, vos Se- ra- phim, da- te
B.c.
[♯]6
47
Presto
A
car- nes hu- ic fa- me- li- co.
T
car- nes hu- ic fa- me- li- co. Me- um pa- nem, me- um De- um, man- du- ca- bo Je- sum
B
car- nes hu- ic fa- me- li- co.
B.c.
[♯]6

115

60

A: Cur- ri- te flu- mi- na san- gui- nis, flu- mi- na
T: Cur- ri- te flu- mi- na san- gui- nis, flu- mi- na si- tis, cur- ri- te, cur- ri-
B: Cur- ri- te, cur- ri- te,

63

A: si- tis, in re- me- di- um mil- le pla- gis, in re- me- di- um mil- le
T: -te, ⟨cur- ri- te, cur- ri- te,⟩
B: ⟨cur- ri- te, cur- ri- te,⟩ in re- me- di- um mil- le pla- gis, in re- me- di- um mil- le

66

A: spi- nis, me- us Pa- stor vul- ne- ra- tus,
T: me- us Pa- stor vul- ne- ra- tus, in re- me- di- um mil- le
B: spi- nis, me- us Pa- stor vul- ne- ra- tus, in re- me- di- um mil- le

117

Sheet music, measures 83–95.

Lyrics:
- A: O ve-re bo-nus Pa-stor,
- T: O ve-re ca-rus A-mor;
- B: -ni. e-di-te er-go, bi-bi-te om-nes, et jam non ho-mi-nes sed di-i vi-vi-
- A (m. 92): e-di-te er-go, bi-bi-te om-nes, et jam non ho-mi-nes sed di-i vi-vi-te,
- T (m. 92): e-di-te er-go, bi-bi-te om-nes, et jam non ho-mi-nes sed di-i vi-vi-te,
- B (m. 92): -te, o

119

110
A
et jam non ho- mi-nes sed di- i vi- vi- te, ex De- o
T
et jam non ho- mi-nes sed di- i vi- vi- te, ex De- o
B
sed di- i vi- vi- te, sed di- i vi- vi- te, ex De- o di- i.
B.c.
113
Prestissimo
di- i.
di- i.
Al- le- lu- ia, ⟨al- le- lu- ia,⟩ al- le- lu- ia, al- le- lu-
120
Al- le- lu- ia, ⟨al- le- lu- ia, al- le- lu- ia,⟩
Al- le- lu- ia, ⟨al- le- lu- ia, al- le- lu- ia,⟩
-ia, ⟨al- le- lu- ia, al- le-

127
A
al- le- lu- ia, al- le- lu- ia, al- le- lu- ia, ⟨al- le-
T
al- le- lu- ia, ⟨al- le- lu- ia,⟩ al- le- lu- ia,
B
-lu- ia, al- le- lu- ia, al- le- lu- ia,
B.c.
134
A
-lu- ia, al- le- lu- ia, al- le- lu- ia,⟩
T
⟨al- le- lu- ia, al- le- lu- ia,⟩ al- le- lu- ia,
B
al- le- lu- ia, al- le- lu- ia,⟩ al- le- lu- ia, ⟨al- le- lu- ia,
B.c.
141
A
al- le- lu- ia,
T
al- le-
B
al- le- lu- ia, al- le- lu- ia,⟩ al- le- lu- ia,
B.c.

148
A
⟨al- le- lu- ia, al- le- lu- ia, al- le- lu- ia, al-
T
-lu- ia, ⟨al- le- lu- ia, al- le- lu- ia, al- le- lu- ia, al-
B
⟨al- le- lu- ia, al- le- lu- ia,
B.c.
155
A
-le- lu- ia, al- le- lu- ia, al- le- lu- ia, al- le-
T
-le- lu- ia, al- le- lu- ia, al- le- lu- ia,
B
al- le- lu- ia, al- le- lu- ia, al- le- lu- ia,
B.c.
162
A
-lu- ia, al- le- - lu- ia,⟩ al- - - le- lu- ia.
T
al- le- lu- ia,⟩ al- le- lu- ia, al- - - le- lu- ia.
B
al- le- lu- ia,⟩ al- le- lu- ia, ⟨al- le- lu- ia.⟩
B.c.

14. Plaudite, cantate

Francesco Cavalli

19
A
can- ta- te, ⟨can- ta- te, can- ta- te, can- ta- te,
T
⟨plau- di- te, plau- di- te, plau- di- te,⟩ can- ta- te, ⟨can- ta- te,
B
plau- di- te, ⟨plau- di- te, plau- di- te, plau- di- te,⟩
B.c.
25
A
can- ta- te⟩ cym- ba- lis, lau- da- te ci- tha- ris, psal- li- te
T
can- ta- te⟩ cym- ba- lis, lau- da- te ci- tha- ris, psal- li- te
B
can- ta- te cym- ba- lis, lau- da- te ci- tha- ris, psal- li- te
B.c.
6
[6]
30
A
or- ga- nis, al- le- - lu- ia, al- le- lu- ia, al-
T
or- ga- nis, al- le- - lu- ia, al- le- lu- ia, al-
B
or- ga- nis, al- le- - lu- ia, ⟨al- le- lu- ia,⟩ al-
B.c.
[6]
6
6

36
A
-le- lu- ia, al- le- lu- ia, al- le- lu- ia.
T
-le- lu- ia, al- le- lu- ia, al- le- lu- ia.
B
-le- lu- ia, ⟨al- le- lu- ia, al- le- lu- ia.⟩
B.c.
42
A
Can-
T
B
Can- ta- te, et au- di- tam fa- ci- te vo- cem lau- dis e-
B.c.
47
A
-ta- te, et au- di- tam fa- ci- te vo- cem lau- dis e- jus,
T
Can- ta- te
B
-jus,
B.c.

52
A
cantate, et auditam
T
et auditam facite vocem laudis ejus, cantate,
B
cantate, ⟨canta-
B.c.
57
A
facite vocem laudis ejus;
T
et auditam facite vocem laudis ejus;
B
-te,⟩ et auditam facite vocem laudis ejus;
B.c.
7 6
62
Allegro
A
venite, venite, et nar-
T
venite, venite, et narrabo vobis,
B
B.c.

127

79
A
ve- ni- te, ve- ni- te, et nar- ra- bo vo- - bis,
T
-te, et nar- ra- bo vo- - bis, ve- ni- te, ve-
B
ve-
B.c.
6
83
A
ve- ni- te, ve- ni- te, et nar- ra- bo vo- bis quan- ta fe- cit
T
-ni- te, et nar- ra- bo, nar- ra- bo vo- bis quan- ta fe- cit
B
-ni- te, ⟨ve- ni- te,⟩ et nar- ra- bo vo- bis quan- ta fe- cit
B.c.
7 [♯]6
87
A
Do- mi- nus a- ni- mae me- ae, quan- ta fe- cit Do- mi- nus
T
Do- mi- nus a- ni- mae me- ae, quan- ta fe- cit Do- mi- nus
B
Do- mi- nus a- ni- mae me- ae, quan- ta fe- cit Do- mi- nus
B.c.

91
A
a- ni- mae me- ae. Spe- ra- te, spe- ra- te, ⟨spe- ra- te, spe-
T
a- ni- mae me- ae.
B
a- ni- mae me- ae.
B.c.
98
A
-ra- te⟩ in e- o gen- tes, spe- ra- te, spe- ra- te, et col- lau-
T
Spe- ra- te, spe- ra- te, spe- ra- te, et col- lau-
B
Spe- ra- te, ⟨spe- ra- te, spe- ra- te,⟩
B.c.
7
103
A
-da- te e- um po- pu- li, et col- lau- da- te e- um po- pu- li, spe- ra-
T
-da- te e- um po- pu- li, spe- ra- te, spe- ra- te, et col- lau- da- te e- um po- pu- li, spe-
B
spe- ra- te, ⟨spe- ra- te, spe- ra- te,⟩ spe- ra- te, ⟨spe-
B.c.

107
A
-te, spe- ra- te, et col- lau- da- te e- um po- pu- li.
T
-ra- te, spe- ra- te, et col- lau- da- te e- um po- - pu- li.
B
-ra- te, spe- ra- te,〉 et col- lau- da- te e- um po- pu- li.
B.c.
112
Allegro e presto
A
Plau- di- te, 〈plau- di- te, plau- di- te, plau- di- te,〉
T
can- ta- te cym- ba- lis,
B
can- ta- te cym- ba- lis,
B.c.
118
A
T
lau- da- te ci- tha- ris, psal- li- te or- ga- nis, al- le- - lu-
B
lau- da- te ci- tha- ris, psal- li- te or- ga- nis, al- le- - lu-
B.c.

124
A
⟨plau- di- te, plau- di- te, plau- di- te, plau- di- te,⟩
T
-ia, ⟨al- le- lu- ia,⟩ plau- di- te,
B
-ia, al- le- lu- ia,
B.c.
130
A
can- ta- te, ⟨can- ta- te, can- ta- te,
T
⟨plau- di- te, plau- di- te, plau- di- te,⟩ can- ta- te,
B
plau- di- te, ⟨plau- di- te, plau- di- te,
B.c.
135
A
can- ta- te, can- ta- te⟩ cym- ba- lis, lau- da- te ci- tha- ris, psal- li- te
T
can- ta- te, can- ta- te cym- ba- lis, lau- da- te ci- tha- ris, psal- li- te
B
plau- di- te,⟩ can- ta- te cym- ba- lis, lau- da- te ci- tha- ris, psal- li- te
B.c.
6
6

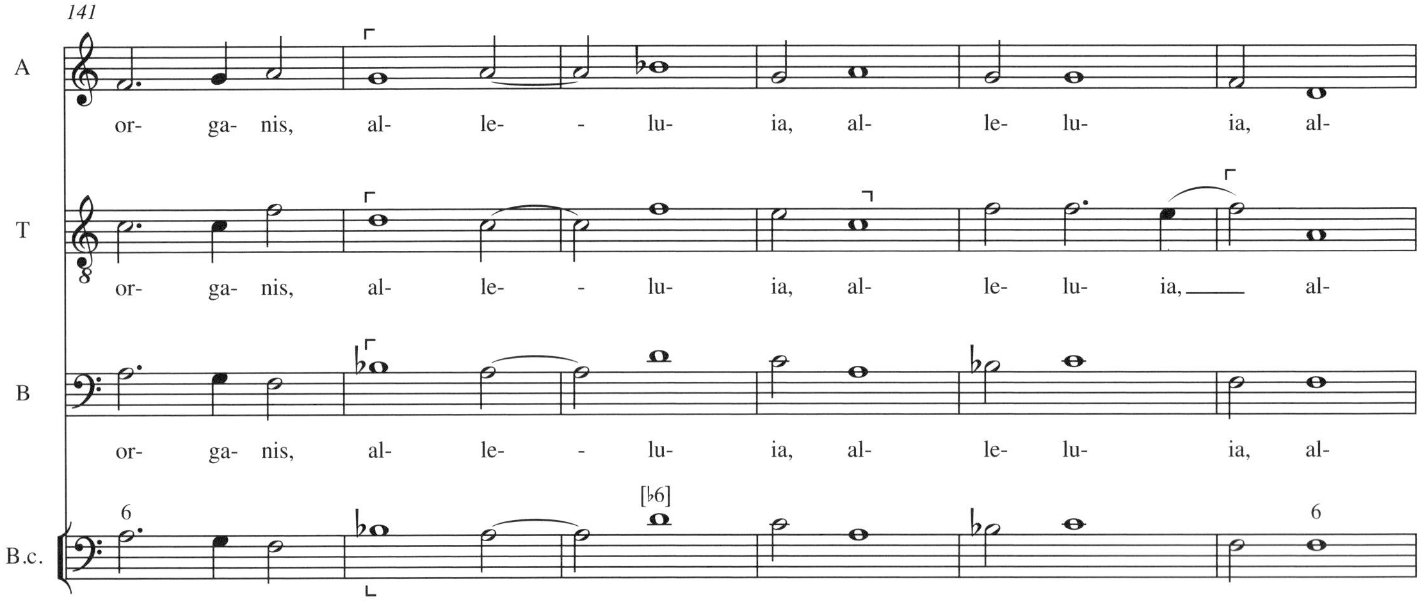
141
A
or- ga- nis, al- le- - lu- ia, al- le- lu- ia, al-
T
or- ga- nis, al- le- - lu- ia, al- le- lu- ia, al-
B
or- ga- nis, al- le- - lu- ia, al- le- lu- ia, al-
B.c.
6
[♭6]
6

147
A
-le- lu- ia, al- le- lu- ia, al- le- lu- ia.
T
-le- lu- ia, al- le- lu- ia, al- le- lu- ia.
B
-le- lu- ia, al- le- lu- ia, al- le- lu- ia.
B.c.
6

15. In virtute tua

Francesco Cavalli

16
A
- a Do- mi- ne lae- ta- bi- tur
T
lae- ta- bi- tur, ⟨lae- ta- bi- tur, lae-
B
lae- ta- bi- tur, ⟨lae- ta- bi- tur,
B.c.
21
A
ju- stus, lae- ta- bi- tur, ⟨lae- ta- bi- tur, lae- ta- bi- tur,⟩
T
-ta- bi- tur⟩ ju- stus, lae- ta- bi- tur, ⟨lae- ta- bi- tur,⟩
B
lae- ta- bi- tur, lae- ta- bi- tur, lae- ta- bi- tur,⟩ in vir-
B.c.
26
A
lae- ta- bi- tur
T
lae- ta- bi- tur ju- stus, lae-
B
-tu- te tu- - a Do- mi- ne lae-
B.c.

32
A
ju- stus, lae- ta- bi- tur, ⟨lae- ta- bi- tur, lae- ta- bi- tur, lae- ta- bi- tur⟩
T
-ta- bi- tur, ⟨lae- ta- bi- tur⟩ ju- stus, lae- ta- bi- tur, ⟨lae- ta- bi- tur⟩
B
-ta- bi- tur ju- stus, lae- ta- bi- tur, lae- ta- bi- tur, ⟨lae- ta- bi- tur⟩
B.c.
37
A
ju- stus, lae- ta- bi- tur, ⟨lae-
T
ju- stus, lae- ta- bi- tur, ⟨lae- ta- bi- tur,⟩ lae- ta- bi- tur, ⟨lae-
B
ju- stus, lae- ta- bi- tur, ⟨lae- ta- bi- tur, lae-
B.c.
42
A
-ta- bi- tur⟩ ju- stus,
T
-ta- bi- tur⟩ ju- stus, et su- per sa- lu-
B
-ta- bi- tur⟩ ju- stus,
B.c.

136

65
A
sa- lu- ta- re tu-
T
- - bit ve- he- men- - ter,
B
ex- sul- ta- bit, ⟨ex- sul-
B.c.
4 ♯
68
A
um ex sul ta bit, ⟨ex sul ta bit,⟩
T
et su- per sa- lu-
B
-ta- bit, ex- sul- ta- bit, ex- sul- ta- bit,⟩ ex- sul- ta-
B.c.
♯
71
A
ex- sul- ta- - bit, ⟨ex- sul-
T
-ta- re tu- um ex- sul- ta- - bit,
B
- bit ve- he- men- ter, ex- sul- ta-
B.c.
♯

75
A
-ta- - bit⟩ ve- he- men- ter.
T
ex- sul- ta- bit ve- he- men- ter.
B
- - bit ve- he- men- ter.
B.c.
80
A
De- si- de- ri- um, ⟨de- si- de- ri- um⟩ a- ni- mae e- jus tri- bu- i- sti, tri- bu-
B.c.
84
A
-i- sti e- i,
T
De- si- de- ri- um, ⟨de- si- de- ri- um⟩ a- ni- mae e-
B.c.
88
T
-jus tri- bu- i- sti, tri- bu- i- sti e- i,
B
De- si- de- ri- um, ⟨de- si- de- ri- um⟩
B.c.

92
A
T
B
B.c.
et vo- lun- ta- te la- bi-
et vo- lun-
a- ni- mae e- jus tri- bu- i- sti, tri- bu- i- sti e- i,
96
-o- rum e- jus non frau- da- sti, non frau- da- sti
-ta- te la- bi- o- rum e- jus non frau- da- - sti, non frau- da- sti e-
99
e- um,
- um, et vo- lun- ta- te la- bi- o- rum e- jus non frau- da-
et vo- lun- ta- te la- bi- o- rum e- jus non frau- da- sti, non frau-

102
A
et vo- lun- ta- te la- bi- o- rum,
T
-sti, non frau- da- sti e- um, et vo- lun-
B
-da- sti, non frau- da- sti e- um, et vo- lun- ta- te la- bi-
B.c.
105
A
⟨et vo- lun- ta- te la- bi- o- rum,
T
-ta- te la- bi- o- rum, et vo- lun- ta- te la- bi- o- rum
B
-o- rum, et vo- lun- ta- te la- bi- o- rum e- jus non frau-
B.c.
108
A
et vo- lun- ta- te la- bi- o- rum⟩ e- jus non frau-
T
e- jus non frau- da- sti, non frau- da- sti e- um, non frau-
B
-da- sti, non frau- da- sti, et vo- lun- ta- te la- bi- o- rum
B.c.

111
A
-da- sti, ⟨non frau- da- sti⟩ e- um.
T
-da- sti, non frau- da- sti e- um.
B
e- jus non frau- da- - sti, ⟨non frau- da- sti⟩ e- um.
B.c.
115
A
Prae- ve- ni- sti, ⟨prae- ve- ni- sti⟩ e- um in
T
Prae- ve- ni- sti, ⟨prae- ve- ni- sti⟩ e- um in be- ne- di- cti- o- ni-
B
Prae- ve- ni- sti, prae- ve- ni- sti e-
B.c.
119
A
be- ne- di- cti- o- ni- bus dul- ce- di- nis, dul- ce- di-
T
-bus dul- ce- di- nis, dul- ce- - di-
B
-um in be- ne- di- cti- o- ni- bus dul- ce- di-
B.c.

124
A
-nis, prae- ve- ni- sti, ⟨prae- ve- ni- sti⟩ e- um in
T
-nis, prae- ve- ni- sti, ⟨prae- ve- ni- sti⟩ e- um in be- ne- di- cti- o- ni-
B
-nis, prae- ve- ni- sti, ⟨prae- ve- ni- sti⟩ e-
B.c.
128
A
be- ne- di- cti- o- ni- bus dul- ce- di- nis, ⟨dul- ce- di-
T
-bus dul- ce- di- nis, dul- ce- - di-
B
-um in be- ne- di- cti- o- ni- bus dul- ce- di-
B.c.
6 ♯ 4 [♯]
133
A
-nis;⟩ po- su- i- sti in ca- pi- te
T
-nis; po- su- i- sti in ca- pi- te e- jus
B
-nis; po- su- i- sti in ca- pi- te e- jus co-
B.c.
♯ ♯6

139
A
e- jus,
T
co- ro- -
B
-ro- - - - nam, ⟨co- ro-
B.c.
144
A
T
- - - nam de la- pi- de pre- ti-
B
- - - nam⟩ de la- pi- de pre- ti-
B.c.
♯ ♯ ♯6
149
A
po- su- i- sti in ca- pi- te e- jus co-
T
-o- so, co- ro- - nam,
B
-o- so, co- ro-
B.c.
♯6

154
A
-ro- - - - nam de la- pi- de
T
co- ro- - - nam de la- pi- de
B
- nam,
B.c.
159
A
pre- ti- o- so, po- su- i- sti in ca- pi- te
T
pre- ti- o- so, po- su- i- sti in ca- pi- te e- jus co-
B
po- su- i- sti in ca- pi- te e- jus
B.c.
4 ♯ ♯6
166
A
e- jus co- ro- - - nam de
T
-ro- - - nam,
B
co- ro- - - - nam de
B.c.

171
A
la- pi- de pre- ti- o- so, po- su- i- sti in
T
po- su- i- sti in ca- pi- te e- jus
B
la- pi- de pre- ti- o- so,
B.c.
♯6
177
A
ca- pi- te e- jus co- ro- - nam, co-
T
co- ro- - nam,
B
co- ro- - nam, co- ro-
B.c.
♯6
5
182
A
-ro- - - - - nam de
T
co- ro- - - nam de
B
- - nam, co- ro- - - nam de
B.c.
6

187
A
la- pi- de pre- ti- o- so, co- ro- nam de la- pi- de, de
T
la- pi- de pre- ti- o- so, co- ro- nam de la- pi-
B
la- pi- de pre- ti- o- so, co- ro- nam de la- pi- de, ⟨co- ro-
6
♯
6
B.c.
194
A
la- pi- de pre- - ti- o- - so.
T
-de, de la- pi- de pre- - ti- o- so.
B
-nam de la- - pi- de⟩ pre- ti- o- - so.
B.c.

16. Peccator, si tu times

Natale Monferrato

-mit daemon fortis, cur-re ad Mariam, cur-re, cur-re ad Mariam, cur-re ad Mariam.

Peccator, si te perdere querit hostis, cur-re ad Mariam, cur-re, cur-re ad

59
Bar
Ma- ri- am, ad Ma- - ri- am.
B.c.
65
C
A
Sur- ge qui dor- mis,
Bar
sur- ge qui ca- -
B.c.
68
C
sur- ge qui pec- - - cas, et
A
et in- vo- ca Ma- ri-
Bar
- dis, sur- ge qui pec- - cas, et in- vo-
B.c.
71
C
in- vo- ca Ma- ri- - am, sur- ge qui pec- cas,
A
- am, Ma- ri- - am, sur- ge qui dor- mis,
Bar
-ca Ma- ri- am, sur- ge, sur- - ge qui ca-
B.c.

74
C
et in- vo-
A
et in- vo-ca Ma- ri- - am,
Bar
- - dis, sur- ge qui dor- mis, qui ca- dis, et
B.c.
7 6
77
C
-ca, et in- vo- ca, ⟨et in- vo- ca⟩ Ma- ri-
A
et in- vo- ca, et in- vo-ca Ma-
Bar
in- vo-ca, ⟨et in- vo-ca,⟩ et in- vo- ca Ma-
B.c.
80
C
- am, sur- - ge, sur- - ge, et in- vo-ca Ma-
A
-ri- am, sur- ge, sur- - ge, et in- vo-ca Ma-
Bar
-ri- am, qui dor- mis, qui ca- dis, qui pec- cas, et in- vo-ca Ma-
B.c.

83
C
-ri- am, Ma- ri- - am, et in- vo- ca Ma- ri- am.
A
-ri- am, Ma- ri- am, et in- vo- ca Ma- ri- am.
Bar
-ri- am, Ma- ri- am, et in- vo- ca Ma- ri- am.
B.c.
87
C
Ma- ri- a tu fons, tu ve- na, tu
A
Ma- ri- a tu fons, tu ve- na, tu vi- ta, tu
B.c.
93
C
vi- ta, tu spes, tu gra- ti- a- rum ma- ter, de- li- ci- a- rum
A
spes, tu gra- ti- a- rum ma- ter, de- li- ci- a- rum
B.c.
100
C
ma- re. o san- ctis- si- ma Ma- ri- a,
A
ma- re. o san- ctis- si- ma Ma- ri- a,
Bar
Am- ple- cte- re me, am-
B.c.

107
C
me pec- can- tem, am- ple- cte- re
A
me fu- gen- tem, am-
Bar
-ple- cte- re me, in- ter bra- chi- a pi- e- ta-
B.c.
114
C
me, sa- na mor- tis vul- ne- ra,
A
-ple- cter- re me, de- le,
Bar
-tis; prae- be la- ctis u- be- ra, am- ple- cte- re me,
B.c.
121
C
de- le, de- le, de- le, de- le,
A
de- le, de- le, de- le, de- le, de- le,
Bar
am- ple- cte- re me, de- le, de- le, de- le
B.c.

128

C: de- le no- stra cri- mi- na,

A: de- le no- stra cri- mi- na,

Bar: no- stra cri- mi- na, o,____ o,____

135

C: o,____ o____ Ma- ri- a.

A: o,____ o____ Ma- ri- a.____ Ma- ri- a, tu es

Bar: o Ma- ri- a.

141

C: Ma- ri- a, tu es il- la glo- ri- o- sa, tu es il- la dul- cis

A: il- la dul- cis ro- sa,

Bar: tu es il- la dul- cis ro- sa, pul- chra

144
C
ro- sa, pul- chra ni- mis et for- mo- sa, tu es il- la glo- ri- o- sa,
A
tu es il- la dul- cis ro- sa, pul- chra ni- mis et for- mo- sa, tu es
Bar
ni- mis et for- mo- sa, tu es il- la glo- ri- o- sa, pul- chra ni- mis et for- mo- sa,
B.c.
147
C
pul- chra ni- mis et for- mo- sa, pul- chra ni- mis et for-
A
il- la glo- ri- o- sa, pul- chra ni- mis et for- mo- sa, pul- chra ni- mis et for-
Bar
pul- chra ni- mis et for- mo- sa, pul- chra ni- mis et for- mo- sa, pul- chra ni- mis et for-
B.c.
150
C
-mo- sa, o Ma- ri- a, o Ma- ri- a, Ma- ri- a.
A
-mo- sa, o Ma- ri- a, Ma- ri- a, o Ma- ri- a, Ma- ri- a.
Bar
-mo- sa, o Ma- ri- a, Ma- ri- a, o Ma- ri- a.
B.c.

155
C
A
Tu es il- la Vir- go quae de- dit cae- lis glo- -
Bar
B.c.
158
C
tu es il- la Vir- go quae de- dit ter- ris De- -
A
- ri- am;
Bar
B.c.
162
C
- um; tu es il- la ter- ra
A
tu es
Bar
tu es il- la ma- jor cae- -
B.c.
6

165
C
for- ti- or, quae so- la ce- pit quem mun- dus,
A
il- la or- be la- ti- or, quem mun- dus, quem
Bar
- - lo quae so- la ce- pit, non ca- pit om-
B.c.
7 6
169
C
quem mun- dus, ⟨quem mun- dus⟩
A
mun- dus non ca- pit om- nis, non ca- pit om- nis, quem
Bar
-nis quem mun- dus non ca- pit om- nis, non ca- pit om- - nis,
B.c.
7 6
173
C
non ca- pit om- nis. Ad Vir- gi- nem er- go pro- pe-
A
mun- dus non ca- pit om- nis. Ad Vir- gi- nem er- go pro- pe-
Bar
non ca- pit om- - nis. Ad Vir- gi- nem er- go pro- pe-
B.c.
[6]

178
C
-re- mus, fe- sti- ne- mus, cur- ra- - mus, cur- ra- mus
A
-re- mus, fe- sti- ne- mus, cur- ra- - mus, cur- ra- mus
Bar
-re- mus, fe- sti- ne- mus, cur- ra- - mus, cur- ra- mus
B.c.
183
C
om- nes, sem- per, sem- per di- cen- tes:
A
om- nes, sem- per, sem- per di- cen- tes: Ma- ri- a tu
Bar
om- nes, sem- per, sem- per di- cen- tes:
B.c.
4
189
C
Ma- ri- a, tu fons, tu ve- na, tu vi- ta, tu spes, tu
A
fons, tu ve- na, tu vi- ta, tu spes, tu
B.c.
195
C
gra- ti- a- rum ma- ter, de- li- ci- a- rum ma-
A
gra- ti- a- rum ma- ter, de- li- ci- a- rum ma-
B.c.

201

C: -re. o san- ctis- si- ma Ma- ri- a,

A: -re. o san- ctis- si- ma Ma- ri- a,

Bar: Am- ple- cte- re me, am- ple- cte- re

B.c.

208

C: me pec- can- tem, am- ple- cte- re me,

A: me fu- gen- tem, am- ple- cte- re

Bar: me, in- ter bra- chi- a pi- e- ta- tis; prae- be

B.c.

215

C: sa- na mor- tis vul- ne- ra,

A: me, de- le, de- le,

Bar: la- ctis u- be- ra, am- ple- cte- re me, am-

B.c.

222
C
A
Bar
B.c.
de- le, de- le, de- le, de- le,
de- le, de- le, de- le, ⟨de- le,⟩
-ple- cte- re me, de- le, de- le, de- le no- stra
229
de- le no- stra cri- mi- na, o, o
de- le no- stra cri- mi- na, o, o
cri- mi- na, o, o,
237
Ma- ri- a. Al- le- lu-
Ma- ri- a. Al- le- lu- ia,
o Ma- ri- a. Al- le- lu- ia, al- le- lu- ia, al- le-

242
C
-ia, al- le- lu- ia, al- le- lu- ia, al- le- lu- ia,
A
al- le- lu- ia, al- le- lu- ia, al- le- lu- ia, al- le-
Bar
-lu- ia, al- le- lu- ia, ⟨al- le- lu- ia,⟩ al- le- lu- ia,
B.c.
246
C
al- le- lu- ia, al- le- lu- ia, al- le- lu- ia, al- le- lu- ia, al- le-
A
-lu- ia, al- le- lu- ia, al- le- lu- ia, al- le- lu- ia,
Bar
al- le- lu- ia, ⟨al- le- lu- ia, al- le- lu- ia,⟩
B.c.
250
C
-lu- ia, ⟨al- le- lu- ia,⟩
A
al- le- lu- ia, al- le- lu- ia, al- le- lu- ia, ⟨al- le- lu- ia, al- le-
Bar
al- le- lu- ia, ⟨al- le- lu- ia,⟩ al- le- lu- ia,
B.c.

253
C
al- le- lu- ia, ⟨al- le- lu- ia,⟩ al- le- lu- ia,
A
-lu- ia,⟩ al- le- lu- ia, al- le- lu- ia, al- le- lu- ia, al- le- lu- ia,
Bar
al- le- lu- ia, al- le-
B.c.
256
C
al- le- lu- ia, al- le- lu- ia, al- lc- lu- ia,
A
al- le- lu- ia, ⟨al- le- lu- ia,⟩ al- le- lu- ia,
Bar
-lu- ia, al- le- lu- ia,
al- le- lu- ia, al- le-
B.c.
7
259
C
al- le- lu- ia, al- le- lu- ia, al- le- lu- ia, ⟨al- le-
A
al- le- lu- ia, al- le- lu- ia, ⟨al- le- lu- ia,⟩ al- le-
Bar
-lu- ia, al- le- lu- ia,
B.c.

263
C
-lu- ia,〉 al- le- lu- ia, al- le- lu- ia,
A
-lu- ia, al- le- lu- ia, al- le- lu- ia, 〈al- le- lu- ia,〉
Bar
al- le- lu- ia, al- le- lu- ia, 〈al- le- lu- ia,〉 al- le- lu- ia, al- le-
B.c.
267
C
al- le- lu- ia, 〈al- le- lu- ia,〉 al- le- lu- ia, al- le-
A
al- le- lu- ia, 〈al- le- lu- ia,〉 al- le- lu- ia, al- le-
Bar
-lu- ia, al- le- lu- ia, al- le- lu- ia, al- le- lu- ia,
B.c.
271
C
-lu- ia, 〈al- le- lu- ia, al- le- lu- ia, al- le- lu- ia,〉 al- le- lu- ia.
A
-lu- ia, al- le- lu- ia, al- le- lu- ia, al- le- lu- - ia.
Bar
al- le- lu- ia, 〈al- le- lu- ia,〉 al- le- lu- ia.
B.c.
6
6

17. Jesu mi dulcissime

Biagio Marini

18
A
spes su- spi- ran- tis a- ni- mae,
T
spes, su- spi- ran- tis a- ni- mae,
B
spes, su- spi- ran- tis a- ni- mae,
B.c.
24
Te
Te quae- runt pi- ae la- cri- mae, Te cla- mor men-
Te quae- runt pi- ae la- cri- mae, Te cla- mor
30
quae- runt pi- ae la- cri- mae, Te cla- mor men- tis in-
- tis in- ti- mae, Te quae- runt pi- ae la- cri- mae,
men- tis in- ti- mae, Te quae- runt pi- ae

36
A
- ti- mae, Te quae- runt pi- ae la- cri- mae, te cla- mor
T
Te quae- runt, te quae- runt pi- ae la- cri- mae,
B
la- cri- mae, Te quae- runt pi- ae la- cri- mae,
B.c.
42
A
men- - tis in- ti- mae, Te quae- runt pi- ae
T
Te quae- runt pi- ae la- cri- mae, Te quae- runt
B
Te cla- mor men- tis in- ti- mae, Te quae- runt
B.c.
48
A
la- cri- mae, Te cla- mor men- - tis in- ti- mae,
T
pi- ae la- cri- mae, Te cla- mor men- tis in- ti- mae,
B
pi- ae la- cri- mae, Te cla- mor men- tis in- ti- mae,
B.c.

54
A
T
B
B.c.
Te cla- mor men- - tis in- ti- mae, Te cla- mor
Te cla- mor men- tis in- ti- mae, Te cla- mor men-
Te cla- mor men- tis in- ti- mae, Te cla- mor
6 7 [♯]6 6
61
[solo]
men- tis in- ti- mae. Je- su dul- cis me- mo- ri- a Dans ve- ra cor- dis
- tis in- ti- mae.
men- tis in- ti- mae.
7 6 6 6
66
gau- di- a; Sed su- per mel et om- ni- a E- jus dul- - cis me- mo- ri-
6
70
-a.
solo
Je- su de- cus an- ge- li-cum, In au- re dul- ce can- ti- cum, In o- re mel mi- ri- fi-
6 6 6

74
T
-cum, In cor- de, in cor- - de ne- ctar cae- li- cum.
solo
B
Je- su so- le se- re- ni- or, Et bal- sa-mo su-
B.c.
78
B
-bli- mi- or, Om- ni dul- co- re du- ci- or, Et cun- ctis, et cun- ctis a- ma- bi- li- or.
B.c.
83
A
Je- su sum- - ma be- ni- gni- tas, Mi- ra cor- dis
T
Je- su sum- - ma be- ni- gni- tas, Mi- ra cor- dis
B
Je- su sum- ma be- ni- gni- tas, Mi- ra cor- dis
B.c.
89
A
ju- cun- di- tas,
T
ju- cun- di- tas, In- com- pre- hen- sa bo- ni- tas, Tu- a me
B
ju- cun- di- tas, In- com- pre-
B.c.

95
A
In- com- pre- hen- sa bo- ni- tas, Tu- a me
T
strin- gat cha- ri- tas, In- com- pre-
B
-hen- sa bo- ni- tas, Tu- a me strin- gat cha- ri- tas,
B.c.
7 ♯ 6 7 6
101
A
strin- gat cha- ri- tas, In- com- pre-
T
-hen- sa bo- ni- tas, Tu- a me strin- gat cha- ri- tas,
B
In- com- pre- hen- sa bo- ni- tas, Tu- a me
B.c.
7 6 6
107
A
-hen- sa bo- ni- tas, Tu- a me strin- gat cha- ri- tas,
T
In- com- pre- hen- sa bo- ni- tas, Tu- a me
B
strin- gat cha- ri- tas, In- com- pre-
B.c.
7 7

169

131
A
-lu- ia, al- le- lu- ia, al- le- lu- ia, ⟨al-
T
-le- lu- ia,
B
al- le- lu- ia, al- le- lu- ia, al- le- lu- ia,
B.c.
7 [♯]6 4 2 6
137
A
-le- lu- ia,⟩ al- le- lu- ia, al- le- lu- ia, al- le-
T
al- le- lu- ia, al- le- lu- ia, al- le-
B
al- le- lu- ia, al- le- lu- ia, al- le-
B.c.
7 ♮6 6 7 ♮6
143
A
-lu- ia, al- le- lu- ia, al- le- lu- ia,
T
-lu- ia, al- le- lu- ia, al- le- lu- ia, al- le- lu-
B
-lu- ia, al- le- lu- ia, al- le- lu- ia,
B.c.
6 7 [♯]6 6 7 6

149
A
T
B
B.c.
— al- le- lu- ia, al- le- lu- ia, al- le- lu- ia, al-
-ia, al- le- lu- ia, al- le- lu- ia, al- le- lu- ia, al-
⟨al- le- lu- ia, al- le- lu- ia, al- le- lu- ia,⟩ al-
6 7 ♯6 6
155
le lu ia, al le lu ia.
-le- lu- ia, al- - le- lu- - ia.
-le- lu- ia, al- - le- lu- ia.
7 [♯]6 ♯ 4 3

18. Obstupescite gentes

Per una Vergine, overo della Madonna

Maurizio Cazzati

18
C1
ca- - ni- te, ca- - ni- te, ca- ni- te
C2
ca- - ni- te, ca- - ni- te, ca- ni- te
B
ca- - ni- te, ca- - ni- te
B.c.
23
C1
Vir- gi- nis tri um phos, ca ni te, ca ni te, ca- ni- te
C2
Vir- gi- nis tri- um- phos, ca- ni- te, ca- ni- te, ca- ni- te
B
Vir- gi- nis tri- um- phos, ca- ni- te, ca- ni- te, ca- ni- te
B.c.
29
C1
Vir- gi- nis tri- um- phos, ca- ni- te Vir- gi- nis tri- um- phos.
C2
Vir- gi- nis tri- um- phos, ca- ni- te Vir- gi- nis tri- um- phos.
B
Vir- gi- nis tri- um- phos, ca- ni- te Vir- gi- nis tri- um- phos.
B.c.

36
C1
fe- sti- na- te in fe- sti- vi- ta- te San- ctae Vir- gi- nis Ma-
C2
Pro- pe- ra- te in so-lem-ni- ta- te, San- ctae Vir- gi- nis N.,
B
San- ctae Vir- gi- nis
B.c.
39
C1
-ri- ae, fe- sti- na- te in fe- sti- vi- ta- te San- ctae Vir- gi- nis N.,
C2
fe- sti- na- te in fe- sti- vi- ta- te San- ctae Vir- gi- nis N.,
B
N., pro- pe- ra- te in so-lem-ni- ta- te, San- ctae Vir- gi- nis N.,
B.c.
43
C1
pro- pe- ra- te in so-lem-ni- ta- te, fe- sti- na- te in fe- sti- vi- ta- te San- ctae Vir-
C2
pro- pe- ra- te in so-lem-ni- ta- te, fe- sti- na- te in fe- sti- vi- ta- te San- ctae Vir-
B
pro- pe- ra- te, fe- sti- na- te, pro- pe- ra- te, fe- sti- na- te, in so-lem-ni- ta- te, San- ctae
B.c.

175

62
C1
po- pu- li de- fer- te lau- des; ca-
C2
po- pu- li de- fer- te lau- des; ca-
B
po- pu- li de- fer- te lau- des;
B.c.
68
C1
- ni- te, ca- - ni- te, ca- ni- te Vir- gi- nis
C2
- ni- te, ca- - ni- te, ca- ni- te Vir- gi- nis
B
ca- - ni- te, ca- - ni- te Vir- gi- nis
B.c.
73
C1
tri- um- phos, ca- ni- te, ca- ni- te, ca- ni- te Vir- gi- nis
C2
tri- um- phos, ca- ni- te, ca- ni- te, ca- ni- te Vir- gi- nis
B
tri- um- phos, ca- ni- te, ca- ni- te, ca- ni- te Vir- gi- nis
B.c.

(m. 79)

C1: tri- um- phos, ca- ni- te Virginis tri- um- phos.
C2: tri- um- phos, ca- ni- te Virginis tri- um- phos.
B: tri- um- phos, ca- ni- te Virginis tri- um- phos.

(m. 85)

C1 [solo]: I- sta, i- sta est, quae im- mun- das de- li- ci- as or- bis cer- to pe-

(m. 89)

C1: - de cal- ca- vit;
C2 [solo]: i- sta est, i- sta est, quae spre- tis A- ver- ni

(m. 93)

C2: prae- mi- is cae- - - lum a- ma- vit;
B solo: i- sta

B: est, ⟨ista est,⟩ quae regna terrena, quae regna terrena despiciens, ad sublimia regna, ad sublimia regna evolavit, ad sublimia regna, ad sublimia regna evolavit.

Allegro

C1: Ridete flores, coronate

C2: Ridete flores, coronate

B: florete, florete lilia, florete,

115
C1
Vir- gi-nem, co- ro- na- te Vir- gi-nem Ma- riam, ri- de-
C2
Vir- gi-nem, co- ro- na- te Vir- gi-nem N., ri- de-
B
flo- re- te, flo-re- - te li- li- a, ri-
B.c.
119
C1
- - te, ri- de- te flo-res, flo- re- te li- li- a, flo-re- te, flo-re-
C2
- - te, ri- de- te flo-res, flo- re- te li- li- a, flo-re- te, flo-re-
B
-de- - te, ri- de- te flo-res, flo- re- te li- li- a, flo- re- te, flo-re- te, flo-
B.c.
123
C1
-te, flo- re- te li- li- a, co- ro- na- te Vir- gi-nem, co- ro- na- te Vir- - gi-nem N.,
C2
-te, flo- re- te li- li- a, co- ro- na- te Vir- gi-nem, co- ro- na- te Vir- - gi-nem N.,
B
-re- te li- li- a, co- ro- na- te Vir- gi-nem, co- ro- na- te Vir- gi-nem N.,
B.c.

127
C1: ri- de- te flo- res, flo- re- te li- li- a, co- ro- na- te, co- ro- na- te, co- ro- na- te

C2: ri- de- te flo- res, flo- re- te li- li- a, co- ro- na- te, co- ro- na- te

B: ri- de- te flo- res, flo- re- te li- li- a, co- ro- na- te, co- ro- na- te

131
C1: Vir- gi- nem N., co- ro- na- te Vir- gi- nem N.

C2: Vir- gi- nem N., co- ro- na- te Vir- gi- nem N.

B: Vir- gi- nem N., co- ro- na- te Vir- gi- nem N.

136 — Largo
C1: Af- fer- te lau- des, le- ga- te pre- ces, con- ce- le- bra- te fe- stum,

C2: Af- fer- te lau- des, le- ga- te pre- ces, con- ce- le- bra- te fe- stum,

B: Af- fer- te lau- des, le- ga- te pre- ces, con- ce- le- bra- te fe- stum,

145
Presto
C1
con- ce- le- bra- - te fe- stum;
C2
con- ce- le- bra- - te fe- stum; ut om- nes cum i- psa lau- da- re, can-
B
con- ce- le- bra- te fe- stum;
B.c.
153
C1
ut om- nes cum
C2
-ta- re, re- gna- re pos- si- mus, al- le- lu- ia,
B
ut om- nes cum i- psa lau- da- re, can-
B.c.
159
C1
i- psa lau- da- re, can- ta- re, re- gna- re pos- si- mus,
C2
ut om- nes cum
B
-ta- re, al- le- lu- ia, al- le- lu- ia, ut
B.c.
4 3

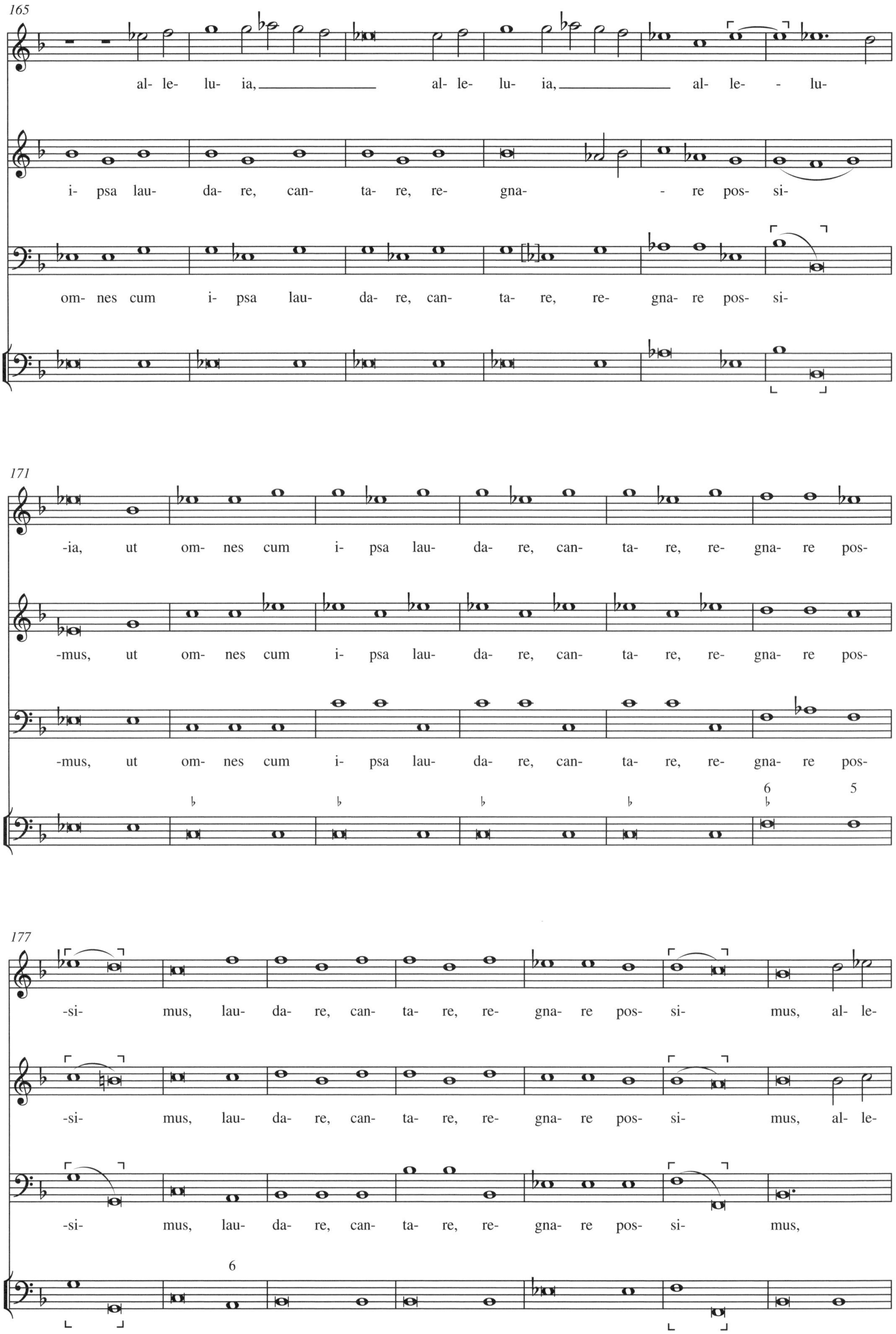
165
C1
al- le- lu- ia, al- le- lu- ia, al- le- - lu-
C2
i- psa lau- da- re, can- ta- re, re- gna- - re pos- si-
B
om- nes cum i- psa lau- da- re, can- ta- re, re- gna- re pos- si-
B.c.
171
C1
-ia, ut om- nes cum i- psa lau- da- re, can- ta- re, re- gna- re pos-
C2
-mus, ut om- nes cum i- psa lau- da- re, can- ta- re, re- gna- re pos-
B
-mus, ut om- nes cum i- psa lau- da- re, can- ta- re, re- gna- re pos-
B.c.
177
C1
-si- mus, lau- da- re, can- ta- re, re- gna- re pos- si- mus, al- le-
C2
-si- mus, lau- da- re, can- ta- re, re- gna- re pos- si- mus, al- le-
B
-si- mus, lau- da- re, can- ta- re, re- gna- re pos- si- mus,
B.c.

184
C1
-lu- ia, al- le- lu- ia, al-
C2
-lu- ia, al- le- lu- ia,
B
ut om- nes cum i- psa lau- da- re, can- ta- re, re-
B.c.
189
C1
- le- - lu- ia, ut om- nes cum i- psa lau-
C2
al- le- - lu- ia,
B
-gna- re pos- - si- mus, al- le- lu- ia, al- le-
B.c.
195
C1
-da- re, can- ta- re, re- gna- re pos- si- mus,
C2
ut om- nes cum i- psa lau-
B
-lu- ia, al- le- lu- ia, ut om- nes cum
B.c.

201
C1
al- le- lu- - ia, ut om- nes cum
C2
-da- re, can- ta- re, re- gna- - re pos- si- mus, ut
B
i- psa lau- da- re, can- ta- re, re- gna- re pos- si- mus,
B.c.
207
C1
i- psa lau- da- re, lau- da- re, can- ta- re, re- gna- - re pos- si-
C2
om- nes cum i- psa lau- da- re, can- ta- re, re- gna- - re pos- si-
B
ut om- nes cum i- psa lau- da- re, can- ta- re, re- gna- re pos- si-
B.c.
214
C1
-mus, lau- da- re, can- ta- re, re- gna- re, re- gna- re pos- si- mus, ut
C2
-mus, lau- da- re, can- ta- re, re- gna- re, re- gna- re pos- si- mus, ut
B
-mus, lau- da- re, can- ta- re, re- gna- re, re- gna- re pos- si- mus, ut
B.c.

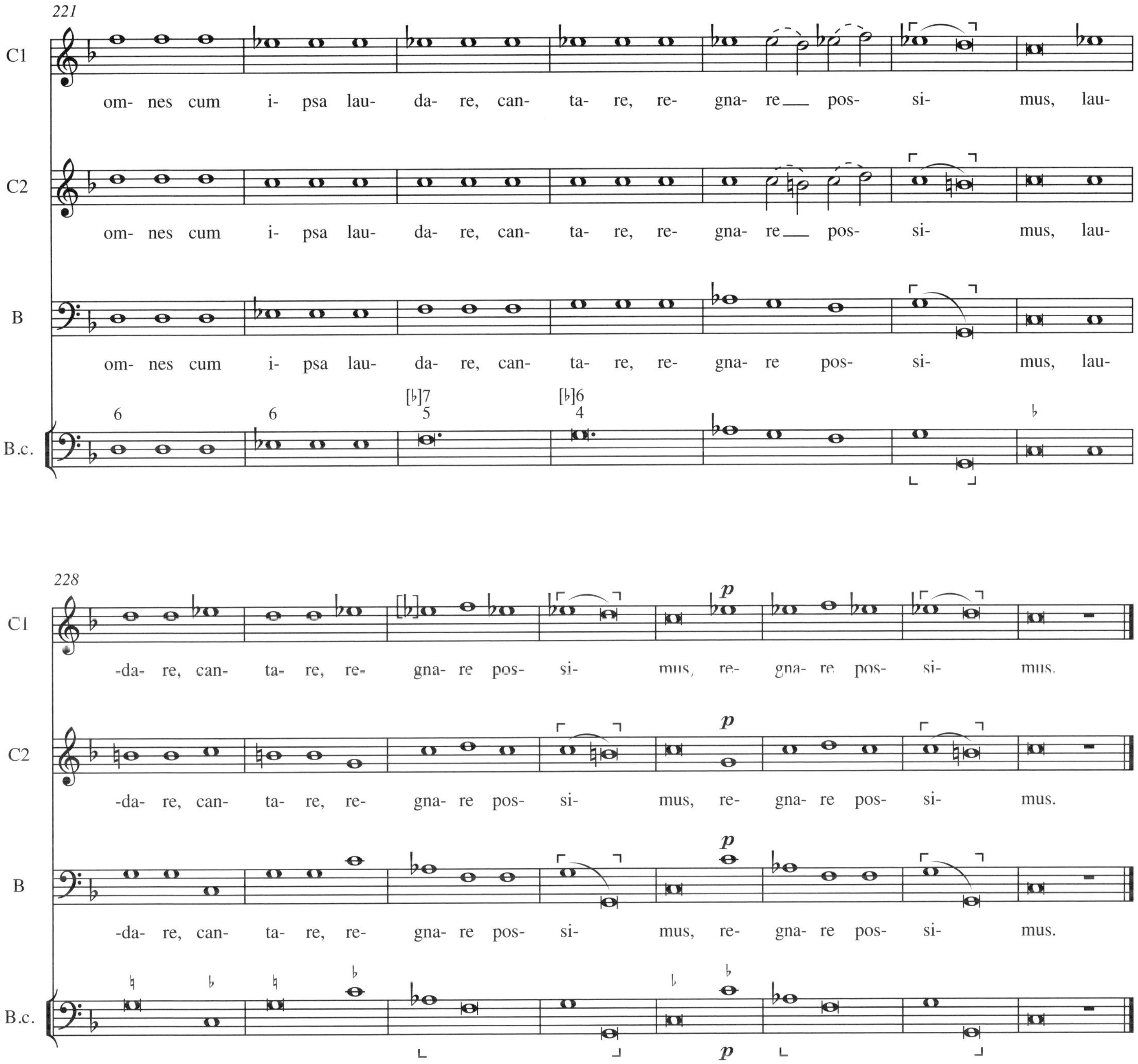
221
C1
om- nes cum i- psa lau- da- re, can- ta- re, re- gna- re pos- si- mus, lau-
C2
om- nes cum i- psa lau- da- re, can- ta- re, re- gna- re pos- si- mus, lau-
B
om- nes cum i- psa lau- da- re, can- ta- re, re- gna- re pos- si- mus, lau-
B.c.
228
C1
-da- re, can- ta- re, re- gna- re pos- si- mus, re- gna- re pos- si- mus.
C2
-da- re, can- ta- re, re- gna- re pos- si- mus, re- gna- re pos- si- mus.
B
-da- re, can- ta- re, re- gna- re pos- si- mus, re- gna- re pos- si- mus.
B.c.

19. Salve Regina

Pietro Andrea Ziani

14
A
spes no- stra, sal- ve, sal- ve, ⟨sal- ve,⟩ sal- ve ma- ter mi- se- ri-
T
sal- ve, sal- ve, ⟨sal- ve,⟩ sal- ve ma- ter mi- se- ri-
B
no- stra, sal- ve, sal- ve, ⟨sal- ve,⟩ sal- ve ma- ter mi- se- ri-
B.c.
18
A
-cor- di- ae. Ad te cla- ma- mus, ex- su- les, fi- li- i, fi- li- i
T
-cor- di- ae. Ad te cla- ma- mus, ex- - su- les, fi- li- i
B
-cor- di- ae. Ad te cla- ma- mus, ex- - su- les, fi- li- i
B.c.
22
A
E- vae, ad te cla- ma- mus, ex- su- les, fi- li- i E-
T
E- vae, ad te cla- ma- mus, ex- - su- les, fi- li- i, fi- li- i E-
B
E- vae, ad te cla- ma- mus, ex- su- les, fi- li- i E-
B.c.

26
A
-vae. Ad te su- spi- ra- mus, ge- men- tes et
T
-vae. Ad te su- spi- ra- mus, ge- men- tes et flen- tes, et
B
-vae. Ad te su- spi- ra- mus, ge- men- tes et flen-
B.c.
31
flen- tes in hac la- cri- ma- rum val- le, ad te, ad
flen- tes in hac la- cri- ma- rum val- le, cla- ma- mus,
-tes in hac la- cri- ma- rum val- le, cla- ma- mus,
36
te, su- spi- ra- mus, ge- men- tes, ge- men- tes et flen-
su- spi- ra- mus, cla- ma- mus, ge- men- tes, in hac la-
su- spi- ra- mus, cla- ma- mus, ge- men- tes et flen- tes in

41
A
-tes in hac la- cri- ma- rum val- le. E- ia er- go, e- ia er- go,
T
-cri- ma- - - rum val- le. E- ia er- go, ⟨e- ia er- go,⟩
B
hac la- cri- ma- rum val- le. E- ia er- go, e- ia er- go,
B.c.
46
A
ad- vo- ca- ta no- stra, ⟨ad- vo- ca- ta no- stra,⟩ il- los tu- os
T
ad- vo- ca- ta no- stra, ad- vo- ca- ta no- stra, il- los
B
ad- vo- ca- ta no- stra, ⟨ad- vo- ca- ta no- stra,⟩ il- los
B.c.
50
A
mi- se- ri- cor- - des o- cu- los ad
T
tu- os mi- se- ri- cor- des o- cu- los ad
B
tu- os mi- se- ri- cor- des o- cu- los ad nos con-
B.c.

54
A
nos con- ver- te, ad nos con- ver- te, ad nos con-
T
nos con- ver- te, ad nos con- ver- te, ad nos con-
B
-ver- te, ad nos con- ver- te, ad nos con- ver- te, ⟨con-
B.c.
59
A
-ver- te, il- los tu- os mi- se- ri- cor- des o- cu-
T
-ver- te, il- los tu- os mi- se- ri- cor- des o- cu-
B
-ver- te,⟩ il- los tu- os, mi- se- ri- cor- des o- cu-
B.c.
64
A
-los ad nos con- ver- te, ad nos con-
T
-los ad nos con- ver- te, ad nos con-
B
-los ad nos con- ver- te, ad
B.c.

69
A
-ver- te, ad nos con- ver- te, con- ver- te, ⟨con- ver- te.⟩
T
-ver- te, ad nos con- ver- te, con- ver- te, ⟨con- ver- te.⟩
B
nos con- ver- te, ⟨con- ver- te,⟩ con- ver- te, ⟨con- ver- te.⟩
B.c.
75
Allegro
A
T
Et Je- sum, be- ne- di- ctum fru- ctum
B
Et Je- sum, be- ne- di- ctum fru- ctum ven- tris tu- i,
B.c.
78
A
Et Je- sum, be- ne- di- ctum fru- ctum ven- tris tu- i,
T
ven- tris tu- i, fru- ctum ven- tris tu- i,
B
et Je- sum, be- ne-
B.c.

81
A
fru- ctum ven- tris tu- i, et
T
et Jesum, be- ne- di- ctum fru- ctum ven- tris
B
-di- ctum fru- ctum ven- tris tu- i, fru- ctum ven- tris
B.c.
[2] [6] ♯4 [6]
84
A
Je- sum, be- ne- di- ctum fru- ctum ven- tris tu- i, no- bis
T
tu- i, no- bis post hoc ex- si- li- um o- sten-
B
tu- i, ⟨fru- - ctum ven- tris tu- i,⟩ no- bis post hoc ex-
B.c.
[♯4] [6]
87
A
post hoc ex- si- li- um o- sten- de,
T
-de, no- bis post hoc ex- si- li- um o- sten-
B
-si- li- um o- sten- - de, no- bis post hoc ex-
B.c.
6 [♯] 2 [6]

90
A
nobis post hoc exsilium ostende.
T
de, ostende.
B
silium ostende, ostende.
B.c.
(93)
A
O clemens, ⟨o clemens,⟩ o pia, o dulcis
T
O clemens, ⟨o clemens,⟩ o pia,
B
O clemens, ⟨o clemens,⟩ o pia,
B.c.
98
A
Virgo, dulcis Virgo Maria,
T
o dulcis Virgo, Virgo Maria, o dulcis
B
o dulcis Virgo Maria,
B.c.

104
A
o dul-cis Vir- go, Vir- go, Vir- - go Ma-ri- a.
T
Vir- go, dul- cis Vir- go, Vir- - go Ma- ri- a.
B
o dul-cis Vir- go, Vir- go Ma- ri- a.
B.c.
110
Adagio
Allegro
Con- ver- te, ⟨con- ver- te.⟩
Con- ver- te, ⟨con- ver- te.⟩ Et Je- sum, be- ne- di- ctum fru- ctum
Con- ver- te, ⟨con- ver- te.⟩
114
Et Je- sum, be- ne- di- ctum fru- ctum
ven- tris tu- i, fru- ctum ven- tris tu- i,
Et Je- sum, be- ne- di- ctum fru- ctum ven- tris tu- i, fru-

117
A
ven- tris tu- i, nobis post hoc ex-
T
nobis post hoc exsilium osten- de,
B
-ctum ventris tu- i, nobis post hoc exsilium o-
B.c.
120
A
-silium osten- - de, nobis
T
nobis post hoc exsilium osten-
B
-sten- - de, nobis post hoc exsilium o-
B.c.
123
A
post hoc exsilium osten- de. O clemens, ⟨o
T
- de, o- sten- de. O clemens, ⟨o
B
-sten- de, o- sten- de. O clemens, ⟨o
B.c.

127
A
clemens,〉 o pi- a, o dul- cis Vir- go, dul- cis
T
clemens,〉 o pi- a, o dul- cis Vir- go,
B
clemens,〉 o pi- a, o dul- cis
B.c.
132
A
Vir- go Ma- ri- a, o dul- cis
T
Vir- go Ma- ri- a, o dul- cis Vir-
B
Vir- go Ma- ri- a,
B.c.
137
A
Vir- go, Vir- go, Vir- - go Ma- ri- a.
T
-go, dul- cis Vir- go, Vir- - go Ma- ri- a.
B
o dul- cis Vir- go, Vir- go Ma- ri- a.
B.c.

20. O Sacramentum

Giovanni Battista Volpe

13
A
- tis_ in- fe- ri, pi-gnus al- mum fi- de- li- um,
T
pi-gnus al- mum fi- de- - li- um,
B
o- nus tre- men-
B.c.
7
17
A
pi-gnus al- mum fi- de- li- um,
T
pi- gnus al- mum fi- de- li- um,
B
- tis_ in- fe- ri, pi-gnus al- mum fi- de- li- um, ho- - nos, ⟨ho-
B.c.
5 6 ♯
21
A
ho- nos,
T
ho- nos, ⟨ho-
B
- nos,⟩ ho- - nos cae- le- stis_ cu- ri- ae, ho- nos,
B.c.
5 6

Presto
A
⟨ho- nos⟩ cae- le- stis cu- ri- ae. Al- le- lu- ia, ⟨al-
T
-nos⟩ cae- le- - stis cu- ri- ae.
B
ho- nos cae- le- stis cu- ri- ae.
B.c.
-le- lu- ia,⟩ al- le- lu- ia, al- le- lu- ia, al- le- lu- ia, al- le-
-lu- ia, al- le- lu- ia, al- le- lu- ia, al- le- lu- ia, al- le- lu- ia, al-
- le- lu- ia, al- - le- lu- ia,
Al- le-
Al- le- lu- ia, al- le- lu- ia, al-

47
A
al- le- lu- ia, al- le- lu- ia, al- le- lu- ia,
T
-lu- ia, al- le- lu- ia, al- le- lu- ia,
B
-le- lu- ia, al- le- lu- ia, al- le- lu- ia, al- - le- lu-
B.c.
53
A
al- - le- lu- ia, al- - le- lu- ia,
T
al- - le- lu- ia, al- - le- lu- ia, al-
B
-ia, al- - le- lu- ia, al-
B.c.
7 [♯]6
60
A
al- le- lu- ia, al- le- lu- ia, al- le- lu- ia, al-
T
- le- lu- ia, al- - le- lu- ia, al- - le- lu- ia, al-
B
- le- lu- ia, al- le- lu- ia, al-
B.c.
[7 ♯6]
♯

66
A
T
B
B.c.
p
-le- lu- ia, al- - le- lu- ia, al- - le- lu- ia.
-le- lu- ia, ⟨al- - le- lu- ia, al- le- lu- ia.⟩
-le- lu- ia, al- le- lu- ia, ⟨al- le- lu- ia.⟩
72
solo
A- ve ci- bus sa- lu- ta- ris, Per- ju- cun- dus sin- gu- la- ris, Vi- ta vir- tus
76
cor- di- um, A- ve, a- ve, a- ve ci- bus sin- gu- la- ris, Per- ju- cun- dus sa- lu-
80
ta- ris, sa- lu- ta- ris, Vi- ta vir- tus cor- di- um, A- ve, ⟨a- ve,⟩ a- ve ci- bus Per- ju- cun- dus sin- gu-
84
-la- ris, Vi- ta vir- tus cor- di- um, Vi- ta vir- tus cor- di- um.
solo
O fru-

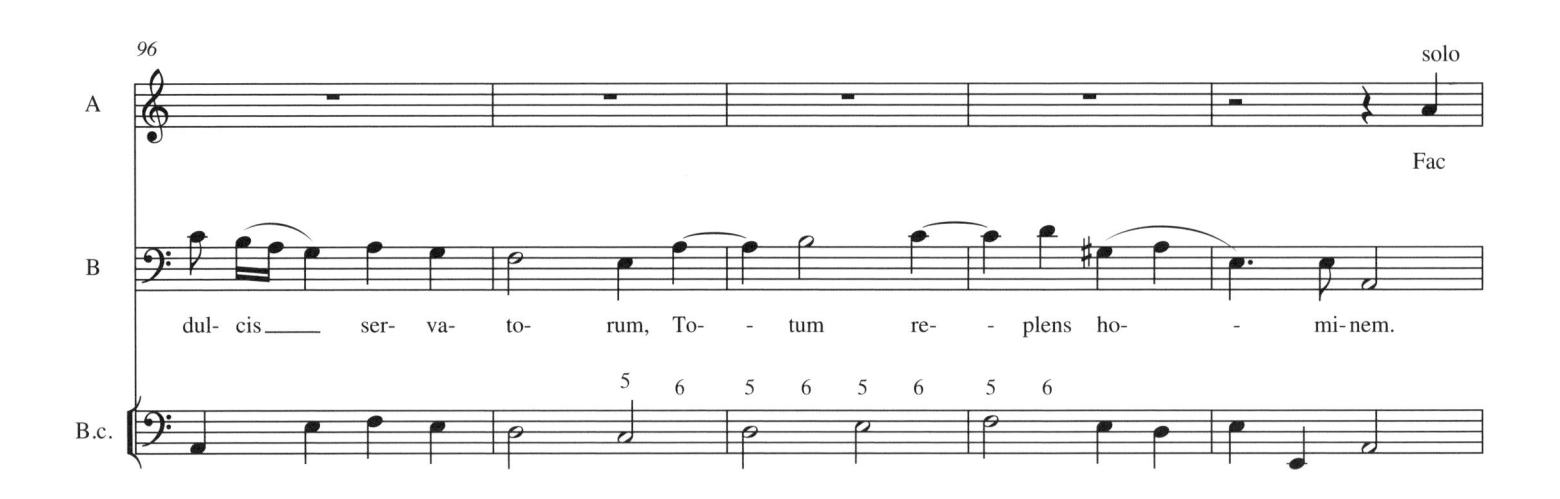

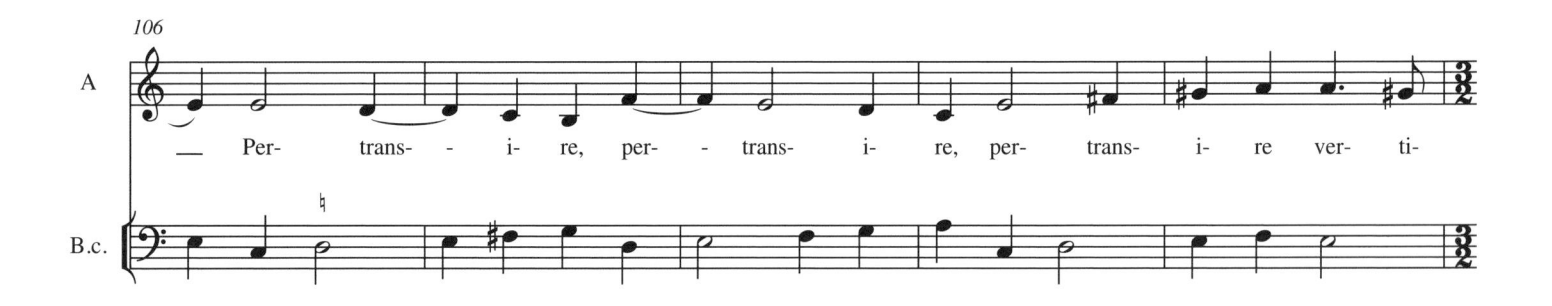

-men- tum, o fru- men- tum e- le- cto- rum, Po- tus dul- cis, po- tus dul- cis ser- va- to- rum, To- tum re- plens ho- mi- nem, Po- tus dul- cis ser- va- to- rum, To- tum re- plens ho- mi- nem.

solo
Fac nos e- sca ta- li pa- stos, Tu- ti sae- cli ni- mis va- stos Per- trans- i- re, per- trans- i- re, per- trans- i- re ver- ti-

111
A
-ces. Al- le- lu- ia, al- le- lu- ia, al- le- lu- ia, al- le- lu- ia, al-
B.c.
4 ♯
117
A
-le- lu- ia, al- le- lu- ia, al- le- lu- ia, al- le- lu- ia, al- le-
B.c.
123
A
-lu- ia, al- le- lu- ia, al- - le- lu- ia, al- - le- lu- ia,
B
Al- le-
B.c.
129
A
al- le- lu- ia, al- le- lu- ia, al- le- lu-
T
Al- le- lu- ia, al- le- lu- ia, al- le- lu- ia,
B
-lu- ia, al- le- lu- ia, al- le- lu- ia, al- le- lu- ia, al- le-
B.c.

135
A
-ia, al- - le- lu- ia, al- - le- lu- ia,
T
al- - le- lu- ia, al-
B
-lu- ia, al- - le- lu- ia, al-
B.c.
142
A
al- le- lu- ia, al- le- lu- ia, al- le-
T
- le- lu- ia, al- - le- lu- ia, al- - le- lu- ia, al- - le-
B
- le- lu- ia, al- - le- lu- ia, al- - le-
B.c.
[7 ♯6] 7 [♯]6 ♯
149
A
-lu- ia, al- - le- lu- ia, al- - le- lu- ia, al- - le- lu- ia,
T
-lu- ia, al- le- lu- ia, al- - le- lu- ia, al- le- lu- ia,
B
-lu- ia, al- le- lu- ia, al- le- lu- ia, al- le- lu- ia,
B.c.
♯
p

156
A
al-
T
al- - le- lu- ia,
B
a[l]- -
B.c.
159
A
- - - le- lu- ia.
T
al- - - - le- lu- ia.
B
- - - le- lu- ia.
B.c.
7 6 5
[♯ 4 ♯]

21. Salve Virgo benignissima

Massimiliano Neri

15
A
Vir- go be- ni- - gnis- si- ma, sal- ve, ⟨sal- ve⟩,
T
Vir- go be- ni- - gnis- si- ma, sal- ve, ⟨sal- ve,⟩
B
Vir- go be- ni- - gnis- si- ma, sal- ve, ⟨sal- ve,⟩
B.c.
7
22
A
sal- ve, ⟨sal- ve⟩ Vir- go cle- men- - tis- si- ma, quae
T
sal- ve, ⟨sal- ve⟩ Vir- go cle- men- - tis- si- ma, quae
B
sal- ve, ⟨sal- ve⟩ Vir- go cle- men- - tis- si- ma, quae
B.c.
7
28
A
no- bis om- ni- bus in te, ⟨in te⟩ spe- ran- ti- bus
T
no- bis om- ni- bus in te, ⟨in te⟩ spe- ran- ti- bus
B
no- bis om- ni- bus in te, ⟨in te⟩ spe- ran- ti- bus
B.c.

34
A
T
mi- se- ri- cor- di- ae tu- ae, mi- se- ri-
B
mi- se- ri- cor- di- ae tu- ae si- num a- pe- ru- i- sti,
B.c.
38
A
mi- se- ri- cor- di- ae tu- ae si- num a- pe- ru-
T
-cor- di- ae tu- ae si- num a- pe- ru- i- sti,
B
B.c.
42
A
-i- sti, ut de ple- ni- tu- di- ne
T
ut de ple- ni- tu- di- ne e- jus ac- ci- pi- ant u- ni- ver- si,
B
ut de ple- ni- tu- di- ne e- jus ac- ci- pi- ant u- ni- ver- si, de
B.c.

46
A
e- jus, de ple- ni- tu- di- ne e- jus ac- ci- pi- ant u- ni-
T
de ple- ni- tu- di- ne e- jus,
B
ple- ni- tu- di- ne e- jus,
B.c.
6
49
A
-ver- si, de ple- ni- tu- di- ne e- jus ac- ci- pi- ant,
T
de ple- ni- tu- di- ne e- jus, de ple- ni- tu- di- ne e- jus, de
B
⟨de ple- ni- tu- di- ne e- jus,⟩ de ple- ni- tu- di- ne e- jus, ⟨de
B.c.
6
52
A
ac- ci- pi- ant u- ni- ver- si.
T
ple- ni- tu- di- ne e- jus ac- ci- pi- ant u- ni- ver- si.
B
ple- ni- tu- di- ne e- jus⟩ ac- ci- pi- ant u- ni- ver- si.
B.c.

56
A
Tu gra- ti- a ple- na,
T
tu nor- ma vir- tu- tis,
B
tu
B.c.
61
A
tu stel- la re- ful- gens, tu
T
tu nor- ma vir-
B
stel- la, tu stel- la re- ful- gens, tu
B.c.
67
A
nor- ma vir- tu- tis, tu gra- ti- a ple- na, tu nor- ma vir-
T
-tu- tis, tu stel- la re- ful- gens, tu stel- la re- ful-
B
gra- ti- a ple- na, tu nor- ma vir- tu- tis, tu stel- la re-
B.c.
5 6 ♯

211

86
A
-a,
T
o Ma-ri- a, in- ven- trix gra- ti-
B
per te Red- em- ptor ad- ve- nit in pre- ti- um, o Ma-ri-
B.c.
7 6 6 7 6
90
A
o Ma-ri- a, ge- ni-trix vi- tae, in- ven- trix gra- ti- ae, ma- ter sa-
T
-ae, in- ven- trix gra- ti- ae, ma- ter sa- lu- tis, ge- ni- trix vi- tae,
B
-a, ma- ter sa- lu- tis, in- ven- trix gra- ti- ae, ma- ter sa- lu- tis, ge- ni- trix
B.c.
7 6 7 6
93
A
-lu- tis, ge- ni- trix vi- tae, o Ma-ri- a, o Ma-ri- a, ge- ni-trix vi- tae.
T
o Ma-ri- a, o Ma- ri- a, ge- ni- trix vi- tae.
B
vi- tae, o Ma- ri- a, o Ma- ri- a, ge- ni- trix vi- tae.
B.c.
3 6 3 4 3

98
A
Stel- la ma- ris, di- ri- ge
T
Stel- la ma- ris, di- ri- ge nos; por- ta cae- li, ex- ci- pe
B
B.c.
105
A
nos; por- ta cae- li, ex- ci- pe nos;
T
nos; tur- ris Da- vid, ⟨tur- ris
B
Stel- la ma- ris, di- ri- ge nos; por- ta
B.c.
111
A
tur- ris Da- vid, ⟨tur- ris Da- vid,⟩ pro- te- ge
T
Da- vid,⟩ pro- te- ge nos; sa- lus mun- di, sa- - lus
B
cae- li, ex- ci- pe nos; tur- ris Da- vid, ⟨tur- ris
B.c.

117
A
nos, ⟨pro- - te- ge nos;⟩ sa- lus mun- di,
T
mun- di, su- sci- pe nos, sa- lus mun- di, di- ri- ge nos,
B
Da- vid,⟩ pro- te- ge nos; sa- lus mun- di, di- ri- ge
B.c.
123
A
ex- ci- pe nos, pro- te- ge nos, sa- lus
T
ex- ci- pe nos, pro- te- ge, ⟨pro- te- ge⟩ nos, sa- lus
B
nos, ex- ci- pe nos, pro- te- ge nos, sa- lus
B.c.
129
A
mun- di, ⟨sa- lus mun- di,⟩ su- sci- pe nos. Al- le- lu- ia, al-
T
mun- di, ⟨sa- lus mun- di,⟩ su- - sci- pe nos.
B
mun- di, ⟨sa- lus mun- di,⟩ su- sci- pe nos.
B.c.

134
A
T
B
B.c.
- le- lu- ia, al- - le- lu- ia,
Al- le-
137
al- le- lu- ia,
-lu- ia, al- - le- lu- ia,
Al- le- lu- ia, al-
140
al- - le- lu- ia,
al- - le- lu- ia, al- - le- lu- ia,
- - le- lu- ia, al- - le- lu- ia, al- le- lu-
♯6

143
A
al- le- lu- ia, al- le- lu- ia, al-
T
al- le- lu- ia, al- le- lu- ia,
B
-ia, al- le- lu- ia, al- le- lu- ia, al-
B.c.
146
A
- le- lu- ia, al- le- lu- ia, al- le- lu- ia.
T
al- le- lu- ia, al- le- lu- ia, al- le- lu- ia.
B
- le- lu- ia, al- le- lu- ia, al- le- lu- ia.
B.c.

22. O vos omnes

Simone Vesi

12
Largo
A
-tes in te- ne- bris et um- bra mor- tis, sur- gi- te,
T
-tes in te- ne- bris et um- bra mor- tis, sur- gi- te, ⟨sur- gi- te,
B
-tes in te- ne- bris et um- bra mor- tis, sur- gi- te, ⟨sur- gi- te, sur- gi- te,⟩
B.c.
16
A
⟨sur- gi- te, sur- gi- te,⟩ sur- gi- te, ⟨sur- gi- te, sur- gi- te, sur- gi- te,⟩ sur- gi- te, ⟨sur- gi- te, sur- gi-
T
sur- gi- te,⟩ sur- gi- te, ⟨sur- gi- te, sur- gi- te,⟩ sur- gi- te, ⟨sur- gi- te, sur- gi- te, sur- gi- te,⟩ sur- gi-
B
sur- gi- te, ⟨sur- gi- te, sur- gi- te,⟩ sur- gi- te, ⟨sur- gi- te, sur- gi- te, sur- gi- te, sur- gi- te,⟩ sur- gi-
B.c.
19
A
-te,⟩ pro- pe- ra- te ad lu- cem; et si fu- i- stis a- li- quan- do
T
-te, pro- pe- ra- te ad lu- cem; et si fu-
B
-te, pro- pe- ra- te ad lu- cem;
B.c.

24
A
te- ne-brae, e- ri- tis lux, ⟨e- ri- tis lux,⟩ et si fu-
T
-i- stis a- li-quan- do te- ne-brae, e- ri- tis lux, et si fu- i- stis a- li-
B
et si fu- i- stis a- li- quan- do te- ne-brae, et si fu- i- stis a- li- quan- do te- ne-brae,
B.c.
28
-i- stis a- li- quan- do te- ne-brae, e- ri- tis lux in Do- mi- no.
-quan- do te- ne-brae, e- ri- tis lux, e- ri- tis lux in Do mi no.
e- ri- tis lux, e- ri- tis lux in Do- mi- no.
32
[solo]
E- ia a- gi- te, a- gi- te, sur- gi- te, pro- pe- ra-
35
- te, ve- ni- te, ve- ni- te, ad Do- mi- num;
40
solo
ve- ni- te, ve- ni- te ad Do- mi-num; il- le e- nim est, qui cor il- lu- mi-nat,

44
A
men- tem e- le-vat, a- ni- mam pu- ri- fi- cat. E- ia, a- gi- te, a- gi- te,
T
E- ia, a- gi- te, a- gi- te,
B
E- ia, a- gi- te, a- gi- te,
B.c.
48
a- gi- te, sur- gi- te, sur- gi- te, ⟨sur- gi- te,⟩ pro- pe- ra- - te, ve- ni- te, ve-
a- gi- te, sur- gi- te, ⟨sur- gi- te, sur- gi- te, sur- gi- te,⟩ pro- pe- ra- te, ve- ni-
a- gi- te, sur- gi- te, ⟨sur- gi- te, sur- gi- te, sur- gi- te, sur- gi- te, sur- gi- te,⟩ pro- pe- ra- te, ve-
51
-ni- te, pro- pe- ra- - te, ve- ni- te, cur- ri- te, can- ta- te, ve- ni- te, lau- da- te, ve-
-te, ve- ni- te, pro- pe- ra- - te, ve- ni- te, cur- ri- te, can- ta- te, ve- ni- te, lau- da- te, ve-
-ni- te, ve- ni- te, pro- pe- ra- te, ve- ni- te, cur- ri- te, can- ta- te, ve- ni- te, lau-

54
A
-ni- te, ⟨ve- ni- te, ve- ni- te,⟩ lau- da- te, lau- da- te e- um di- cen- tes:
T
-ni- te, ve- ni- te, ve- ni- te, lau- da- te, lau- da- te e- um di- cen- tes:
B
-da- te, ve- ni- te, ve- ni- te, ⟨ve- ni- te,⟩ lau- da- te, lau- da- te e- um di- cen- tes:
B.c.
58
solo
A
O quam su- a vis es Do- mi- ne, lae-
B.c.
63
A
tan- - - -
B.c.
67
A
- ti- bus in te. O quam su- a- vis, su- a- vis es Do- mi- ne,
T
O quam su- a- - vis es Do- mi- ne,
B
O quam su- a- - vis es Do- mi- ne,
B.c.

73
A
T
B
B.c.
lae- tan- -
lae- tan- - -
lae- - tan- ti- bus, lae-
77
- - - -
- - - -
-tan- - - -
81
- ti- bus in te.
- ti- bus in te.
solo
- ti- bus in te. Ec- ce De- us, Sal- va- tor no- ster; ac- ce- di- te ad

(sheet music)

110
solo
A
Ac- ce- di- te ad il- lum, et fa- ci- es ve- strae non con- fun- den-
T
-um.
B.c.
113
A
- - tur, non con- fun- den-
B.c.
116
A
-tur; hic est e- nim De- us, lar- gi- tor bo- no- rum om- ni- um, sal- vans
B.c.
119
A
a- ni- mas, per- du- cens il- las ad cae- le- sti pa- tri- am.
B.c.
122
A
Cur- ra- mus er- go, pro- pe- re- mus, fe- sti- ne- mus, cur- ra- mus er- go, pro- pe- re- mus, fe- sti- ne- mus,
T
Cur- ra- mus er- go, pro- pe- re- mus, fe- sti- ne- mus, cur- ra- mus er- go, pro- pe- re- mus, fe- sti- ne- mus,
B
Cur- ra- mus er- go, pro- pe- re- mus, fe- sti- ne- mus, cur- ra- mus er- go, pro- pe- re- mus, fe- sti- ne- mus,
B.c.

126
A
can- te- - - mus, can- te- mus:
T
can-te- - - mus, can- te- mus:
B
can-te- - - mus, can- te- mus:
B.c.
131
solo
A
O quam su- a- - vis es Do- mi- ne, lae-
B.c.
136
A
-tan- - - -
B.c.
140
A
- ti- bus in te. O quam su- a- vis, su- a- vis es Do- mi- ne,
T
O quam su- a- - vis es Do- mi- ne,
B
O quam su- a- - vis es Do- mi- ne,
B.c.

146
A
T
B
B.c.
lae- tan- - -
lae- tan- - - -
lae- - tan- ti- bus, lae- tan-
6
151
A
T
B
B.c.
- - - - ti- bus in te.
- - - - ti- bus in te.
- - - - ti- bus in te.
6

23. Laetare Mater Ecclesia

Stefano Filippini

18
A
du- ci- te cho- - ros, cho- -
T
du- ci- te cho- - ros, cho-
B
du- ci- te cho-
3
B.c.
23
A
- - ros fi- li- ae Je- ru- sa- lem,
T
- - ros fi- li- ae Je- ru- sa- lem,
B
- - ros fi- li- ae Je- ru- sa- lem,
B.c.
29
A
du- ci- te cho- - ros, du- ci- te
T
du- ci- te cho- - ros fi- li- ae Je- ru- sa- lem,
B
fi- li- ae Je- ru- sa- lem,
B.c.

35
A
cho- - - ros fi- li- ae Je- ru- sa- lem,
T
fi- li- ae Je- ru- sa- lem,
B
du- ci- te cho- - ros fi- li- ae Je- ru- sa- lem,
B.c.
40
A
fi- li- ae Je- ru- sa- lem, fi- li- ae Je- ru- sa- lem;
T
fi- li- ae Je- ru- sa- lem, fi- li- ae Je- ru- sa- lem;
B
fi- li- ae Je- ru- sa- lem, fi- li- ae Je- ru- sa- lem;
B.c.
46
A
qui- a al- te- rum A- fri- ca pro- tu- lit An- ni- ba- lem,
T
qui- a al- te- rum A- fri- ca pro- tu- lit An- ni- ba- lem,
B
qui- a al- te- rum A- fri- ca pro- tu- lit An- ni- ba- lem,
B.c.
6

sed pro Roma strenue pugnantem.

Non hic aceto fregit Alpes, sed suae matris fractus est lacrimis, sed suae matris fractus est lacrimis.

Alterum Africa protulit Annibalem,

sed pro Roma strenue pugnantem. (A, T, B, B.c., m. 71)

Habuit ille venenum in anulo, hic antidotum in calamo; habuit ille hic virus evomuit. (T, B.c., m. 77)

Alterum Africa protulit Annibalem, (A, T, B, B.c., m. 85)

sed pro Roma strenue pugnantem.

Ille Romanos apud Cannas profligavit; hic Pelagium convicit, et evertit Erebum.

Alterum Africa protulit Annibalem, sed pro

110
A
T
B
B.c.
Ro- ma stre- nu- e pu- gnan- tem. Lae- tus
Ro- ma stre- nu- e pu- gnan- tem. Lae- tus
Ro- ma stre- nu- e pu- gnan- tem. Lae- tus
116
er- go tri- um- phet in cae- lis, qui tam for-
er- go tri- um- phet in cae- lis, qui tam for-
er- go tri- um- phet in cae- lis, qui tam for-
122
- - tis pu- gna- vit in ter- ris;
- - - tis pu- gna- vit in ter- ris;
- - - tis pu- gna- vit in ter- ris;

128

A: af- fer- te pal- mas pae- a- - na ca- - nen- tes,
T: af- fer- te pal- mas pae- a- - na ca- - nen- tes,
B: af- fer- te pal- mas pae- a- - na ca- - nen- tes,

134

A: e- jus tem- po- ra cin- - gi- te lau- re- is.
T: e- jus tem- po- ra cin- gi- te, cin- gi- te lau- re- is.
B: e- jus tem- po- ra cin- - gi- te lau- re- is.

140

A: Gau- de- at tel- lus, plau- dant An- ge- li, psal- lant fi- de- les in
T: Gau- de- at tel- lus, plau- dant An- ge- li, psal- lant fi- de- les in
B: Gau- de- at tel- lus, plau- dant An- ge- li, psal- lant fi- de- les in

146
A
so- no tu- bae. Gau- de- at tel- lus, plau- dant
T
so- no tu- bae. Gau- de- at tel- lus, plau- dant
B
so- no tu- bae. Gau- de- at tel- lus, plau- dant
B.c.
152
A
An- ge- li, psal- lant fi- de- les in chor- dis et or- ga- no.
T
An- ge- li, psal- lant fi- de- les in chor- - dis et or- ga- no.
B
An- ge- li, psal- lant fi- de- les in chor- - dis et or- ga- no.
B.c.
159
A
Gau- de- at tel- lus, plau- dant An- ge- li, psal- lant fi- de- les in
T
Gau- de- at tel- lus, plau- dant An- ge- li, psal- lant fi- de- les in
B
Gau- de- at tel- lus, plau- dant An- ge- li, psal- lant fi- de- les in
B.c.

165
A
tim- pa- no et cho- ro. Om- nis spi- ri- tus lau- det Do- mi-
T
tim- pa- no et cho- ro.
B
tim- pa- no et cho- ro.
B.c.
170
A
-num, om- nis spi- ri- tus, om- nis
T
Om- nis spi- ri- tus, om- nis spi- ri- tus lau- det Do- mi- num,
B
Om- nis spi- ri- tus,
B.c.
174
A
spi- ri- tus, om- nis spi- ri- tus, om- nis
T
om- nis spi- ri- tus lau- - det, om- nis
B
om- nis spi- ri- tus lau- det, ⟨lau- det,⟩
B.c.

178
A
spi- ri- tus lau- det Do- mi- num, om- nis spi- ri- tus lau- det Do- mi-
T
spi- ri- tus lau- det Do- mi- num, om- nis spi- ri- tus lau- det Do- mi-
B
lau- det Do- mi- num, om- nis spi- ri- tus lau- det Do- mi-
B.c.
183
A
-num, om- nis spi- ri- tus lau- dct Do- mi- num.
T
-num, om- nis spi- ri- tus lau- det Do- mi- num.
B
-num, om- nis spi- ri- tus lau- det Do- mi- num.
B.c.

Critical Report

Sources

Complete Editions

The first edition of the *Sacra Corona*, printed in Venice by Francesco Magni in 1656, serves as the principal source for this edition:

> Magni 1656: CANTO Primo | SACRA | CORONA | MOTETTI A Due, e Trè voci Di Diversi Eccellentissimi | Autori moderni, Novamente raccolti & dati in luce | Da Bartolomeo Marcesso | DEDICATI | AL MOLTO ILL.RE SIGNORE | SIGNOR E PATRON COL.MO | IL SIG. FEDERICO SCULAZZON | [coat of arms] | In VENETIA MDCLVI Apresso Francesco Magni[1]

The only known copy of this print is held at US-Wc (shelfmark M1490.M185 S2 Case). This exemplar is in excellent condition and survives complete, consisting of five partbooks: Canto Primo, 77 pages (p. 61 erroneously numbered 91); Canto Secondo, 79 pages (p. 65 erroneously numbered 67); Basso, 62 pages; and Basso Continuo, 61 pages. The more recent provenance of the volume is not difficult to reconstruct; on the inside of its front cover, it bears the bookplate of the distinguished British music historian Godfrey Edward Pellew Arkwright (1864–1944).[2] On 13 February 1939 much of his considerable library, including several works of great age, rarity, and value, went up for auction; the copy of the *Sacra Corona* was purchased by the Library of Congress at that time.[3] So far it has not been possible to identify conclusively the previous owners of the Arkwright copy; it may be the same copy of *Sacra Corona* that belonged to the French musician and music scholar Adrien de La Fage, but this is impossible to verify.[4] A second bookplate, apparently much older than that of Arkwright, also appears on the inside front cover, but it is difficult to decipher; it is partially torn off, and a second name ("Ioannis [illegible]") has been written in ink over the name printed on the bookplate ("DOMINICI MAF . . . [missing]"). On the publication history of this source, see "The Printer" and "The Compiler" in the introduction.

Magni's edition was reprinted in 1659 in Antwerp by the heirs of Pierre Phalèse:

> Phalèse 1659: SACRA | CORONA, | MOTETTI | A II. III. VOCI | Di diversi Eccellentissimi Autori moderni, Novamente | raccolti & dati in luce, Da Bartolomeo Marcesso. | BASSO CONTINUO. | IN ANVERSA, | Presso i Heredi di PETRO PHALESIO, | Al Re David. | M. DC. LIX[5]

Three partbooks of this edition survive at GB-Och (shelfmark Mus. 284–8[2]): Cantus I, 77 pages (p. 11 erroneously numbered 9); Cantus II, 79 pages; and Basso Continuo, 61 pages. The vocal Bassus partbook is lacking. Another copy of the Cantus I partbook survives at B-Bc (shelfmark II 64.625 A).

Phalèse 1659 is part of a series of similar reprints this publisher produced of collections previously published by the Gardano-Magni firm in Venice.[6] The Gardano (Gardane) family, which had French origins, moved to Venice during the first half of the sixteenth century and is known even then to have had professional relations with the Phalèse family—relations that were likely continued after Bartolomeo Magni acquired the firm (see "The Printer" in the introduction).[7] The eventual dissemination of some pieces in the collection to northern Europe was probably via Phalèse 1659, and indeed some compositions were copied in north European manuscript collections.[8]

Phalèse 1659 is closely dependent on the Magni edition, as evidenced by several *errores significativi*. These include some erroneous pitches or rhythms (see, e.g., the CNs to no. 14, mm. 6 and 29; and no. 20, m. 70) and missing measures, resting or otherwise (e.g., in no. 8, m. 42; no. 9, m. 143; and no. 11, m. 70). The Phalèse print also introduces a few new errors; in no. 7, for example, the alto has g' instead of a' as the first note of measure 24. At the same time, it offers corrections to some errors in the Magni edition. When musically valid, these corrections are implemented in the edition and reported in the critical notes below.[9] The most obvious and noteworthy difference between the two sources is that ₵ in Magni 1656 is universally replaced with ₵ in Phalèse 1659, though the change of meter has no major implications for performance at this period. This edition uses ₵ for all duple-meter passages, following Magni 1656.

Partial Editions

Eight motets from the collection (nos. 2, 3, 5, 6, 8, 9, 13, and 14) appeared in an anthology of 1668 by the Bolognese printer Giacomo Monti:

> Monti 1668: [partbook name]. | SACRI CONCERTI | OVERO MOTETTI | A due, e trè voci di diversi Eccellentissimi | Autori; | *Raccolti, e dati in luce da Marino Silvani, e* | CONSACRATI | al Molt'Illustre Signor | GIACOMO MARIA | MARCHESINI. | [floral vignette] | IN BOLOGNA, per Giacomo Monti. MDCLXVIII. | *Con licenza de' Superiori*.[10]

This anthology, printed by a Bolognese printer with strong Roman connections,[11] was the first of a well-known series of music publications edited by Marino Silvani.[12] It survives today in copies in GB-Lbl, I-Baf, I-Bc, and I-BRs and consists of four partbooks (Canto Primo, Canto Secondo, Basso, Organo). The I-Bc copy (shelfmark V.178) was consulted for this edition. Since the Monti 1668 versions of the eight motets listed above do not differ greatly from those in Magni 1656, the former source has been consulted only for purposes of comparison in ambiguous passages.

A few individual compositions from the *Sacra Corona* also appeared later in single-author printed collections published by their respective composers. These sources have been consulted only for purposes of comparison to resolve errors or ambiguities that appear in both Magni 1656 and Phalèse 1659 for those pieces. For example, a later version of Tarditi's "Victoriam, victoriam" (no. 10) appears as the fourth piece in the following print:

> Tarditi 1663: CONCERTO | IL TRIGESIMO QUINTO | DI MOTETTI | A DOI, E TRE VOCI, | Con alcuni con Violini, Et una Messa Concertata à tre Voci | DI | HORATIO TARDITI | DEDICATO | Al | Reverendissimo Padre Don | PIETRO FERRACCI | DA CREMONA | Abbate Generale Apostolico della Congregatione | Camaldolense | Eletto dalla Santità di N.S. Alessandro VII. [printer's mark] | IN VENETIA, M. DC. LXIII. | Appresso Alessandro Vincenti.[13]

Complete exemplars of this print survive in I-Bc (shelfmark CC.6; consulted for this edition) and I-FZac (shelfmark 32); both feature six partbooks (Canto, Basso, Terza Parte, Basso continuo, and two unlabeled violin partbooks). Another exemplar, at S-Uu, lacks the second violin partbook. The version of "Victoriam, victoriam" included in this print varies in several passages from the version that appears in *Sacra Corona*; these variant readings are detailed in the critical notes.

A later version of Neri's "Ad charismata caelorum" (no. 4) appears as the second piece in the following print:

> Neri 1664: [partbook name] | MOTETTI | A DUE E TRE VOCI Libro Primo | DI MASSIMILIANO NERI | Organista nella *Serenissima* Ducale di S. Marco | Degl'Accademici Erranti di Brescia | Opera Terza. | VENETIA MDCLXIIII Appresso Francesco Magni detto Gardano[14]

This print survives in an incomplete single copy at PL-WRu (shelfmark 50659 Muz; Alto and Basso Continuo partbooks only). Its version of "Ad charismata caelorum" varies significantly from the version that appears in *Sacra Corona* and is included in the appendix to this edition. Because the sole surviving copy of the source is incomplete, the canto part has been reconstructed by the editor. Whenever possible, the canto part is borrowed from the *Sacra Corona* version of the piece; in two passages where the *Sacra Corona* version does not correspond well to the surviving parts of Neri 1664 (mm. 29–30 and 81–87), new material has been supplied by the editor in brackets.

Cazzati's "Obstupescite gentes" (no. 18) was later published as the eleventh piece in the following print:

> Cazzati 1670: [partbook name] | MOTETTI | a Due, Trè, e Quattro, | DEDICATI ALL'ILLUSTRISSIMO SIGNOR | CO. ANTONIO ORSI | DA | MAURITIO CAZZATI | Maestro di Capella in S. PETRONIO di Bologna, | & Accademico Eccitato, | OPERA TERZA | Ristampata, et ampliata con nuove aggiunte. | [ornament] | In Bologna, Con licenza de' Superiori. 1670.[15]

This print survives in a single, complete exemplar at I-Bc (shelfmark X.259) and consists of five partbooks (Canto, Alto, Canto Secondo, Basso, and Organo). Tenor vocal parts are included in the Canto Secondo partbook. Its version of "Obstupescite gentes" features a only few minor variations and corrections (see the critical notes).

Editorial Methods

The compositions of the *Sacra Corona* employ a variety of sometimes conflicting notational conventions, and there seems to have been no attempt at standardization or homogenization on the part of the compiler, Bartolomeo Marcesso.[16] This edition aims to strike a balance between maintaining distinctive notational features, especially those typical of other surviving works of individual composers, and standardizing the appearance and presentation of the compositions in the interest of visual and notational consistency.

The titles of the motets are based both on their textual incipits and on the titles given in the *tavola* of the source's Basso Continuo partbook, with the Latin orthography tacitly emended as described below. Numbering is editorial and is based on the order in which the motets appear in the Basso Continuo partbook, the only partbook to include all twenty-three pieces. The vocal part names used in the edition are based on the scoring rubrics in the *tavola* and at the beginning of pieces and are left in their original Italian. Those rubrics, which also include the names and titles of composers and sometimes indicate topic or occasion (e.g., "Della B.V.M." in no. 8), have been removed to the critical notes, with minor textual variations noted. Because some rubrics indicating topic or occasion appear in the source only above the music and not in the *tavola* (e.g., in no. 18), all rubrics of this sort are also given as subtitles within the music.

The use of clefs for the vocal parts is consistent throughout the sources and always based on the voice type (soprano = C1 or G2, alto = C3, tenor = C4, bass = F4). In the edition, all canto and alto parts have been transcribed in treble clef, all tenor parts in transposing treble clef, and bass and baritone parts have been transcribed in bass clef. F4 (bass) clef is the clef most commonly used in the basso continuo part, with occasional use of C4 for higher passages; this part is transcribed chiefly in bass clef, with very high passages set in treble clef. Original clefs are shown as clef incipits.

Meters, especially triple meters, are notated variously throughout the anthology. While the composers of the Venetian group (see "The Composers" in the introduction) tend to favor more modern meters like $\frac{3}{2}$ and $\frac{3}{1}$ with the occasional use of **3** (usually but not always indicating a signature of three minims to the measure), those of the non-Venetian group, particularly Filippini and Cazzati (see, e.g., no. 8), occasionally indicate triple time with archaic signatures like O^3_1 and C^3_2, which appear also in some of their other works (as well as in those of some composers of the Roman school at this period). When such meters occur, they have been replaced with their modern equivalents: $\frac{3}{2}$ for C^3_2; and either $\frac{3}{4}$ or $\frac{3}{2}$ for $\mathbf{3}$, depending on context, with the original meter shown above the staff. The meter O^3_1 has been transcribed in most instances as $\frac{3}{1}$, though no. 8 uses $\frac{6}{2}$ (and halved note values; see below) for two passages in O^3_1. All other meters have been adopted from the source.

Rhythmic values are transcribed in a 1:1 ratio, except for two passages in no. 8 (mm. 71–98 and 107–34), both featuring the meter O^3_1, in which rhythmic values are halved for clarity. The slurring of the source have been retained in the edition. In the vocal parts, tied notes within a measure are combined into an equivalent single note value where appropriate; similarly, a few note values from the source have been split into tied notes where necessary in modern engraving practice. In the basso continuo part, as in other basso continuo parts of this period, tied notes within the same measure may imply the rearticulation of a harmony (see, e.g., no. 10, mm. 16–17) and have therefore been maintained in the edition. Editorial ties and slurs (usually added for consistency between voices or parallel passages) are dashed. All other editorially added elements are placed in brackets. The visual presentation of rests has been adjusted to accord with modern notational conventions. Coloration (the use of black notes in triple-meter passages to indicate syncopation and/or hemiolas) is indicated with open horizontal brackets. Fermatas have been filled in tacitly on resting measures where necessary; additional fermatas are supplied by the editor in brackets.

Both accidentals and basso continuo figures are handled variously in the sources. In general, the composers of the Venetian group (see "The Composers and Their Music" in the introduction) are very generous in their application of both accidentals and bass figures, often signing the same accidental multiple times within the same major rhythmic unit; see, for example, no. 2, measures 34 (C, notes 1 and 3) and 41 (C, notes 1 and 3); no. 3, measures 9 (C, notes 1–3), 11 (C, notes 1–4), and 12 (C, notes 1–3); and no. 6, measure 59 (C1, notes 1, 3, and 4), among others. The composers of the "non-Venetian" group, in contrast, apply fewer accidentals, tending to treat a greater proportion of inflections and figures as implied; see, for example, no. 9 (Tarditi), measures 28 (B) and 30 (C).[17] In order to make this distinction in practice clear, this edition retains all source accidentals, even those that are redundant by modern standards; however, all accidentals are assumed to be valid through the end of the measure, per modern notational practice. When the source signs ♯ or ♭ are equivalent to ♮ in modern practice, they have been transcribed in the edition as ♮. Editorially added accidentals are placed in brackets and are valid throughout the measure. When an editorial accidental precedes the first inflection of the same pitch in the source, both accidentals are given in the edition. Cautionary accidentals added by the editor are placed in parentheses.

All bass figures are placed above the staff regardless of their position in the sources. Figures are placed metrically to correspond to the indicated harmonic changes. Minor inaccuracies in the alignment of figures have been corrected tacitly; changes to the positioning of figures is reported in the critical notes only in cases where a figure is obviously assigned to the wrong note in the source. Inflections of intervals are regularized to precede the numeral (e.g., ♯6 instead of 6♯); inflections typically follow the figures in the source. Figure numerals are stacked from highest to lowest in accordance with modern practice. As with accidentals, the symbols ♯ and ♭ are rendered as ♮ when functioning as cancellations of previously flatted or sharped notes, respectively. Thirds are notated variously in the sources, whether with the figure 3 (when no inflection is necessary), with an inflection (♯, ♭, or ♮), or with both. In the edition, the numeral 3 is used when no inflection is needed; when one is needed, the appropriate accidental alone is used, substituting for the numeral. Editorial figures are added in brackets. No realization of the basso continuo part is provided.

Repeat signs are used in three compositions (nos. 1, 19, and 21). While some controversy still remains about the interpretation of repeat signs in seventeenth-century music,[18] it seems likely that double barlines flanked by dots did not necessarily have the same meaning as their modern counterparts; depending on the style and genre of the composition, they were employed not necessarily to signify an actual repeat but rather to delineate a principal section (which might or might not be repeated). Repeat signs from the sources are retained in the edition, and their interpretation is left to performers. Superfluous or erroneous repeat signs are reported in the critical notes, as are those that are added by hand but not present in any later sources (e.g., in no. 5, m. 89; see plate 2). When the source indicates the repetition of a section with a verbal rubric such as "ut supra" (as in no. 18, mm. 50–84) or a text incipit (as in no. 19, mm. 125–41, which, incidentally, appears in conjunction with the repeat signs in mm. 93–125), the music is written out in full with no further indication in the critical notes.

Because barlines are notated inconsistently in the sources, barring has been regularized in the edition. Double barlines are used to delineate major musical sections in the works by Monferrato (nos. 2 and 16), Ziani (nos. 6 and 19), and Cazzati (nos. 8 and 18), as well as in no. 4 (by Neri), no. 20 (by Volpe), and the version of no. 4 taken from Neri 1663 (in the appendix). They are retained in the edition if they are present in at least one vocal part; double barlines that appear only in the basso continuo have been removed and reported in the critical notes. Because the use of double barlines seems, for the most part, to be associated only with a few specific composers in the collection (see above), no further double barlines have been added.

The appearance, orthography, and placement of all verbal elements—tempo markings, directives, and dynamic markings—have been standardized, and all abbreviations have been expanded (e.g., "adag." for "adagio"). In the source, tempo markings do not consistently appear in all parts; in the edition, all tempo markings are considered to apply to the entire musical texture and are therefore placed accordingly (i.e., at the top of the system instead of in individual parts). Where necessary, the original placement and appearance of tempos and section labels is reported in the critical notes. Since tempo markings appear in the source typically only in sounding parts, notes reporting missing tempos only account for sounding parts. Voicing cues (such as "A." for alto) that appear only in the basso continuo part have been eliminated tacitly, as have text incipits that appear as cues in all of the parts, since such indications are rendered superfluous in score format. Similar cues that appear in multiple other parts (such as "Solo"), when assumed to apply to the entire ensemble, are retained and placed above the topmost staff. The spelling, punctuation, capitalization, and syllabification of sung texts have been standardized in accordance with modern Latin usage (see "Texts and Translations" for details). Where necessary, commas have been added to clarify text repetitions. Text repetitions indicated by the shorthand *ij* in the source have been realized within angle brackets; text supplied by the editor is enclosed in square brackets.

In "Obstupescite gentes" by Maurizio Cazzati (no. 18), which is given the heading "Per una Vergine, overo della Madona" (for a virgin or for the Madonna) in the source (see plate 3), the rubric *N*. appears frequently to allow the insertion of the saint's name of choice; "Mariae," however, is specified in the canto 1 part in measures 38–39. Although the edition reproduces both the name and the *N*. as they appear in the source, performers should feel free to replace the name "Mariae" with the name of another virgin saint if desired, and to make slight adjustments to note values as necessary to accommodate the name chosen.

Critical Notes

The notes below record differences between the edition and the source not otherwise covered in the editorial methods. They are organized into paragraphs that detail (1) the original scoring information and composer credits given in the source for each piece (based on the *tavola* of the source's Basso continuo partbook); (2) the disposition of vocal parts within the source partbooks for those vocal parts whose names differ from those of the partbooks; and (3) emended readings (corrections of errors in the source). In the emended readings, measures are counted consecutively from the beginning of each piece. Notes are counted consecutively within each measure, including both noteheads of tied notes; rests are counted separately.

The following abbreviations are used in the notes: C = Canto; A = Alto; B = Basso; Bar = Baritono; B.c. = Basso Continuo; m., mm. = measure(s). Pitches are identified according to the system in which c' denotes middle C. Later collections containing works first printed in *Sacra Corona* are referred to by author (or publisher, as convenient) and year of publication (e.g., "Phalèse 1659," "Cazzati 1670").

1. Nigra sum (Rovetta)

"2 Canti | Del Sig. Gio: Rouetta Maestro di Capella della Serenissima Republica Di Venetia."

Canto 1 in Canto Primo partbook; canto 2 in Canto Secondo partbook.

2. Dulce sit vobis pati (Monferrato)

"Canto è Alto | Del Sig. Natal Monferato Vice Maestro di Capella della Serenissima Republica di Venetia."

Canto in Canto Primo partbook; alto in Canto Secondo partbook.

M. 119, B.c., note 1, first figure is $\frac{5}{4}$.   M. 218, C, note 1 is half–half rest.

3. O bone Jesu (Cavalli)

"Canto è alto | Del Sig. Francesco Caualli Organista di S. Marco in Venetia."

Canto in Canto Primo partbook; alto in Canto Secondo partbook.

M. 84, C1, note 1 has augmentation dot.

4. Ad charismata caelorum (Neri)

"Canto è Alto | Del Sig. Maximiliano Neri. Organista di S. Marco."

Canto in Canto Primo partbook; alto in Canto Secondo partbook.

M. 26, B.c., note 2 has figures 4–♭3 above and ♭ on fourth staff space.   M. 48, B.c. has double barline at end of measure.   M. 53, B.c., note 2, figure moved from m. 54, note 2.

5. Jesu mi, Jesu benignissime (Volpe)

"Due Canti | Del Sig. D. Gio. Battista Volpe detto Rouetta."

Canto 1 in Canto Secondo partbook; canto 2 in Canto Primo partbook.

M. 10, C2, notes 2–3 are both 8ths.   M. 65, C1, notes 4–5 are d" dotted quarter.   M. 83, C2, note 2 is 8th.   M. 89 preceded by handwritten repeat sign in all parts.

6. Exsultate, gaudete, jubilate (Ziani)

"Canto e Tenore | Del Sig. D. Pietr'Andrea Ziani."

Canto in Canto Primo partbook; tenore in Canto Secondo partbook.

M. 113, B.c., note 1, figure is 7.   M. 128, B.c., note 2 has sharp.

7. Surge propera (Marini)

"Alto è Basso | Del Sig. Cauaglier Biagio Marini, Maestro Di Capella del Domo di Vicenza."

Alto in Canto Secondo partbook.

M. 6, B.c., note 1, figures are stacked (as $\frac{7}{6}$).   M. 27, B, note 3 through m. 28, note 1, text is "languet."   M. 66, B, note 7 has sharp.   M. 78, B.c., note 2 has natural.   M. 86, B.c., note 1, figure is ♯.   M. 110, B, note 1 is quarter.   M. 129, B.c., note 3 has figure ♯.   M. 133, B has superfluous repeat sign after final barline.

8. Salve mundi triumphatrix (Cazzati)

"Alto è Basso. Della B.V.M. | Del Sig. D. Mauritio Cazzati Maestro di Capella, in Santa Maria maggiore di Bergamo."

Alto in Canto Secondo partbook.

Mm. 42–55, A, only thirteen measures of rest (instead of fourteen). M. 55, B is d dotted half–d dotted half. Mm. 63–67, A, only three measures of rest (instead of five). M. 84, B.c., note 1 preceded by extraneous sharp. M. 94, B, notes 4–5 are g–f♯. M. 104, A has rubric "Si seguita la seconda strofa se piace"; B has rubric "Si seguita per la seconda strofa, se piace"; B.c. has "Si seguita per la seconda stroffa."

9. Spargite flores (Tarditi)

"Canto e Basso | Del Sig. Horatio Tarditi Maestro di Cappella di Faenza."

Canto in Canto Primo partbook.

M. 1, B.c. has meter **3**. M. 9, B is d whole. M. 14, B.c., note 1, figure is ♭5. M. 138, B, note 1 is f. M. 140, B.c., note 1, figure is ♭6. M. 143 lacking in B.c. (edition follows B part). M. 207, B.c., tempo appears on note 2.

10. Victoriam, victoriam (Tarditi)

"Canto è Basso | Del Sig. Horatio Tarditi Maestro di Cappella di Faenza."

Canto in Canto Primo partbook.

M. 7, C, note 5, rhythmic value unclear (edition follows Phalèse 1659). M. 13, B.c., note 1, figure unclear (edition follows Phalèse 1659). M. 18, C, B.c., dynamic *p* lacking (edition follows Tarditi 1663). M. 23, tempo lacking in B.c. (edition follows Tarditi 1663). M. 30, C, notes 4 and 6 are both dotted 8ths (edition follows Tarditi 1663). M. 44, C, note 6, augmentation dot lacking (added by hand and printed in Phalèse 1659). M. 66, B lacks fermata (edition follows Tarditi 1663). Mm. 67–69, B, rests corrected by hand. Mm. 71–73, C, rests obscured by attempt to correct by hand; "3" written below. Mm. 74–75, B, rests corrected by hand. Mm. 76, 79, and 82, C, rest is probably half (in each case corrected to whole rest by hand, with "1" written below the staff). Mm. 77–78, B, rests corrected by hand.

Variants (Tarditi 1663). Mm. 1–2 lacking in all parts. M. 3, B.c. is g–f♯–g. M. 4, B, notes 7–8 are dotted 8th–16th; B.c., note 1 is g. M. 6, B, notes 5–6 are both 8ths. M. 9, B.c., notes 1–2 are c half. M. 13, B, note 7 and rest 1 are reversed. M. 13, B.c., note 1 lacks figure. M. 14, B.c., note 3 has figure sharp. M. 17, B.c., beats 1–2 have dynamic *f*, beats 3–4 have dynamic *p*. M. 18, B lacks dynamics; B.c., note 3 is 8th–8th. M. 19, B.c., note 2 has dynamic *f* and lacks notehead. M. 22 lacking in B.c. M. 23, B.c. has tempo "adagio." M. 24, B.c., note 1 has figure ♯. M. 25, B.c., note 1 lacks figures. M. 28, B.c., note 3 has figures 4–3. M. 30, B.c. has tempo "adagio." Mm. 30–31, B.c. lacks tie. M. 34, C, note 7 has sharp. M. 37, C, note 5 is a'. M. 40, B.c., note 1 has figure 6. Mm. 42–44 as in example 1. M. 45, C, B, tempo is "Allegro assai"; B, notes 5–6 are slurred; notes 7–8 are slurred; B.c. lacks tempo; B.c., note 1 is G quarter–g quar-

Example 1. Tarditi, "Victoriam, victoriam," mm. 42–44 (reading from Tarditi 1663).

ter; note 2 is c' half. M. 46, B.c. is b half–a half. M. 49, C, notes 1–2 are both d". M. 50, C, notes 3–4 are slurred; notes 5–6 are slurred. M. 50, B, notes 2–3 are both 8ths. M. 51, B, 3–4 are slurred; notes 5–6 are slurred. M. 52, C, notes 3–4 are dotted 8th–16th. M. 54, B, notes 1–2 are both 8ths. M. 55, C, notes 2–3 are both 8ths; B, note 9 lacks sharp. M. 56, C, notes 1–2 are both 8ths. M. 57, B, notes 1–2 are both 8ths. M. 58, B, note 8 has sharp; B.c., note 2 is d. M. 59, B.c. is A half (with figure 6)–G half; note 3 is lacking. M. 60, C, notes 1–2 are both 8ths; B.c., note 5 is slurred to m. 61, note 1. M. 61, B, notes 2–3 are both 8ths. M. 62, C, notes 1–2 are both 8ths; note 3 has figure ♯. M. 64, C, note 3 is barely legible. M. 65, C, note 2 is g'; notes 3–4 are both 8ths. M. 66, C, note 1 lacks fermata. Mm. 67–89 as in example 2. M. 90, meter is $\frac{16}{12}$. Mm. 90–91, B.c. lacks dynamics. M. 91, B, note 2 lacks dynamic *f*. M. 95, B, note 7 is f. M. 97, C, notes 2–3 are dotted 8th–16th. M. 102, C, notes 4–7 are barely legible. M. 104, B, note 7 has sharp; B.c., note 3 has figure ♯. M. 105, C, note 9 is 8th–8th (with syllable "-mus" on second 8th). Mm. 106–7, C, beat 3 has dynamic *p*, beat 4 has dynamic *f*. M. 106, B.c., note 1 is d; note 2, dynamic is *p*; note 3 lacks dynamic. M. 107, B.c., note 1 has dynamic *f*; note 2 lacks dynamic; note 3 has dynamic *p*; note 4 lacks dynamic. M. 108, C, B, note 1 is 8th–8th (with syllable "-mus" on second 8th); C, note 1 has dynamic *f*; note 2 lacks dynamic. M. 109, C, note 1 has dynamic *p*; note 4 is f".

11. Stellae discedite (Filippini)

"Due Canti | Del Molto Reu. P. Baccillier Stefano Filippini detto l'Argentina."

M. 19, B.c., note 2, figure is 6–5. M. 22, B.c., note 1, figure is 6–5. M. 56, C1, note 3 is b♭'.

12. Quis dabit mihi tantam charitatem (Strozzi)

"A 3. Alto Tenore è Basso. | Della Virtuosissima Signora Barbara Strozzi."

Alto in Canto Primo partbook; tenore in Canto Secondo partbook.

M. 21, A has meter **3**. Mm. 34–35, A, slur moved from m. 35, note 1, through m. 36, note 1. Mm. 47–48, A, slur spans m. 47, notes 1–2. M. 57, A, note 1 is barely legible. M. 61, T, B, B.c., meter is **3**; B is f whole–half rest. M. 64,

Example 2. Tarditi, "Victoriam, victoriam," mm. 67–89 (reading from Tarditi 1663).

Example 2 continued

T, B, B.c., meter is **3**. M. 74, B.c., beat 3, figures are 6–4. M. 85, B.c., beat 3, figures are 4–2. Mm. 89–90, A, slur begins m. 89, note 7. M. 99, B.c., note 1 is lacking (edition follows Phalèse 1659). Mm. 100–102, T, position of slurs is ambiguous. M. 101, T, note 3 is quarter–8th. M. 104, A, B, B.c., "Adagio" moved from m. 103, beat 2. M. 140, A, dynamic *p* moved from m. 141, beat 1. M. 143, A has superfluous meter 𝄴; B.c., rubric is "Aria A. solo." M. 184, B.c., note 3 is b. M. 194, T, note 2 has dynamic *p*.

13. O quando suavissimum (Rovetta)

"A 3. Alto Tenor è Basso. | Del Sig. Gio. Rouetta Maestro di Capella della Serenissima Republica di Venetia."

Alto in Canto Secondo partbook; Tenore in Canto Primo partbook.

M. 15, B.c., meter is $\frac{3}{1}$. M. 73, A, meter is $\frac{3}{1}$ (corrected by hand to $\frac{3}{2}$). M. 113, tempo indication is "presto" in B.

14. Plaudite, cantate (Cavalli)

"A 3. Alto Tenore e Basso | Del Sig. Francesco Caualli Organista di S. Marco in Venetia."

Alto in Canto Primo partbook; Tenore in Canto Secondo partbook.

M. 5, T, B, tempo is lacking. M. 6, B.c., notes 1–2 are c'–c'. M. 29, B.c., notes 1–2 are both halves. M. 30, A, notes 2–3 are f'–g'. M. 32, B.c., note 2 has figure ♭. M. 35, B.c., note 2 is g. M. 62, A lacks tempo. M. 84, A, note 2 is a. M. 116, T, B, tempo is lacking. M. 120, B, notes 1–2 are both halves.

15. In virtute tua (Cavalli)

"A 3. Alto Tenore è Basso | Del Sig. Francesco Caualli Organista di S. Marco."

Alto in Canto Primo partbook; Tenore in Canto Secondo partbook.

M. 155, A, note 3, sharp moved from note 2.

16. Peccator, si tu times (Monferrato)

"A 3. Canto Alto è Baritono. | Del Sig. D. Natal Monferato Vice Maestro di Cappella della Serenissima Republica Di Venetia."

Canto in Canto Primo partbook; Alto in Canto Secondo partbook; Baritono in Basso partbook.

M. 55, B.c., note 1 is barely legible. M. 77, C, note 1 is e'. M. 206, A is f' dotted whole.

17. Jesu mi dulcissime (Marini)

A 3. Alto Tenore e Basso. | Del Sig. Cauaglier Biagio Marini, Maestro di Capella del Domo di Vicenza.

Alto in Canto Primo partbook; tenore in Canto Secondo partbook.

M. 3, T, note 2, syllable "-su" moved from note 3. M. 4, B.c., figures are 6–4–3 (6 moved to m. 3, note 2). M. 7, T, note 1 lacks augmentation dot. M. 10, T, note 1 lacks augmentation dot. M. 13, B.c., note 2, figures are 4–7–3. M. 17, A is dotted breve. M. 19, A, note 1 lacks augmentation dot. M. 26, B.c., note 1 has figure 6. M. 31, B.c., note 2, figures are $\frac{7}{\#}$–6. M. 39, B.c., note 1 has figure 6. M. 40, B, notes 1–2 are d'–b. M. 52, B.c., note 2, figures are $\frac{7}{\#}$–6. M. 53, T is dotted breve. M. 58, T is whole–half rest–half rest; B is dotted breve. M. 64, B.c., note 2, figure moved from note 1. M. 81, B.c., note 1 has figure ♯. M. 83, B, meter is **3**. M. 106, B.c., note 1 lacks augmentation dot. Mm. 111–12, B.c., notes lack augmentation dots. M. 131, B.c., note 1, first figure is $\frac{7}{\#}$. Mm. 133–41 lacking in T (edition follows Phalèse 1659). M. 144, B.c., note 1, first figure is $\frac{7}{\#}$. M. 155, B.c., note 1, first figure is $\frac{7}{\#}$.

18. Obstupescite gentes (Cazzati)

"A 3. due Canti, e Basso. | Del Sig. D. Mauritio Cazzati, Maestro di Capella, in Santa Maria maggiore di Bergomo."

M. 47, C1, note 1 has text "-ae." Mm. 109–10 lacking in C1. M. 110 lacking in C2. M. 120, C2, note 7 is g' (edition follows Cazzati 1670). M. 130, C2, note 1 is e" (edition follows Cazzati 1670). M. 168, B, note 3 has flat.

19. Salve Regina (Ziani)

"A 3. Alto Tenore è Basso | Del Sig. D. Pietr'Andrea Ziani."

Alto in Canto Primo partbook; tenore in Canto Secondo partbook.

M. 32, T, note 6 has flat. M. 50, A, notes 2–3 are barely legible. M. 119, A, note 4 is e'. M. 122, B.c., note 3, figures are 6–7.

20. O Sacramentum (Volpe)

"A 3. Alto Tenore e Basso | Del Sig. D. Gio. Battista Volpe detto Rouetta."

Alto in Canto Primo partbook; tenore in Canto Secondo partbook.

M. 15, B.c., note 4, figure is 7. M. 63, T, note 2 has dynamic "pian." M. 70, T, note 1 is quarter. M. 109, A, note 2 has augmentation dot. M. 155, B.c. has double barline at end of measure.

21. Salve Virgo benignissima (Neri)

"A 3. Alto Tenore e Basso | Del Sig. Maximilliano Neri. Organista di S. Marco in Venetia."

Alto in Canto Primo partbook; tenore in Canto Secondo partbook.

Title given in all source *tavole* as "Salve Virgo clementissima" (edition follows text incipit of A). Mm. 25–27, B, text is "benignissima." Mm. 80–81, B.c., notes lack augmentation dots. M. 81, A, T, note 1 lacks augmentation dot. M. 82, T, meter change moved from m. 81. M. 104, A, note 1 lacks augmentation dot; B.c., note 1 is missnig (edition follows T part). M. 139, T has double barline at end of measure.

22. O vos omnes (Vesi)

"A 3. Alto Tenore e Basso | Del Sig. D. Simon Vesi, Maestro di Capella Di Padoua."

Alto in Canto Primo partbook; tenore in Canto Secondo partbook.

Mm. 35–39, B.c., notes lack augmentation dots. M. 56, T, slur spans notes 2–3. M. 87, B, note 3, sharp moved from note 2. M. 117, A, notes 5 and 6 are both 8ths (edition follows Phalèse 1659). M. 152, A, note 1 has flat.

23. Laetare Mater Ecclesia (Filippini)

"A 3. Alto Tenor è Basso. | Del Molto Reu. P. Baccillier Stefano Filippini detto l'Argentina."

Alto in Canto Primo partbook; tenore in Canto Secondo partbook.

Appendix: Ad charismata caelorum (version from Neri 1664)

M. 29, A, note 4 has handwritten flat above. M. 40, A is dotted whole. M. 111, B.c., meter change moved from m. 112; note 1 has augmentation dot.

Notes

1. RISM B/I 1656[1]; *Catalogue de la bibliothèque musicale de feu M. J. Adr. de la Fage ancien maitre de chapelle, etc.* (Paris: L. Potier Libraire, 1862), no. 1638; Robert Eitner et al., *Bibliographie der Musik-Sammelwerke des XVI. und XVII. Jahrhunderts* (Berlin: Leo Liepmannssohn, 1877), 287. On the collation and bibliographical details of the collection, see also Stanley Boorman, "Bibliographical Aspects of Italian Printed Music of the Sixteenth and Seventeenth Centuries," *Studies in Bibliography* 56 (2003–4): 203.

2. See *NG2*, s.v. "Arkwright, G(odfrey) E(dward) P(ellew)" (p. 4), by Edward Van Der Straeten, which lists his principal works of scholarship.

3. The *Sacra Corona* copy is listed in the catalog of the auction, *Catalogue of a Selected Portion of the Well-Known Collection of Old and Rare Music and Books on Music: The Property of Godfrey E. P. Arkwright Which Will Be Sold by Auction by Sotheby & Co.* (London: Sotheby & Co., 1939), no. 193. The description corresponds to the copy now owned by US-Wc: "The 4 partbooks . . . in 1 vol., each with separate title, half morocco." Unfortunately, there is no indication in the catalog of where and when Arkwright acquired the volume, even though that information is given for several other items in the catalog. The acquisition of the Arkwright copy of *Sacra Corona* is also recorded in *Annual Report of the Librarian of Congress for the Fiscal Year Ended June 30, 1939* (Washington, D.C.: United States Government Printing Office, 1940), 193, where it is listed under the name of the editor, Bartolomeo Marcesso. The report makes note of both bookplates: "one of Godfrey E. P. Arkwright, the other unidentified."

4. La Fage's collection went up for auction on 15 December 1862 in Paris. *Sacra Corona* is listed as no. 1638 in the auction catalog (see note 1 above).

5. RISM B/I 1659[2]; Aloys Hiff, *Catalogue of Printed Music Published Prior to 1801 Now in the Library of Christ Church, Oxford* (London: Humphrey Milford, 1919), 62. Complete bibliographical information is given in the online catalog of GB-Och (http://library.chch.ox.ac.uk/music/).

6. Several of Giovanni Rovetta's works were reprinted by Phalèse shortly after the appearance of their Venetian first editions: *Motetti Concertati a due e tre voci con le letanie della Madona a quattro . . . opera quinta* (Venice: Alessandro Vincenti, 1639; RISM R 2967), reprinted as *Motetta concertata duabus, et tribus vocibus, adiunctis litaniis Beata Virginis quatuor vocibus . . . opus quintum* (Antwerp: heirs of Pierre Phalèse, 1640; 2nd ed., 1648; RISM R2968 and R2969); *Gemma musicalis diversis cantionibus*

sacri (Antwerp: Magdalène Phalèse, 1694; RISM R2977); *Novi concentus sacrae Philomelae* (Antwerpen: heirs of Pierre Phalèse, 1653; RISM R2979). Maurizio Cazzati too had some reprints of his Venetian editions by the Antwerp Phalèse firm.

7. Although no documentation has surfaced about possible commercial relations between the Magni and Phalèse firms, it is worth noting that Biagio Marini's *Corona melodica ex diversis sacrae musicae floribus concinnata* (op. 15, 1644; RISM A/I M666) was published by "Haeredes PETRII PHALESII." Indeed, Marini's personal involvement with the Phalèse edition of *Sacra Corona* seems suggested by the appearance in Phalèse 1659 of a lengthy correction to a corrupt passage in his motet "Jesu mi dulcissime" (no. 17; T, mm. 133–41; see the critical notes). The change from ₵ to ¢ is perhaps the most noteworthy difference between the Magni and Phalèse editions of the *Sacra Corona*.

8. Some manuscript copies once preserved in the library of the Thomaskirche in Leipzig are known from their incipits transcribed in two eighteenth-century inventories; see Arnold Schering, "Die alte Chorbibliothek der Thomasschule in Leipzig," *Archiv für Musikwissenschaft* 1 (January 1919): 275–88, where the titles and attributions are given as "Ad caris[si]mata coelorum. à 2" (p. 283), "Ad carismata coelorum accedite. à 3" (ibid.), and "Dulce sit vobis pati. à 2" (p. 286, listed under "Monteverdi [Monteferd]"). Since Monteverdi is not known to have composed a piece with the title "Dulce sit vobis pati," the setting by Monferrato is almost certainly meant; similarly, although no attribution is listed for "Ad carismata coelorum," the rarity of the text makes it likely that the setting in question is that of Neri from the *Sacra Corona*.

9. A few attempted corrections in Phalèse 1659 are not valid; e.g., in no. 18, C2, m. 130, note 1 (e" in Magni 1656) is replaced in the Phalèse print with the equally erroneous d".

10. Gaspari, 2:360; RISM B/I 1668[2].

11. Monti was the official printer of the Sant'Uffizio in Bologna; see *DBI*, s.v. "Monti, Giacomo" (pp. 263–65), by Roberto Marchi.

12. In his dedication to Giacomo Maria Marchesini, Silvani mentions the fact that his anthology includes works culled from previously published volumes: "A comun beneficio, & à publica curiosità de' Professori di Musica, hò raccolto buon numero di Motetti Sacri, composti da i più celebri, e rinomati Maestri, che fioriscono in questi tempi in Italia, considerando, che sarà per riuscire di com[m]odo non ordinario, haver raccolto in un Volume quel, che in molti si trova disperso" (For the common benefit, and for the public curiosity of those who practice music, I have collected a good number of sacred motets, composed by the most celebrated and renowned masters flourishing in Italy at this time, considering that it will be of more than ordinary advantage [to the reader] to have collected in one volume things that were scattered across many).

13. RISM A/I T211; RISM B/I 1663[3]; Gaspari, 2:502.

14. RISM A/I N404; I thank Mirosław Osowski of the Biblioteka Uniwersytecka, Wrocław, for providing information about this copy. See also Oscar Mischiati, Mariella Sala, and Ernesto Meli, *Bibliografia delle opere dei musicisti bresciani pubblicate a stampa dal 1497 al 1740* (Florence: Leo S. Olschki, 1992), no. 371; the inscription "De gli Academici Erranti di Brescia L'Affaticato" appears on all of Neri's music prints, stating his membership in the renowned Brescian Accademia degli Erranti and suggesting that he may have had Brescian origins.

15. Gaspari, 2:397; RISM A/I C1581.

16. Perhaps owing to the relative haste with which the collection seems to have been prepared; see "Possible Occasions" in the introduction.

17. Accidentals are also handled this way in some of the works by Venetian composers, however: see, e.g., no. 13 (Rovetta), mm. 2 (A) and 3 (B).

18. See, e.g., Robert Donington, *The Interpretation of Early Music*, rev. ed. (London: Faber, 1974), 377–81; and Michael Talbot, review of Giovanni Legrenzi, *The Instrumental Music of Giovanni Legrenzi: Sonate a due, tre e quattro stromenti, libro quarto, opus 10*, ed. Stephen Bonta; Biagio Marini, *Per ogni sorte di strumento musicale, libro terzo, opera XXII (1655)*, ed. Ottavio Beretta; and Biagio Marini, *Sonate, sinfonie, canzoni, passamezzi, balletti, correnti, gagliarde, & ritornelli . . .* , ed. Maura Zoni, *Notes* 63, no. 2 (December 2006): 425.

Appendix

Ad charismata caelorum

Version from *Motetti a due e tre voci* (1664)

Massimiliano Neri

C
A
B.c.
Ve- ne- ra-
ve- strum qui vos pa- - scit, con- so- la- tur, vos e- nu- trit, vos e- nu- trit, con- vi- va- tur,
- mi- ni De- um ve- strum qui vos pa- scit, con- so- la- tur, vos e- nu- trit, con- vi- va- tur,
ve- ne- ra-
ve- ne- ra- mi- ni De- um ve- strum qui vos pa- scit, con- so- la- tur, qui vos pa-
- mi- ni De- um ve- strum qui vos pa- scit, con- so- la- tur, vos e- nu- trit, vos e- nu- trit, qui vos pa-
- scit, con- so- la- tur, vos e- nu- trit, [vos e- nu- trit, con- vi- va-] tur. O
- scit, con- so- la- tur, vos e- nu- trit, vos e- nu- - trit, con- vi- va- tur. O

253

55
C
-stra- vit. Ac- cur- ri- te lae- tan- tes,
A
-stra- vit. ac- ce- di- te ve- ne-
B.c.
61
C
ac- cur- ri- te lae- tan- tes, lae- tan- tes, ac- - cur- ri- te,
A
-ran- tes, ac-
B.c.
67
C
lae- tan- tes,
A
-ce- di- te ve- ne- ran- tes, ac- - ce- di- te ve- ne-
B.c.
72
C
lae- tan- - tes, ac- - cur- ri- te,
A
-ran- tes, ve- ne-
B.c.

77
C
laetantes, [laetan-
A
-rantes, ⟨venerantes,⟩ accedite laetantes, lae-
B.c.
82
C
tes, laetantes, laetantes, lae-
A
-tantes, laetan-
B.c.
87
C
-tantes,] accurrite.
A
-tes, accurrite. Alleluia, al-
B.c.
92
C
Alleluia, allelu-
A
-leluia,
B.c.

97
C
-ia, al- le- lu- ia, al- le- lu- ia, al- le- lu- ia, al- le-
A
al- le- lu- ia, al- le- lu- ia, al- le-
B.c.
102
C
-lu- ia, al- le- lu- ia, al- le- lu- ia, al- le- lu- ia, al-
A
-lu- ia, al- le- lu- ia, ⟨al- le- lu- ia,⟩ al- le- lu- ia, al-
B.c.
108
C
-le- lu- ia, al- le- lu- ia, al- le- lu- ia.
A
-le- lu- ia, ⟨al- le- lu- ia,⟩ al- le- lu- ia.
B.c.